FORD MADOX FORD'S MODERNITY

Edited by
Robert Hampson
and
Max Saunders

Rodopi

Amsterdam - New York, NY 2003

The Ford Madox Ford Society

The publication of this volume of International Ford Madox Ford Studies was made possible thanks to the generous support of the Joseph Conrad Society (UK) and the Juliet McLauchlan Bequest.

Illustration on this page: William Henry Hyde, 'The Nerves of London' - one of Hyde's illustrations for Ford's trilogy *England and the English* (New York: McClure, Phillips & Co., 1907) - reproduced by kind permission of Mrs Auriol Earle and Mrs Joan Hamilton

Title page illustration: Ford c.1915, pen and ink drawing, © Alfred Cohen, 2000

Cover illustration: Luigi Russolo, 'I Ricordi di una Notte' (1911). Oil on canvas, 39¾ x 39?. Reproduced with kind permission of Miss Barbara Jane Slifka, New York.

THE NERVES OF LONDON

The paper on which this book is printed meets the requirements of "ISO 9706:1994, Information and documentation - Paper for documents - Requirements for permanence".

ISBN: 90-420-1187-4
©Editions Rodopi B.V., Amsterdam - New York, NY 2003
Printed in The Netherlands

CONTENTS

CONTENTS

CONTENTS

FORD MADOX FORD'S MODERNITY

A quick appreciation, a power of observing, or perhaps of feeling, are patent in all his works, just as they are obvious in his person. It is the sort of vibrating nervousness of a man who, having had many sensations, has lived much. It is, in fact, modernity – for what separates the life we live today from the lives that all former men have lived is the fact that we are surrounded by such an infinite number of little and transitory facts – the tram-tickets of life, as it were – and of little transitory objects. If we fail in quickness of apprehension we fall short of being modern.

Ford, 'Literary Portraits: XIV. Mr. Maurice Hewlett', *Tribune* **(26 Oct. 1907), 2.**

The aspect of the world must be vastly different to those born within the last quarter of a century. My existence began, consciously at least, in the country. Rounded limbs of horses progressed there before rounded hay-wains; cherries hung upon boughs; speech was slow; brooks gurgled very gently. That was the normal basis of human life. But, for those born since the 'nineties the earth is a matter of hurtling, coloured squareness, of the jar of telephone bells, of every kind of rattle and bang, of every kind of detonation, of every kind of light in shafts, in coronets, in whirls and blaze and flash. The ocular and phonetic break between today and the historic ages is incredible. To all intents and purposes the Kent of my childhood and adolescence differed very little from the Greece where Sappho sang. There were railway trains, but one used them little; there was gunpowder, but one saw its effects seldom enough. Nowadays, ten times a day we are whirled at incredible speeds through glooms, amidst clamours. And the business of the young artist of today is to render those glooms, those clamours, those iron boxes, those explosions, those voices from the metal horns of talking-machines and hooters.

Upon this task the Vorticists have set out, quite tentatively. And I repeat that I find a certain strangeness in their effects. I imagine that I should prefer to be where Christobel low-lieth and to listen to the song the sirens sang. But I am in London of the nineteen tens, and I am content to endure the rattles and the bangs—and I hope to see them rendered. And I certainly do not hope to see them rendered with the palette-effects of the late Lord Leighton or the verbal felicities of the late Lord Tennyson. I am curious – I am even avid – to see the method that shall make grass grow over my own methods and I am content to be superseded. I think that that should be the attitude of the composed and reasonable human being.

Ford, 'On a Notice of "Blast"', *Outlook,* **36 (31 July 1915), 143-44.**

It is, for instance, perfectly safe to say that no writer after today will be able to neglect *Ulysses*. Writers may dislike the book, or may be for it as enthusiastic as you will; ignore it they cannot, any more than passengers after the 'forties of last century could ignore the railway as a means of transit.

Ford, '*Ulysses* **and the Handling of Indecencies',** *English Review,* **35 (Dec. 1922), 538-48.**

GENERAL EDITOR'S PREFACE

Max Saunders

Ford Madox Ford has as often been a subject of controversy as a candidate for literary canonization. He was, nonetheless, a major presence in early twentieth-century literature, and he has remained a significant figure in the history of modern English and American literature for over a century now. Throughout that time he has been written about – not just by critics, but often by leading novelists and poets, such as Graham Greene, Robert Lowell, William Carlos Williams, Gore Vidal, A. S. Byatt, and Julian Barnes. His two acknowledged masterpieces have remained in print since the 1940s. *The Good Soldier* now regularly figures in studies of Modernism and on its syllabuses. *Parade's End* has been increasingly recognized as comparably important. It was described by Malcolm Bradbury as 'a central Modernist novel of the 1920s, in which it is exemplary'; by Anthony Burgess as 'the finest novel about the First World War'; and by Samuel Hynes as 'the greatest war novel ever written by an Englishman'.

During the last decade or so, there has been a striking resurgence of interest in Ford and in the multifarious aspects of his work. As befits such an international and internationalist phenomenon as Ford himself, this critical attention has been markedly international, manifesting itself not only in the United Kingdom and the U. S. A., but in Continental Europe and elsewhere. Many of his works have not only been republished in their original language, but also translated into more than a dozen others.

The founding of the International Ford Madox Ford Studies series reflects this increasing interest in Ford's writing and the wider understanding of his role in literary history. Each volume will normally be based upon a particular theme or issue. Each will relate aspects of Ford's work, life, and contacts, to broader concerns of his time.

GENERAL EDITOR'S PREFACE

This second volume, *Ford Madox Ford's Modernity*, explores Ford's complex engagements with his own times, and with historical, cultural and technological change. The main emphases are on his most experimental novels, *The Good Soldier* and *Parade's End*. But a wide range of his writing is discussed, bringing out the extent of his involvements with contemporary literary, artistic, and intellectual, developments.

The series is published in association with the Ford Madox Ford Society. Forthcoming and projected volumes will be announced on the Society's web site, together with details of whom to contact with suggestions about future volumes or contributions. The address is: **www.rialto.com/fordmadoxford_society**

FOREWORD

Sir Frank Kermode

Ford Madox Ford died over sixty years ago. He had published a great many books, not all of them of high quality, though a few have proved capable of inspiring champions in each successive generation.

He had a wide acquaintance and his name continually crops up in literary history and gossip about the arts in the early years of the twentieth century. As the editor of an important literary journal, he was the first to recognise and celebrate the talent of D. H. Lawrence. He was a link between the traditional and the new: a friend of Henry James and a collaborator with Conrad, he was an admired colleague of Ezra Pound, and an associate, albeit uneasily, of Hemingway. In his last years he was a sort of battered hero to the American poets Allen Tate and Robert Lowell. As Max Saunders showed in his excellent book, the biography of Ford involves many other biographies as well.

His private life, especially in respect of his complicated dealings with women, inevitably retains its interest. He presents biographers as well as critics problems of unusual complexity; he often failed to distinguish between truth and fiction, to the extent that some perfectly truthful statements of his have been disbelieved.

The claims to canonical status of *The Good Soldier* and the tetralogy *Parade's End* (or, in the opinion of some critics, three quarters of it) have been made more or less confidently ever since their publication, but over the years one has been conscious of an element of uncertainty about the higher claims made for Ford. He has somehow hovered on the threshold of immortality. Lately, however, we have probably come to understand him better, and come to terms with the paradoxes of his life and work. No one critic or scholar can claim all the credit for this development, but it is fair to say that the publication of Saunders's biography gave a new stability to the novelist's reputation. His and Robert Hampson's calling the conference that brought together the expert contributors to the present volume, and the subsequent foundation of a society for the study of Ford, further secured Ford's standing, and we witness here yet another decisive advance.

It is hardly surprising that *The Good Soldier* should be the topic of so many of these chapters. Its great merits apart, it contains many fascinating puzzles. One of these, perhaps the most difficult, concerns the implausible ubiquity in the narrative of the date August 4. Martin Stannard, in the essay here included, takes us a good bit nearer a solution than he did in his fine edition of *The Good Soldier* (1995), though the final proof of his argument seems to remain tantalisingly out of reach. Many other aspects of this masterpiece are here illuminated, for example by Roger Poole's latest assertion of his radical view of the matter, which at once simplifies and complicates the issues.

For the rest, one can say that it is enriching to know more about Ford and the use of the newfangled telephone, about his *deuxième carrière* as a market gardener, and, not least, about his position as an old-style cultivated English gentleman with strong notions of proper behaviour, pitched into the ungentlemanly iconoclasm of a new world, the world of Futurism, Vortex, Impressionism, Post-Impressionism and the other scandals of the Edwardian avant-garde. We are also offered more light on his relations with Violet Hunt and Stella Bowen, and, perhaps more important, on his reading. Ford was, he said, mad about books; he also loved writers, and perhaps fared better with books and writing than he did with affairs of the heart.

Roger Poole declares, in this volume, that Ford, whom he regards as technically at least the equal of James, Conrad and Joyce, 'even now remains a figure in the shadows, off-stage, waiting'. This splendid collection may well change all that; Ford is now close to centre stage, and lit with increasing brilliance.

INTRODUCTION

Max Saunders

Ford Madox Ford has often been characterized as a throwback. To his first biographer he appeared *The Last Pre-Raphaelite*. It was perhaps the price he paid for his support of the avant-garde – *les jeunes*, as he called them – that its members like Ernest Hemingway, Jean Rhys, or Wyndham Lewis would portray him as a representative of the old guard. There is an element of truth in this version of him, of course. His historical romances, his recreations of feudalism and the values of 'the gentleman' or 'the Tory' can seem anachronistic when set beside the fractured high modernism of Eliot and Pound. Yet from another point of view, that modernism's neo-classicizing bent is no less historically-minded. Eliot and Pound shared Ford's love of the Provençal Troubadours. Eliot's admiration for Lancelot Andrewes; Joyce's fascination with Aquinas; Pound's redactions of Renaissance translations of Homer, Anglo-Saxon or Chinese lyric – all these are no less nostalgic than Ford's historic sense.

In his essay 'Literary History and Literary Modernity', Paul de Man argues that modernity always needs to assert its destruction of literary history, but this necessarily fails since it thus takes its place in that literary history.[1] Ford's modernity lies perhaps in his awareness of the complex dialectic of the modern and the historic. He slyly hints at it in calling Conrad an Elizabethan or Pound a modern re-incarnation of Bertran de Born. This leads us towards a complementary truth: that Ford is exemplary in his engagement with modern history, culture, and of course literary developments. We see this in his openness to the contemporary technologies of communication, the media, and transport; to the political and social changes of his era, especially as these relate to the women's movement, crises of Englishness and Imperialism, and the First World War; and to modernist experimentation in art and literature. We see it also in his interest in contemporary popular forms such as the detective story. This is the version of Ford that is to the fore in this collection of essays. It enables fresh perspectives on how Ford was, as he said (with a characteristically paradoxical flourish) the novelist should be, the 'historian' – not of the past, but 'of his own time'.[2] And, as he was one of the first Anglophone modernists to recognize, this implied a new, if ambivalent, aesthetic. He wrote in 1910: 'nothing is more difficult, nothing is more terrible than to look things in the face. We have to be ready to recognise, and if we are strong enough to acclaim, that things seeming to us hideous may embody a New Beauty'.[3]

Critical work on Ford has begun some exciting transformations. He has always been championed by creative writers – Ezra Pound, Rebecca West, Sinclair Lewis, W. H. Auden, Graham Greene, William Carlos Williams, Robert Lowell, Anthony Burgess, Alison Lurie, Malcolm Bradbury, Ruth Rendell, Gore Vidal, A. S. Byatt, Julian Barnes. Literary criticism has been more sporadic in its attentions. The 1960s and early 1970s saw a renewal of interest. Ford's technical self-consciousness; his mastery of unreliable narration; his advocacy of *le mot juste*, the 'time shift', and the *progression d'effet* suited the New Criticism, which fostered studies of his 'technique'. Then there was a lull. Perhaps the reductive Freudianism of Arthur Mizener's 1971 biography, *The Saddest Story*, deterred prospective scholars with its projection of a damaged fantasist. Perhaps the Marxism and Feminism of the 1970s and 1980s didn't know what to make of Ford's paradoxical positions (or didn't approve of what they made). Was he a feudal Tory or a radical anarchist? How could the cosmopolitan socialite live on the land, befriending the rural poor. How could the creator of fictional sublime bitches such as Sylvia Tietjens or Florence Dowell also be an advocate of the Suffragettes?

Nevertheless, this period challenged the hegemony of the 'classic' modernists and recovered the diversity of writing in the Edwardian period, during the First World War, and in the 1920s and 1930s. We tend now to talk of 'modernisms'. Ford's differences from Conrad or Joyce or Eliot are no longer reasons for dismissing him. Indeed, the very qualities that troubled New Critics seeking 'concreteness' and 'sincerity' are what make him seem modern now – his psychological impressionism; his ludic qualities; even his accessibility.

Critical interest in him is currently flourishing, and (as with any major literary figure about whom people have been writing for over a century) the secondary bibliography is already extensive.[4] He is increasingly studied world-wide. There have been three full-length biographical studies since Mizener's (and further biographical investigations appear here). Carcanet Press's ambitious 'Millennium Ford' project, which aims to republish the major novels, poetry, autobiography and essays, is now well-established. Major critics are increasingly acknowledging Ford's stature. Besides those represented here one could mention Samuel Hynes, George Steiner, John Sutherland, and the late Tony Tanner.

This collection of nineteen essays by leading American, British and European Ford scholars reflects the latest developments in Ford studies as well as in contemporary literary criticism. They are all based on papers given at the first British conference on Ford, held at the Centre (now Institute) for English Studies, University of London, in November 1996.[5] As Ford's role in modernist movements becomes better established, the volume will also be of interest to scholars and students in the broader area of literary modernism. It is intended to contribute to the on-going major reconsideration of modernism and modernity in works such as *Edwardian Fiction: An Oxford Companion*; in recent studies by Christopher Butler, Peter Nicholls, Lawrence Rainey, and David Ayers; and in the journal *Modernism/Modernity*.[6] Above all, it seeks to support Malcolm Bradbury's claim that Ford is 'a central figure, artistically and influentially, in the modern movement'.[7]

The book explores Ford's engagement with 'modernity' by approaching his work with a range of current critical approaches including narrative theory, post-colonial criticism, gender studies, psychoanalysis, new historicism, the study of life-writing, and the new bibliography. At the heart of the volume are essays on Ford's major works, *The Good Soldier* and *Parade's End*, offering a range of significant new work on both texts. These are supported by essays on Ford and modernity; by comparative essays on Ford and other major modern writers; and by sophisticated readings of lesser-known works.

The essays in the volume have been arranged into four sections; though, as the following brief summaries show, there are numerous continuities and interactions between essays in different sections.

(1) Conditions of Modernity: Technology, Gender, and the City

The first group of four essays investigates Ford's responses to crucial modern changes in technology, city experience, the perception of intimacy, space, and gender. These essays are placed first because these concerns recur throughout the volume.

Philip Horne's essay argues that the telephone, like other technological developments, 'offers the writer new metaphors for experience, but also alters the experience for which metaphors are to be found'. A survey from some of the earliest written responses to the device to Proust, explores the philosophical and theological implications of telephonic presence and the telephone's transformation of the social meaning of space. This provides a context for a discussion of *A Call* and the opening of *A Man Could Stand Up –*.

Sara Haslam shows how trains loom large in Ford's *oeuvre*, providing scenes, impressions, and sometimes plots for his fiction and memoirs. In particular, Ford uses the train to focus anxieties about the experience of modernity. She relates this thematic presence to the nineteenth century study of trauma associated with train accidents – 'railway spine' and 'railway brain' – demonstrating that Ford's association of railway travel and mental stress is part of a larger turn-of-the-century discourse of degeneration. Against this, Haslam sets Ford's sense of the train as offering opportunities for the writer. Not only does Ford represent his literary 'training' in terms of reading, or collaborating with Conrad, on trains, but, as Haslam's argument shows, railway travel also had an impact on his aesthetics: his impressionism was informed by the experience of train-travel, in particular, the experience of viewing successions of fragmentary and fleeting views.

Giovanni Cianci's essay affirms the importance of Italian Futurism as a context for Ford's formal experiments in the decade leading up to *The Good Soldier*. He shows how, in *The Soul of London* (1905), the discontinuities and fragmentation of modern city life produce a crisis of representation, to which 'impressionism' is Ford's response. Futurist manifestos similarly affirm the link between modernity and urban experience, while Futurist paintings provide a way of representing the multiplicity of urban experience and the revolution in the categories of space and time as a result of trains, trams, and motorcars. Cianci finally considers Futurism as a neglected context for *The Good Soldier*.

In contrast, Robin Peel's essay shows how Ford's engagement with modernity is by no means confined to the urban environment. He considers Ford's brief involvement in a rural Fabian community, which he went on to satirise in *The Simple Life Limited*. Peel argues that the view of Ford as 'urban, cosmopolitan modernist and urbane radical Tory' doesn't do justice to his complex development and neglects his attraction to subversive questions of class and gender. An account of turn of the century 'simple lifers', such as Tolstoy, Morris, Edward Carpenter, and C. R. Asbee, enriches a reading of *The Simple Life Limited*. The discussion closes on a consideration of *Women & Men*, which Ford started writing next, and in which he reflected contemporary sexological debates, as well as anticipating recent critiques of the construction of gender in life and in literature.

(2) *The Good Soldier*: Desire, Text, and History

The next six essays focus on *The Good Soldier*. Davida Pines takes up this issue of gender. Drawing on D. A. Miller's *Narrative and Its Discontents*, she explores the narrative role of marriage in *The Good Soldier*. She shows how, instead of the traditional plot in which marriage means the satisfaction of desire and the end of experience, in *The Good Soldier* marriage enables the proliferation of possible relations and significations. This leads to a reappraisal of the dynamics of the Ashburnham marriage. As Pines demonstrates, even Leonora's 'successful marriage' to Bayham fails to satisfy the traditional marriage plot, since, like other relations in *The Good Soldier*, it fails to find resolution in a couple but rather in a stable triad.

Caroline Patey's essay is also concerned with familial and marital structures, but moves criticism of *The Good Soldier* into the field of post-colonial theory. She explores the imperial resonances of the terms 'heart' and 'darkness', arguing that Ford's language places the novel at the heart of the Edwardian debate on empire and nationality. She further relates the novel's anxiety about sexuality to contemporary discourses of ethnology and argues that the American Dowell's bafflement in the face of English social and familial customs reflects the ethnographer's problems in attempting to represent kinship and cultural practices in other cultures.

Sally Bachner's essay places *The Good Soldier* within the detective tradition of Conan Doyle to show how it addresses an epistemological crisis, figured as the inaccessibility of the human heart, and finds a solution in identification. Bachner shows how, in opposition to Freud, *The Good Soldier* operates on a model in which identification is inseparable from desire. From this basis she explores Ford's impressionism as a theory of perception, cognition and response.

Roger Poole's essay is also concerned with detection. He offers a radical re-reading of *The Good Soldier* as potentially a detective story, through a re-interpretation of Dowell's character and the nature of his unreliable narration. Poole argues that Ford means us to notice Dowell's inconsistencies and that he is using and abusing the modalities of *vraisemblance* in order to parody and subvert the Jamesian novel. Drawing on the model of James's *The Golden Bowl*, Poole argues for the possibility of a criminal Dowell who has conspired with Leonora to obtain Florence's money and Ashburnham's estate. Through this strategy of 'radical doubt', the essay confronts Frank Kermode's assertion of 'the illusion of the single right reading'.

Martin Stannard's essay also considers the problem of 'errors' in a text with an unreliable narrator. In particular, he addresses the interpretative problems posed by Ford's insistence on the date 4 August in relation to the events of *The Good Soldier*. He draws upon his experience of editing the Norton Critical Edition and shows how this novel challenges conventional theories of the copy-text.

Bernard Bergonzi develops his reading of Stannard's edition to discuss *The Good Soldier* as a war-novel. He places it in a European context, showing how, like Mann's *The Magic Mountain* and Musil's *The Man Without Qualities*, *The Good Soldier* can be read as representing a world about to be swept away by World War I. It is an account of the novel suggesting its continuities with *Parade's End*.

(3) Ford, the War and the post-War: Englishness, Society, History
The third group contains three essays offering fresh perspectives on Ford's responses to the First World War and to the social and historical change produced by the war and its after-effects. In the first of a pair of essays focusing on *Parade's End*, Dennis Brown reads Ford's tetralogy against two contexts: the recent critical explorations of the idea of 'Englishness' and psycho-analytic concepts of 'containment', group leadership, and masculinity. Brown places *Parade's End* in the long sequence of writings questioning Englishness, foregrounding Ford's subjection of its representative, Christopher Tietjens, to strains which take his sanity and masculinity near breaking-point. It is a reading which brings out the parallels between *Parade's End* and recent fiction such as Kazuo Ishiguro's *The Remains of the Day* and Pat Barker's *Ghost Road* trilogy.

In the second essay on *Parade's End*, Robert L. Caserio starts from Lionel Trilling's argument that modern literature pursues 'the bitter line of hostility to civilization' to explore the paradoxical modernity of Ford's great war fiction, arguing that the tetralogy upholds the ideal of the civilized state as the guarantor of public virtue. Through comparison with Kipling's post-war story, 'The Church That Was At Antioch', Caserio argues for a line in modernism able to imagine public virtue without succumbing to authoritarianism.

Cornelia Cook's essay concentrates on Ford's first sustained response to the aftermath of the war: *No Enemy*. Ford called this complex work a 'Reconstructionary Tale'. Cook demonstrates how the war reminiscence calls attention to itself as a literary construction and to a range of constructions and reconstructions – of memory, history, political programmes, propaganda, even military engineering – which shape the experience of its central figure, the poet 'Gringoire'. *No Enemy* implicitly sets the post-war political agenda of Reconstruction in a context where the needs and desires of society and the individual call forth continuing activities of reconstruction including those of the artist.

(4) Ford and Modern Writing: Biography, Intertextuality, and Style

The final group consists of six comparativist studies of Ford in relation to other writers: partners, friends, influences, contemporaries.

In the first of a pair of essays treating of Ford's literary relationship with his significant others, Joseph Wiesenfarth considers the intertextual hostilities between Ford and Violet Hunt. Hunt's memoir of their relationship, *The Flurried Years*, has been quarried by biographers as source-material. It is also well-recognised that both Florence Dowell and Sylvia Tietjens are at least in part based upon Hunt. Wiesenfarth's study instead reads their work in terms of a sustained exchange between Ford and Hunt. Thus *The Flurried Years* and Hunt's novel *The House of Many Mirrors* are read as her literary revenge upon Ford for his faithlessness, while nonetheless demonstrating Ford's influence as writer and critic. Wiesenfarth is also able to show how Ford's memoirs, though they don't mention Hunt, nonetheless respond to her portrayal of him.

INTRODUCTION

Ros Pesman's essay re-appraises *Drawn from Life,* the memoir by Stella Bowen, Ford's companion from 1919-1929. Pesman explores Bowen's motives for writing her autobiography, which is also a biography of Ford from the end of the war to his death. The essay offers a valuable re-appraisal of a work too many biographers have simply taken at face value. Pesman shows how Bowen 'mythologised' Ford and her relationship with him and, in particular, the painful process of separation.

Elena Lamberti considers Ford's relationship with one of his protégés from this period, Ernest Hemingway. She offers a meditation on the fraught relationship between the two writers when Ford took on the young Hemingway as an assistant editor for his *transatlantic review.* Moving between biography, allegory, and comparative criticism, Lamberti uses the encounter to focus a series of contrasts: between age and youth; between the pre-war modernists and the 'Lost Generation'; between British and American; between two styles, fabulation and reportage; and between the views of life presented by each writer. In particular Ford's combination of historical nostalgia and optimism that society can be reconstructed is contrasted with what Calvino describes as Hemingway's 'existential vacuity'.

Comparative studies of Ford have tended to focus on his relations with American writers (James, Crane, Pound) or the influence of Flaubert and Turgenev. But the next two essays open up new comparative territory. W. B. Hutchings' essay explores Ford's engagement with another major writer, one of his main 'precursors', Guy de Maupassant. Ford often cited Maupassant as an example of a true novelist. But this is the first sustained investigation of Maupassant's impact on his work. Hutchings argues that Ford's notion of literary impressionism derives from Maupassant's quest for objective presentation of concrete facts that convey states of mind. The essay then uses a range of texts to compare the two writers' 'sense of place as a visual experience'. The second half concentrates on Maupassant and *The Good Soldier* and, in particular, on the detailed echoes of the novel of another quasi-incestuous passion Ford said he had in mind, *Fort comme la mort*.

Vita Fortunati's essay is another pioneering comparison of *The Good Soldier* – and *Heart of Darkness* – with Luigi Pirandello's *Quaderni di Serafino Gubbio operatore* and Italo Svevo's *La coscienza di Zeno*. The essay establishes a shared *zeitgeist* in these fictions of the turn of the century and focuses on the use of unreliable narrators as a response to an epistemological crisis. All four authors tell stories of alienation, using fragmented time-schemes and multiple viewpoints to disturb and challenge our sense of reality. They develop a new form of the novel and a poetics of cognitive relativism, which produces, in short, the end of the naturalistic novel.

In the concluding essay, Paul Skinner considers Ford's style, contrasting it with that of other, obscurer modernists. He examines Ford's writing in relation to his dictum that style should be 'unnoticeable' and argues that his success in 'keying [his] prose down' has often worked against his reputation. His style doesn't announce its own virtuosity and complexity; nor does it progress by allusion and obscurity. His books don't require the 'reader's guides' or 'companions', the annotation-industries devoted to Joyce, Pound, and Eliot. Paradoxically, this 'readerly writer' has not been as widely read as the other major modernists precisely because his works don't require exegesis.

This collection, then, reflects many of the developments in literary studies since the 1970s. It is perhaps appropriate to indicate here, by way of conclusion, other configurations that the editorial arrangement of the essays might otherwise obscure. There is obviously a thread of analyses of gender trouble that can be traced through the essays by Peel, Pines, Bachner, Brown, and Wiesenfarth. A psycho-analytic thread could be traced through those by Haslam, Peel, Pines, Bachner, and Brown. And Skinner shows Ford negotiating, in the very texture of his writing, that most modernist dialectic of consciousness and the unconscious. The collection also inaugurates some new approaches to

Ford, notably an ethnological perspective and approaches in terms of detective-fiction theory and the impact of technology. We begin to see what postcolonial Ford criticism might look like in the pieces by Patey, Brown, and Caserio. And Fordian eco-criticism emerges in the essays by Cook, Patey, Peel, and Skinner.[8] Finally, the volume also advances other key areas of Ford criticism, such as the study of his aesthetics (Bachner, Cianci, Horne, Poole, Skinner); studies of his engagement with public debates and values (Brown, Caserio, Cook, Patey, Peel); and comparative studies.

Most of the present essays are comparative to some extent. New readings are offered of Ford's relationships with other writers such as Conrad, Hemingway, Violet Hunt, and Stella Bowen, but there is also work on some unusual suspects: Maupassant, Kipling, Conan Doyle, Proust, Pirandello, Mann, Svevo, Italian Futurists, Musil, Ishiguro, and Pat Barker. The comparativist work here combines British, American and European criticism of Ford, and shows him a presence in all three traditions. He emerges as a writer of international stature, worthy of comparison with other major figures.

The critical consensus – that Ford's best-known works are his best – is strengthened by the invigorating new criticism of *The Good Soldier* and *Parade's End* here. Poole and Skinner make new cases for Ford's conscious craftsmanship, countering the charge (explored once more here, by Stannard) of authorial insouciance. But the collection also gives ground-breaking attention to the fascinations of some of his less well-known books – though perhaps those which could be seen as most closely allied to his masterpieces: works such as *The Soul of London, A Call, The Simple Life Limited,* and *No Enemy.*

What, finally, comes across in all these essays is the breadth and alertness of Ford's intelligence, as demonstrated in his extraordinary receptivity to complexities and nuances of the discourses of technology, social change, and the human sciences; in short, to the experience of modernity.

NOTES

1. Paul de Man, *Blindness and Insight: Essays in the Rhetoric of Contemporary Criticism*, second edition (London: Methuen, 1983), pp. 150-1.

2. Ford Madox Ford, *It Was the Nightingale* (London: Heinemann, 1934), p. 180.

3. 'The Critical Attitude: On the Objection to the Critical Attitude', *English Review*, 4 (February 1910), 531-42; reprinted in *The Critical Attitude* (London: Duckworth, 1911), pp.8-9.

4. See D. D. Harvey, *Ford Madox Ford [. . .]A Bibliography of Works and Criticism* (Princeton: Princeton University Press, 1962); and Max Saunders, 'Ford Madox Ford: Further Bibliographies', *English Literature in Transition*, 43:2 (2000), 131-205.

5. Two other fine papers given at the conference have been published elsewhere. Eugene Goodheart, 'The Art of Ambivalence: *The Good Soldier*', *Sewanee Review*, 106 (1998), 619-29; and Trudi Tate, 'Rumour, Propaganda, and *Parade's End*', *Essays in Criticism*, 47:4 (October 1997), 332-53; revised into pp. 50-62 of Tate, *Modernism, History and the First World War* (Manchester: Manchester University Press, 1998).

6. *Edwardian Fiction*, ed. Sandra Kemp, Charlotte Mitchell, and David Trotter (Oxford: Oxford University Press, 1997). Christopher Butler, *Early Modernism* (Oxford: Clarendon Press, 1994). Peter Nicholls, *Modernisms* (Basingstoke: Macmillan, 1995). Lawrence Rainey, *Institutions of Modernism* (New Haven: Yale University Press, 1998). David Ayers, *English Literature in the 1920s* (Edinburgh University Press, 1999).

7. Malcolm Bradbury, 'A Good Soldier on Parade', *Guardian* (26 January 1996), *Friday Review*, 14.

8. See also the following essays in *Antæus* no. 56 (Spring 1986): Samuel Hynes, 'The Genre of *No Enemy*', 125-42; Elissa Greenwald, '*No Enemy*: Ford's "Reconstructionary War"', 143-56; Edward Krickel, 'Notes upon Sheepfolds: Ford's Agricultural Testament', 157-78; Kingsley Widmer, 'From Great War to Little Garden: Ford's Ford', 179-90. Also see Jonathan Bate, 'Arcadia and Armageddon: Three English Novelists and the First World War', *Études Anglaises*, 39:2 (April-June 1986), 150-62; and two essays from *Agenda*, 27:4-28:1 (Winter 1989-Spring 1990): Cornelia Cook, '*Last Post*: "The Last of the Tietjens Series"', 23-30; and Paul Skinner, 'Just Ford – An Appreciation of *No Enemy: A Tale of Reconstruction*', 103-9.

I

CONDITIONS OF MODERNITY:
TECHNOLOGY, GENDER,
AND THE CITY

ABSENT-MINDEDNESS: FORD ON THE PHONE[1]

Philip Horne

Alexander Graham Bell, the educator of the deaf, to whom it was of no direct use, invented the telephone in Boston in 1875. Herbert Casson, an American historian of the telephone writing in 1910, seems to have been not sufficiently thinking of Bell's other line of work when he wrote that 'The disadvantage of being deaf and dumb to all absent persons, which was universal in pre-telephonic days, has now happily been overcome'.[2]   Bell demonstrated the 'Electrical Speaking Telephone' to the public for the first time at the Centennial Exhibition in Philadelphia in 1876. The Transcendentalist poet and preacher Jones Very, not operating at his former visionary intensity, was moved to record it on 23 February 1877 as

> The marvel of our age, the Telephone!
> What is the Telephone, do you inquire?
> The marvel of our time, before unknown,
> The human voice speaks through the electric wire!
> The distant city hears the spoken word,
> In waves of sound, transmitted o'er the line...[3]

It was only eight days after this first literary rendering that any public mention of the new invention was made in Britain, in the *Athenaeum*; and although the London *Times* was converted later in the year – 'Suddenly and quietly the whole human race is brought within speaking and hearing distance. Scarcely anything was more desired and more impossible'[4] – Britain strikingly lagged behind America for decades in introducing and extending telephone systems. The American historian I have cited declares – in 1910, the year of Ford's novel *A Call* – that 'From first to last, the story of the telephone in Great Britain has been a "comedy of errors"'[5]. Haunting the

extraordinary technological developments of the Electrical Speaking
Telephone, and the high public rhetoric about it as 'the marvel of our
age', there has indeed been from the first, a spectre of error and
confusion, not all of it comic.

Another progressivist American poet, Christopher Pearse Cranch,
also a painter and Unitarian clergyman and an acquaintance of
Browning, made in 1887 rather more imaginative headway in his
grand, suggestive claims for the new lines:

> Fleeter than Time, across the Continent,
> Through unsunned ocean depths, from beach to beach,
> Around the rolling globe Thought's couriers reach.
> The new-tuned earth like some vast instrument
> Tingles from zone to zone; for Art has lent
> New nerves, new pulse, new motion – all to each
> And each to all, in swift electric speech
> Bound by a force unwearied and unspent. . . [6]

Cranch in his mystical optimism imagines the whole world as
transformed and retuned, made an 'instrument', by being strung with
sounding wires – and perhaps as eroticised ('Tingles from zone to
zone'). The empire covering the earth in this vision is that of
capitalised – and maybe 'capitalised' should be a pun – 'Thought'.
This sonnet, 'The Telegraph and Telephone', ends sweepingly: 'And
Time and Space are naught. The mind is all'. The new medium of the
telephone is seen here then as offering a kind of immediacy,
establishing the primacy of the mind over the physical laws of bodily
existence. Technology has become instrumental to intellect.

However, even within this salute to the new possibilities of global
communication there lurks a darker suggestion, of telephonic
connection as a doom:

all to each
And each to all, in swift electric speech
Bound by a force unwearied and unspent.

This promiscuous binding together can sound hellish; and why is electricity described as '*un*wearied and *un*spent' if someone isn't liable to be 'wearied and spent' in the process? The effort imaginatively to accommodate the telephone took some strange forms. To an English Protestant, William Coldbrook, in 1891, the new institution heralded the last days: he wrote an ingenious pamphlet, *The Invention of the Telephone / Predicted by St. John in the Book of Revelation*, identifying the telephone with the sixth angel's sixth plague in Chapter 16, the 'unclean spirits, as it were frogs', which come out of the mouth of the dragon and the beast and the false prophet to gather the kings of the earth to the battle of Armageddon. Coldbrook foresees, in the build-up of military technology and the accelerated communications of the time, the conditions for a great war, which he says will happen in the Middle East. He makes a special point of '*as it were* frogs' – the frog symbolises only the mode of transmission of the summons to war, he says, and is *not* 'a symbolical representation of the spirits; for no Jew or Christian, and it must be assumed that St. John was either, would liken an infernal spirit to one of the most harmless and timid creatures in creation'.[7] And he notes, 'It is a remarkable fact that the same animal which symbolised the transmission of the summons to war in the vision was equally effective in directing the attention of Galvani to the action of the electric current, under circumstances more providential than accidental.'[8]

The telephone's purported abolition of 'Time and Space' in Cranch's poem 'The Seven Wonders of the World', which has rather an apocalyptic sound, is only of course a half-measure; everyone physically remains where he or she is; but in a telephonic exchange the persons speaking to each other are imaginatively in two places at once, their selves divided in a way which disturbs previous conceptions of *presence*. Where, really, *is* a person speaking on the telephone?

The question troubled religious thinkers at the other end of the spectrum from the Protestant Coldbrook. On the way to Ford we may pause again to consider another pamphlet, from 1887, this one called *La Confession par Téléphone, ou, si, dans un cas extrême, un prêtre pourrait confesser & absoudre validement par le téléphone un absent* by le Père Abbé Eschbach de la Congrégation du Saint-Esprit et du Saint Coeur de Marie, Docteur en Théologie, Supérieure du Séminaire Français de Rome ('Confession over the Telephone, or, whether, in an extreme case, a priest could validly confess and absolve an absent person by telephone'). Eschbach is following up Berardi, the learned priest of Faenza, in his *Praxis Confessariorum*, whose Latin he quotes: 'Curiosa fit quaestio,... an absolutio data ope telephonii (ita ut sacerdos per instrumentum istud suam vocem pertingere faciat usque ad aures poenitentis) valida sit?'[9] ('It is a curious question whether absolution given by means of the telephone [provided the priest makes his voice reach the ears of the penitent through that instrument] be valid?')

Berardi thinks it may be valid, Eschbach disagrees. There is an unavoidably Shandean, seemingly disproportionate solemnity to Eschbach's proceedings in this tract, which is larded with further Latin and copious authorities – a 1602 decree by Pope Clement VIII against absolution through letters becomes central – and which takes a severe line with the liberals he is refuting. The theological issue, however, is a serious one. The matter of *presence* here is crucial, as it will determine the saving or not of souls. 'Inter absentes non potest dari absolutio pro peccatis'[10] ('Absolution for sins cannot be given between absent persons'): we must be sure about the case of our 'prêtre' and our 'mourant'. Even if,

Dans un instant, le fil téléphonique va recevoir et transmettre de l'un à l'autre, avec la rapidité de l'éclair, leurs moindres paroles; créera-t-il aussi entre eux la présence spécifiquement exigée pour l'administration du sacrement de pénitence?

In an instant, the telephone wire will receive and transmit from one person to another, with the speed of lightning, their smallest utterances; will it also create between them the presence specifically demanded for the administration of the sacrament of penitence?[11]

Eschbach's answer is no. For sacramental purposes a telephone connection does not constitute a real presence.

Marcel Proust appears at first to be on a different line in *Le côté de Guermantes* (1920-21), where his narrator Marcel, waiting for a call from his grandmother, is eloquent about

l'admirable féerie à laquelle quelques instants suffisent pour qu'apparaisse près de nous, invisible mais présent, l'être à qui nous voulions parler et qui, restant à sa table, dans la ville qu'il habite (pour ma grand'mère c'était Paris), sous un ciel différent du nôtre, par un temps qui n'est pas forcément le même, au milieu de circonstances et de préoccupations que nous ignorons et que cet être va nous dire, se trouve tout à coup transporté à des centaines de lieues (lui et toute l'ambiance où il reste plongé) près de notre oreille, au moment où notre caprice l'a ordonné.

the wonderful sorcery by which a few moments are enough to cause the appearance beside us, invisible but present, of the being to whom we wish to speak and who, without leaving his own table, in the town where he lives (for my grandmother it was Paris), under a sky different from ours, in weather which is not necessarily the same, amid circumstances and preoccupations of which we know nothing and of which this being will tell us, finds himself suddenly transported to hundreds of leagues away (he and all the atmosphere in which he remains fixed) – just next to our ear, at the moment decreed by our whim.[12]

'Invisible but present' *seems* to assert that not all the senses need be satisfied for presence to occur (a question discussed by Eschbach). The double location of telephone speakers, their simultaneous partaking in two sets of circumstances, two realities, leads Marcel to treat the telephone as an 'admirable féerie', a wonderful sorcery (not the sort of image that would appeal to the clerical Catholic stickler, Eschbach); and the next moment Marcel compares the 'miracle' of the telephone to the magical conjurings-up of fairytale sorceresses. So far so marvellous, perhaps.

But, for Proust, the relation between people, between subject and loved object, is a kind of sacrament, and he goes on to tease out, like Eschbach, some of the philosophical and theological ramifications of the telephonic situation. Does the telephone create in *Proust*'s terms the 'presence specifically demanded'? The sensitive Marcel too, soon after this, dramatising the successful connection of a 'phone call, presses the point and finds something unsatisfactory, a source of exquisite pathos, in the quality of the experience:

> Et aussitôt que notre appel a retenti, dans la nuit pleine d'apparitions sur laquelle nos oreilles s'ouvrent seules, un bruit léger – un bruit abstrait – celui de la distance supprimée – et la voix de l'être cher s'adresse à nous.
>
> C'est lui, c'est sa voix qui nous parle, qui est là. Mais comme elle est loin! Que de fois je n'ai pu l'écouter sans angoisse, comme si devant cette impossibilité de voir, avant de longues heures de voyage, celle dont la voix était si près de mon oreille, je sentais mieux ce qu'il y a de décevant dans l'apparence du rapprochement le plus doux, et à quelle distance nous pouvons être des personnes aimées au moment où il semble que nous n'aurions qu'à étendre la main pour les retenir. Présence réelle que cette voix si proche – dans la séparation effective! Mais anticipation aussi d'une séparation éternelle!

And as soon as our call has rung out, in the darkness full of apparitions to which our ears alone are open, a faint noise – an abstract noise – the noise of distance being suppressed – and the voice of the dear one is addressing itself to us.

It is she, it is her voice which is speaking, which is there. But how far away it is! How many times I have been unable to listen to it without anguish, as if, confronting the impossibility of seeing, without long hours of travel, her whose voice was so close to my ear, I felt more acutely the deceptiveness of the appearance of the tenderest proximity, felt more at what a distance we may be from our loved ones at the very moment when it seems we only have to stretch out our hand to keep them by us. A real presence, that voice so close to us – but in actual separation! An anticipation too of an eternal separation!

Distance is suppressed – 'Time and Space are naught', or anyhow seem naught – and the other person's voice is *there*; '*But* how far away it is!' What we hear is in fact only a reproduction; the real voice stays where it is. Distance seems abolished but remains in place. The sacramental is explicitly invoked: 'Présence réelle que cette voix si proche', 'A real presence, that voice so close to us'. The theological doctrine of the Real Presence maintains the actual redeeming presence of Christ's body and blood in the sacrament, against those who regard them as present only symbolically or figuratively; the presence is 'real' in spirit, even while the physical attributes of bread and wine are unchanged. On the secular front, between mortals, however, 'actual separation' is more painful, anticipating 'eternal separation'. Marcel goes on to recount his frequent sense when speaking to his grandmother on the 'phone that 'cette voix clamait des profondeurs d'où l'on ne remonte pas', 'that voice was calling from the depths out of which one does not rise again'; and that, in its inaccessibility to his baffled longing, the voice is a ghost: 'J'aurais voulu l'embrasser; mais je n'avais près de moi que cette voix, fantôme aussi impalpable que celui qui reviendrait peut-être me visiter quand ma grand'mère serait morte'. ('I would have tried to embrace her; but all I had next to me was that voice, as impalpable a phantom as the one which would perhaps return to visit me when my grandmother was dead.') The other speaker on the telephone can be already like a memory, half real and half unreal. And thus when we ourselves speak on the telephone we may forfeit some of our own grasp on identity.

The telephone, then, casts reality into doubt; it offers in the present something analogous to what memory offers from the past: a vivid intangibility, a paradoxical half-reality. Even before Proust, Ford Madox Ford, quirky Catholic convert and diagnostician of modernities, seems alive to this dimension of the 'phone. In *A Call*, which has a claim to be the first serious telephone novel, Ford has his hero plagued by 'the unreal sounds of voices on the telephone'.[13] And when Tietjens, in *Some Do Not . . .* (1924), remembers words he has spoken in the past, 'His voice – his own voice – came to him as if from the other end of a long-distance telephone. A damn long-distance one! Ten years...'.[14] Ford is also alive to the telephone's potential for psychological disturbance and intimate intrusion, for its literal invocation of unwanted presences (a kind of witchcraft).

A Call was subtitled 'A Tale of a Passion' in the *English Review* of 1909 and 'A Tale of Two Passions' in the Chatto and Windus book of February 1910. Later that year, Virginia Woolf was to say, notoriously, 'human character changed'. Ford's 'Epistolary Epilogue' spells out what he meant by calling the novel *A Call*:

> what I meant was that Mr Robert Grimshaw, putting the earpiece to
> his ear and the mouthpiece to his mouth, exclaimed, after the decent
> interval that so late at night the gentleman in charge of the exchange
> needs for awaking from slumber and grunting something intelligible
> – Mr Grimshaw exclaimed 'Give me 4259 Mayfair'. (*Call* 163)

Robert Grimshaw is the novel's brilliant, confused, 'meddling fool at the other end of the telephone' (*Call* 104), a half-Greek English gentleman or part-'dago' as he calls himself. He is, at least early on, in love with his strong, passionate cousin Katya Lascarides but has quarreled with her, and she has gone to America to work as a psychotherapist. He has subsequently fallen in love with another woman, the gentler, saintly Pauline Lucas, but the novel starts with Grimshaw – talking much about the requirements of civilisation and to save himself from betraying what he takes to be his duty to Katya – deliberately and sacrificially marrying off this new love Pauline to his large, rather dim, malleable, incongruously hypochondriacal English best friend Dudley Leicester (who 'had been Robert Grimshaw's fag at school' [*Call* 19]). 'I suppose what I really want,' says Grimshaw, 'is both Katya and Pauline' (*Call* 23). Max Saunders notes, on this two-passion theme, that such a 'pattern, of feeling bound to one woman and infatuated with another was one [Ford] re-enacted through his life'.[15] The telephonic connection, then, may be that Grimshaw, with his 'two passions', could be described as wanting to be in two places at once, as over-extending himself.

Grimshaw's sacrificial scheme goes predictably wrong. Pauline Lucas and Dudley Leicester marry each other with decent intentions, but for Grimshaw's sake. The self-deceiving Grimshaw is plagued with guilt and can't stop pining for Pauline. When he happens to see Dudley Leicester in the street one night apparently escorting home, apparently with adulterous intentions, the notorious Lady Etta Hudson, an old flame of Dudley Leicester's, he is maddened. He goes home to bed, but under the strain of passionate emotion his civilised repressions fall away, and he can't sleep for wondering what is happening at Lady Etta's. (Strikingly, 'the thought of Pauline Leicester made his hands toss beneath the sheets' [*Call* 154].) At Grimshaw's bedside

> the telephone instrument, like a gleaming metal flower, with its
> nickel corolla and black bell, shone with reflected light [. . . .]
> suddenly his whole body stirred in bed. The whites of his eyes
> gleamed below the dark irises, his white teeth showed, and as he

clasped the instrument to him he appeared, as it were, a Shylock who clutched to his breast his knife and demanded of the universe his right to the peace of mind that knowledge at least was to give him. (*Call* 155)

This extraordinary passage associates the sexual stirrings of the bedroom and their imaginative projection into the world with the connective power of the telephone network; the telephone itself becomes a weapon, a knife, with the Greek 'dago' becoming a vindictive Shylock, a Jew, in the overheated account rendered by the narrative voice.

Meanwhile the dim, confused Dudley Leicester has been drawn into Etta Hudson's hall in a daze, very possibly with no adulterous intent:

And suddenly, in the thick darkness, whirring as if it were a scream, intermitted for a moment and again commencing, a little bell rang out at Dudley Leicester's elbow.

Etta Hudson laughs down at him: 'Tell whoever it is ... that Sir William is in Paris and Lady Hudson in bed. Say "sir" when you speak, and they'll think it's the second footman, Moddle!'

Dudley Leicester put the receiver to his ear. A peremptory 'Are you 4259 Mayfair?' made him suddenly afraid, as if a schoolmaster had detected him in some crime. (*Call* 47)

He answers, as Etta Hudson has said, with a 'sir':

Then suddenly – still low, distinct, stealthy, and clear – the voice of the invisible man asked: 'Isn't that Dudley Leicester speaking?'
He answered 'Yes', and then with a sudden panic he hung the receiver upon the hook. (*Call* 48)

Grimshaw has assumed that Dudley Leicester will recognise his voice, but in fact his victim 'was too stupid, and the tinny sound of the instrument had destroyed the resemblance of any human voice' (*Call* 155). The telephone call throws Dudley Leicester into what Ford calls 'a world of dread' (*Call* 50), and he becomes obsessed – rather beyond credibility – with the emotional damage the putative blackmailer may do Pauline by revealing his compromising presence at Etta Hudson's. He starts rushing up to grab strangers and demand with menaces, 'Are you the chap who rang up 4259 Mayfair?' (*Call* 80). Then he becomes completely silent, 'his eyes gazing upon nothing' (*Call* 83). On the other side, watching this process becomes a torment to Robert Grimshaw, once he discovers from Etta Hudson that she and Dudley Leicester *weren't* having an affair.

A Call is not a successful work. Ford's plotting problems are serious, only partly because of the difficulties of expanding what had originally been a short story. I have recounted the story's events in chronological order; Ford's narration does not tell us till near the end that Robert Grimshaw was the caller who has driven Dudley Leicester mad, though we might guess. Whether we guess or not, the whodunnit suspense to which Ford commits himself forestalls any close notation of Grimshaw's consciousness – the regular handicap of whodunnits – and he is described mostly from the outside (turning 'ashy pale' and so on). Dudley Leicester is a vivid caricature of stupid English decency in the first part of the book; when he stops speaking, he becomes a dummy in the corner. The whole Katya aspect of the plotting is strained (her motives are contrived and perverse). The decisions Ford makes about the handling of point of view, in other words, and his elaborately ingenious striving for surprises, cumulatively damage the credibility of the characterisation in general. Arnold Bennett in his Journals saw *A Call* as 'slick work', but felt Ford 'doesn't get down to the real stuff', and, reviewing it in the *New Age,* declared it 'profoundly and hopelessly untrue to life'.[16] Bennett ends his review, though, by saying, 'But regard *A Call* as an original kind of fairy-tale, and it is about perfect'.[17]

Bennett's comment may prompt us to recall Proust's description of the telephonic apparatus as 'féerie', as sorcery, and to see the brilliance of Ford's tragic, grotesque, farcical main idea, the idea of Dudley Leicester's paralysed horror at having his voice recognised, as by a wizard, when he is in the wrong place. In fact, by speaking into the telephone, through this modern magic, Dudley Leicester is plunged into a state of speechlessness, of drastic absent-mindedness, which destroys his sanity. The telephone's division of presence – its extensions of agency and transformation of the social meanings of space, so to speak, its creation of new forms of power and surveillance – is potently expressed in Robert Grimshaw's meddling, quasi-authorial intervention here and Dudley Leicester's prostration under it.

The situation and the incident here are not only tragic but also farcical, farce being a genre peculiarly concerned with comic division and presence, the ironies of a person's physical location as registers of double or multiple commitment. With its sensory deprivation – apart from the aural – the faceless telephone can foster the uncertainties and kinds of misunderstanding about identities and situations which are the stuff of farce. In April 1878, a year after the telephone was heard of in Britain, we already have *The Telephone: a Farce in One Act* by Arthur Clements, a dismally incoherent knockabout in which a scientist-telephonist-villain's scheme is thwarted by crossed wires (he proposes to the wrong woman).

The French order these things better, and *Le Téléphone: vaudeville en un acte* in 1882, by the seasoned *farceurs* Hippolyte Raymond and Paul Burani, is a polished adaptation of the new technology to a classic French format: the telephone is 'une invention superbe . . . pour les cocottes'[18] ('a superb invention for tarts'). The Raymond-Burani intrigue is that the enterprising heroine makes separate rendez-vous by 'phone with her old rich lover and her young poor one, who are in the same building, but the operator puts her through to them in the wrong order. Such farcical misconnection occurs even in Proust, after the scene quoted above, when Marcel is summoned back to the telephone office from his hotel to take a call from his grandmother:

> "C'est toi, grand'mère?" Une voix de femme avec un fort accent anglais me répondit: "Oui, mais je ne reconnais pas votre voix." (*Call* 165)

> 'Is that you, grandmother?' A woman's voice with a strong English accent replied, 'Yes, but I don't recognise your voice'.

The joke is *non*-recognition: 'Yes, but ...'. The comic but disturbing contradiction turns out to arise from a 'simple coincidence': the Englishwoman's grandson has a name almost identical to Marcel's and lives in an annexe of the hotel. Marcel is psychologically primed for this upset because he has been in anguish at his unwonted separation from his grandmother.

Separation-anxiety, a state which the telephone feeds but cannot satisfy, is peculiarly intense and widespread in modern war. It is not only in the mind of the apocalyptist William Coldbrook that the telephone is connected to the cataclysm of a globe-spanning conflict. Max Saunders, who calls Ford 'the novelist of spatial dualities, one of whose great subjects was how the mind is usually somewhere quite other' (Saunders vol. 2, 201), cites 'A Day of Battle', a 1916 essay written in the Ypres Salient, on the displaced soldier's displaced anxiety, not fears about the danger of imminent death but home thoughts about things back in England:

> he is indeed *homo duplex*: a poor fellow whose body is tied in one place, but whose mind and personality brood eternally over another distant locality. (Saunders vol. 2, 197)

The soldier is thus long-distance man: a formula which could nicely define the brooding Robert Grimshaw or the shattered Dudley Leicester. Saunders regards this essay as a key document in the genesis of *Parade's End*, and for my purpose it helps to put our concern with telephonic dislocation through from the pre-War world to the post-War, from *A Call* to *Parade's End*, the work in which Ford's characteristic modes and preoccupations find subject-matter offering their fullest public correlatives.

In the bravura kaleidoscopic opening chapters of *A Man Could Stand Up* – (1926), the third of the tetralogy, the tumultuous celebrations of the Armistice find Valentine Wannop a gym teacher in a London suburb. The novel begins – and, as V. S. Pritchett says, Ford is 'best at beginnings'[19] –

> Slowly, amidst intolerable noises from, on the one hand the street and, on the other, from the large and voluminously echoing playground, the depths of the telephone began, for Valentine, to assume an aspect that, years ago it used to have – of being a part of the supernatural paraphernalia of inscrutable Destiny ... Valentine with the receiver at her ear was plunged immediately into incomprehensible news uttered by a voice that she seemed half to remember. Right in the middle of a sentence it hit her. . . (*PE* 503)

The archness and personification here – and the syntactic elaboration – suggest that Ford has learned since *A Call* from reading Proust, whom he had thought of translating ('depths' echoes Proust's 'profondeurs'). What is peculiarly Fordian is the stunning, invasive impact of the call, the modern state of shock it produces; the fragmentation of the sentence and its consequent incomprehensibility; the psychological confusion of the *half*-remembered voice – which speaks of a 'he' that Valentine cannot at first identify. Diverse realities, their sounds and fractured voices, dazzlingly overlap and collide in the rendering of her consciousness: Valentine is distracted by noises in playground and street, while 'The ... voice in the telephone ... came as if from caverns' (*PE* 504). The 'wicked telephone' (*PE* 505) has made her miss the actual Armistice signal, has deflected her from inhabiting her own rightful place in history. The manipulative voice turns out to be that of the slimy Edith Ethel Duchemin, now Lady Macmaster. Ford renders the strands of Valentine's experience through virtuoso multi-tracking:

> The hissing, bitter voice from the telephone enunciated the one address she did not want to hear:
> 'Lincolns.s.s . . . Inn!'
> Sin! . . . Like the Devil!
> It hurt.
> The cruel voice said:
> 'I'm s.s.peaking from there!'
> Valentine said courageously:
> 'Well; it's a great day. I suppose you're bothered by the cheering like me. I can't hear what you want. I don't care. Let 'em cheer!'
> She felt like that. She should not have. (*PE* 507)

Pritchett says that much of Ford's art is based on 'an analysis of talk, the way it plunges and works back and forth',[20] and this passage breaks for jagged paragraphs between narrator's third-person point-of-view narration, Edith Ethel's remote, hissing, telephonic speech, Valentine's replies, and Valentine's internal monologue. The telephone, with its peremptory demands of attitude and emotion, becomes a potent emblem of *homo duplex*.

In such a thorough-going rendering of telephonic consciousness, with the whole thing there, we might say 'The mind is all' – but without the cheerfulness of Christopher Cranch. Valentine is pinned and wriggling at the end of the line, in a traumatic, farcical perversion of 'all to each / And each to all, in swift electric speech / Bound'... Indeed, in due course, her horrified passivity evokes a surreal image, worthy of *Nightmare on Elm Street,* for Edith Ethel's eventual low sexual-financial proposition:

> She was still breathless; the telephone continued to quack. She wished it would stop, but she felt too weak to get up and hang the receiver on its hook. She wished it would stop; it gave her the feeling that a strand of Edith Ethel's hair, say, was penetrating nauseously to her torpedo-grey cloister. Something like that! (*PE* 518)

And it is only after twenty-five pages of looping, complex, embedded narration that Valentine brings Edith Ethel's call to a definitive end, with an act which seems to speak for Ford's own sense of the advantages of being 'deaf and dumb to all absent persons'. *His* motto might be 'Only disconnect':

> She marched straight at the telephone that was by now uttering long, tinny, night-jar's calls and, with one snap, pulled the receiver right off the twisted, green-blue cord. . . . Broke it! With incidental satisfaction. (*PE* 528)

NOTES

1. A different and slightly fuller version of this essay, 'On the Phone: Some Connections', appeared in *Raritan*, Winter 1999 (XVIII: 3). I am grateful to *Raritan* for permission to use it here. I am also grateful to various people for their helpful criticisms and suggestions, including Steve Clark, Judith Hawley, Danny Karlin, Max Saunders, John Sutherland, Peter Swaab, David Trotter, and Melissa Zeiger.

2. Herbert N. Casson, *The History of the Telephone* (Chicago: A.C. McClurg & Co., 1910), p. v.

3. Jones Very, 'The Telephone', 'c. 23 February 1877', Chadwyck-Healey *American Poetry* database.

4. Cited in *The History of the Telephone*, p. 250.

5. *Ibid.,* p. 255.

6. Christopher Pearse Cranch, *Ariel and Caliban, with other poems*, 'Seven Wonders of the World, XIV. The Telegraph and Telephone' (Boston & New York: Houghton, Mifflin & Co., 1887), p. 145.

7. William Coldbrook, *The Invention of the Telephone Predicted by St. John in the Book of Revelation* (London: John Snow & Co., 1891), p. 10.

8. *Ibid.,* p. 11.

9. *La Confession par Téléphone, ou, si, dans un cas extrême, un prêtre pourrait confesser & absoudre validement par le téléphone un absent* par le P.A. Eschbach de la Congrégation du Saint-Esprit et du Saint Coeur de Marie, Docteur en Théologie, Supérieure du Séminaire Français de Rome (Tournai: Vve. H. Casterman, 1887).

10. *Ibid.,* p. 18.

11. *Ibid.,* p. 17.

12. Marcel Proust, *A la recherche du temps perdu III: Le côté de Guermantes I*, edited by Pierre Clarac & André Ferré (Paris: Gallimard, 1954), p. 159. Max Saunders kindly reminds me of Freud's very germane remarks in *Civilization and Its Discontents* (1930): 'With every tool man is perfecting his own organs, whether motor or sensory, or is removing the limits to their functioning . . . With the help of the telephone he can hear at distances which would be respected as unattainable even in a fairy tale . . . These things do not only sound like a fairy tale, they are an actual fulfilment of every – or of almost every – fairy-tale wish.' (London: The Hogarth Press, 1975), pp. 27-8.

13. Ford Madox Ford, *A Call: A Tale of Two Passions*, with an Afterword by C. H. Sisson (Manchester: Carcanet, 1984), p. 156. Subsequent references are to this edition.

14. Ford Madox Ford, *Parade's End*, with an introduction by Robie Macauley (Harmondsworth: Penguin, 1982), p. 281.

15. Max Saunders, *Ford Madox Ford: A Dual Life*, 2 vols (Oxford: Oxford University Press, 1996), vol. 1, p. 303.

16. *The Journals of Arnold Bennett*, selected and edited by Frank Swinnerton (Harmondsworth: Penguin, 1954), p. 216; Arnold Bennett, review of *A Call*, *The New Age*, reprinted in *Ford Madox Ford: The Critical Heritage*, edited by Frank MacShane (London: Routledge and Keegan Paul, 1972), p. 34.

17. *Ford Madox Ford: The Critical Heritage*, p. 35.

18. Hippolyte Raymond and Paul Burani, *Le Téléphone: vaudeville en un acte* (Paris: Tresse, 1883), p. 9.

19. V.S. Pritchett, 'Fordie', *The Working Novelist* (London: Chatto & Windus, 1965), p. 9.

20. *Ibid.*, p. 11.

FORD'S TRAINING

Sara Haslam

This chapter is called 'Ford's Training' not simply because Ford was fascinated by the transport revolution that surrounded him. He was also fascinated by the impressionist possibilities such matters presented to him in his role as novelist. In addition Ford's apprehension of his literary training is often bound up with images of the train: one oft-repeated memory of his collaborations with Conrad recalls a journey by rail to London. As Conrad, in deep concentration, corrects the proofs of *Romance* Ford interrupts him. He is rewarded by an instinctive spring at his throat.[1] Max Saunders has interpreted the 'scene in the train' as exposing 'Ford's suppressed doubts about what Conrad really thought about him',[2] and, presumably, his writing. More confident in the analysis of his training is an autobiographical passage from *Return to Yesterday* in which he explains his youthful, and continuing, understanding of the reflexive relationship between reading and writing. Ford remembers reading Kipling on a train approaching Winchelsea:

> More plainly than the long curtains of the room in which I am writing I see now the browning bowl of my pipe, the singularly brown grey ashes, the bright placards as the train runs into the old-fashioned station.[3]

With the memory of the train and in the second memory of it as he writes comes the balance and control of older and younger, literally differentiated selves. In the visual image Ford achieves access to an older self: he travels, and joins a train less traumatic than that associated with his collaboration.

Historian Llewllyn Woodward tells us that the 'building of the railways was the greatest physical achievement carried out by the human race within a comparatively short space of time.' He indicates that a work of this kind was likely to touch almost every aspect of the national life, but centres his argument on the way in which the railways broke down what he calls the 'caste system and isolation' of rural England.[4] Ford attends to the sociologically fragmentative effects of the train, believing that with 'the ease of locomotion came the habit of flux'.[5] Such flux related to the relentless succession of new sights from a railway window as much as to where people could now work or send their children to school. This is an important and historically obvious factor, but it does not quite explain the extent and variation of the symbolic power of the train in this period. It is only one of many reasons why the image of the train, in Ford and in many writers, became a totem. The train signified the death-knell to the old world: it was sounded as such with noticeable regularity.

In Francois Truffaut's 'Belle Epoque', set in Paris in 1918, the vision of a train, screaming through the countryside, begins the action. Aboard, the inventor of the moving walk-way hears the attempted murder of a woman by her mentally ill husband. He rescues her and they fall in love. The themes of entrained psychological dysfunction, violence and sex are later joined by that of politics as an anarchist, whose threat to the status quo has been realized in an assassination, is arrested in spectacular style on a train. Trains too appear perfectly 'on time' when there is trauma to be found in Ford's writing. The opening scenes of the Wellsian tale of time-travel, *Ladies Whose Bright Eyes*, depict Sorrell's sense of decorum under attack. He is violently rescued from the social solecisms of an intensely demanding woman – there is an added implication of sexual intimidation – when the train on which they are travelling crashes. The movement of the train has served in Sorrell's mind as a mirror to his growing unease. Describing it provides him with a critical language, explaining his unrest as his ontological security is further assaulted: 'The smooth running of the train had changed into a fantastic, hard jabbing'.[6] Over this he has no control. In Dowell, narrator of *The Good Soldier*, the lack of ability to control the running of trains, and the 'frenzy' into which this drives him, is a thinly disguised parallel to the fact that he can neither understand nor harness twentieth-century sexual demands and existence. This reading is supported by a passage from a turn of the century work, *The Soul of London*, in which the railway is said to 'crash through' the world, 'boring straight ways into the heart of it with a fine contempt for natural obstacles'.[7] Obstacles such as, metaphorically speaking, the ignorance, modesty and fear of Dowell. The following revelation, acute in its resonances, occurs after Leonora's desperate outburst at the secessionist shrine of the tower, where the might of two women, flanked by the armies of Catholicism and Protestantism, has collided. Dowell provides us with his idiosyncratic comparison:

> I have been exceedingly impatient at missing trains. The Belgian state railway has a trick of letting the French trains miss their connections at Brussels. That has always infuriated me. I have written about it letters to *The Times* that *The Times* never printed; those that I wrote to the Paris edition of the *New York Herald* were always printed, but they never seemed to satisfy me when I saw them. Well, that was a sort of frenzy with me.[8]

Satisfaction would be denied. Dowell's slightly paranoid response indicates his impotent and incomplete grasp of the existential fight between the women. His subconscious has translated the boundary between knowledge and ignorance into a language he can understand. He cannot control trains, and this fact provides the language. The modern age, modern knowledge, push on without him, and he is shown as emasculated by this experience.

Ford displays similar irritation at the unpredictability of train services, thus invoking his own feelings of impotence.[9] In *The Marsden Case*, Jessop's disillusionment with the army and its persistent undermining of himself and his battalion comes to a head at Hazebrouck station in February, 1917. He notices a dusty, bedraggled translation of one of his own books at the station bookstall, symptomatic of the fact, he surmises, that 'no human soul ... would ever think of me again'. His train moves out of the station, and it is immediately bombed by the Germans. He loses consciousness, perhaps gratefully. His sense of himself is both epitomized and justified in this definitively situated response to his psychological flailing, for after the 'great crash', opines the later Jessop, 'I have nothing personal to record, and indeed after that I was not much good'.[10] The war-laboured Ford undertook just such a journey in 1917. He stopped at Hazebrouck and spied one of his works. The bombing of his train meant Ford had to wait in the carriage, without doors and windows, for the night. Such lack of control signified by encounters with trains and endless waiting, informs a state of mind. It drove Dowell into a 'frenzy', it made Jessop generally miserable, it helped to rupture Ford's sense of himself.

Freud too was anxious about train travel. He 'confesses' this new addition to his self-analyzed neurotic make-up in a letter to Fleiss in August, 1897. The reason he gives is his position as a parent assailed by 'daily reports of train accidents'.[11] Another reason, I would contend, is revealed in a letter to Fliess six weeks later, at the beginning of October, when Freud is uncovering the awakening of his arousal towards 'matrem'. The occasion for this awakening was a train journey from Leipzig to Vienna, during which, he writes, he and his mother 'spent a night together' and he must have seen her naked or 'nudam'.[12] As this memory was surfacing, though still repressed, Freud discovered 'new' anxieties, bred of Martha's excitement at the coming August holiday.

The work of a nineteenth-century surgeon provides a more widely applicable analysis of this phenomenon of anxiety about train travel. John Erichsen is the doctor most commonly associated with the terms 'railway-spine' and 'railway brain' – used to describe nervous disorders incurred nominally, though not exclusively, as a result of train crashes. He relates his interest firstly to the increase in railway traffic, and accordingly to the increase of such injuries of the nervous system, but, perhaps more significantly, also to the 'insidious character of the early symptoms'. *On Railway and Other Injuries of the Nervous System* was published in 1866, to remedy, as Erichsen states in the preface, the woeful lack of attention devoted by the medical profession in general to such an important subject. He wrestles with the inherited ignorance of the psychological ramific-ations of the trauma, but simultaneously compounds the problem:

> In those cases in which a man advanced in life, of energetic business habits, of great mental ability and vigour, in no way subject to gusty fits of emotion, or to local nervous disquietudes of any kind, – a man, in fact, active in mind, accustomed to self-control, addicted to business, and healthy in body, suddenly, and for the first time in his life, after the infliction of a severe shock to the system, finds himself affected by a *train of symptoms* indicative of serious and deep-seated injury to the nervous system, – is it reasonable to say that such a man has suddenly become 'hysterical', like a love-sick girl?[13]

Erichsen betrays a reluctance to accept what such trauma could do to men. In the cultural climate of the time, he was being asked to accept that it turned men into women. Although, in a new edition in 1875, Erichsen was able to admit the qualified existence of hysteria in men – it would *only* occur as a result of a railway accident[14] – Freud writes in 1886 of the continuing 'lively opposition' of the German authorities to 'regard neuroses arising from trauma' in men as hysteria.[15]

The fictional association of trains with impotence and frag-mentation is partly explained, I believe, by such contemporary debates as these. In the strength of its connection to what eventually became known as male hysteria, the train was unique. In Freud's letters, the leading psycho-analytical thinker of the day is seen to assume that a fundamental psychological experience, at an Oedipally important age, happened on a train. A more practical demonstration of the enormity of the threat the train posed is provided by the *Lancet*. Experiments were showing that animals in whom epilepsy had been induced by wilful damage of the spinal cord could transmit the disease to their off-spring. The spinal cord was involved in all cases of railway spine and railway brain. Assumptions were made that humans could suffer similar genetic results.[16] Travel on the railway, and the image of the train itself, therefore provide a system of critical languages and culturally translatable assumptions. Translations abound between psychology, medicine, fiction and history. Perhaps not surprisingly, morality too joins the fray.

In the somewhat extreme view taken by Max Nordau, the 'fin-de-siècle disposition' was caused primarily by the technological revolution. The 'new nervous diseases', bearing names such as 'railway spine and railway brain' were directly attributable to aspects of modern civilization. They were diseases, in his opinion, of degeneracy and hysteria. The demands placed upon the mental capabilities of humanity by the increasing possibilities of travel, by the extended sensual forays and by the nervous activity endemic to the terrain, caused the damage.[17] And although his tone is exaggerated, and frankly disturbed at times, he can be compared with Ford and others in his concentration on the splintering properties of the new speed and new sights.[18] Ford distinguishes between the railway as a metaphor for modern society, and as indicative of a more individual problem posed by the time. Train travel prescribes swift experience of fragmentative sights, the undergoing of fragmentative moments, the speed of which precludes any restorative gain. In *The Soul of London*, the current of life is compared to a journey by train at uncontrollable speed and enforced distance. The train carries one relentlessly forward, ever further from real sight, and the railway window becomes symptomatic of the self and its role in modern society. One travels, one watches, one does not engage (*SL* 120-1).

Ford experiments with the disjunctive space thus created. It is a space peculiar to the modern age, and what Peter Gay calls the 'propulsive power of erotic and aggressive urges' finds its locus on the railway.[19] Nordau makes explicit his belief in a link between train travel and sexual immorality: the example from Truffaut identified a relationship, at least. Ashburnham's first public, and portentous, indiscretion occurs with a young woman on a train journey. This locomotive symbol seems to incite, or at least to contain, his sexual impropriety. The fact of its incitement of such action is not in doubt in

Wells's *Tono-Bungay*, as Ponderevo relates an evening trip home with Marion:

> We were alone in the carriage, and for the first time I ventured to put my arm about her.
> "You mustn't", she said feebly.[20]

Their situation both encourages his action, and sanctions the feebleness of her 'resistant' response. Dowell judges Ashburnham's action as 'ill-timed' due, one could surmise, to the accelerated temporality which comes with the train (*GS* 41). The coachman who exhaustively drives Emma Bovary and Leon cannot understand their 'furious desire for locomotion', though the reader, presumably, can.[21] But such an intimate space not only encourages sexual behaviour; it is also seen to inform much more subtle subversions of the norm.

Tietjens and Macmaster conduct their most expressive and revelatory conversations whilst watching England hurtle by. Unable to concentrate on correcting the proofs of his book, Macmaster's brain wanders, and, only then, aboard the train, does he recognize the extent of Tietjens' shock at Sylvia's imminent return. A discussion ensues in which Macmaster feels patently uncomfortable. This degenerates into a row, on the merits of monogamy, divorce, the class system, Malthusian political economy and war. A hostage to fortune and the close quarters of the carriage, Macmaster cannot escape Tietjens' treacherous polemic, and as the train pulls into a station, he puts his head out of the window to call for a porter before either the train, or Tietjens, have stopped.[22] The confinement during the discussion, and the areas into which the conversation has strayed, means that the legacy of this passage is one of intimacy which has been forcibly stretched. A train journey Ford undertook with Arthur Marwood, which precipitated strikingly similar conversations, also precipitated much of the plot which became *Parade's End*.[23] Such encounters seem to be creatively productive; they are more so, perhaps, when the protagonists are strangers.

SARA HASLAM

According to John Stallworthy's biography of Wilfred Owen, an untitled poem of 1917 signifies Owen's 'latent or suppressed homosexuality'.[24] It begins in a train:

> It was a navy boy, so prim, so trim,
> That boarded my compartment of the train.
> I shared my cigarettes and books to him.
> He shared his heart to me. (Who knows my gain!)

The nature of the space is conceivably erotic, and the speaker expects to be seduced by the invader of what is *his* compartment. The train produces a striking physical proximity of different classes and ages, but the encounter is, nonetheless, obviously anonymous. The anonymous encounter in confined space was of course hugely significant. Ford is similarly proprietorial in an incident in a compartment related in 1907, but his initial distaste quickly transmutes into interest as he guesses the couple are on their honeymoon. He watches them closely, and considers what effect his presence is having on their as yet delicate relationship. His novelist's eye learns, secretly, from the experience (*SP* 110). An encounter involving a quiet indulgence of fictional identity is recorded by Mary (Mrs. Humphry) Ward, in 1888. As she sits in her compartment at Waterloo a lady jumps into the same carriage. Hugely excited by the fact that she has got hold of a library copy of *Robert Elsmere*, she 'breathlessly' informs her friend who waits to see her off of her success. Mrs. Ward does not reveal her identity but 'leaves her to read'.[25] In a paradoxically public and intimate setting, she has heard herself talked of by a stranger, and has resisted making herself known.

And so trains seem to encourage as well as to symbolize the extension of dimensions. They produce new levels of knowledge and experience, which inspire anxiety as well as opportunity. The train also connotes a constantly changing picture. In Ford the framing of the railway window, despite the speed of the sights, can be interpreted as a necessary organization of that picture, the very wholeness of

42

which is only just beginning to be seen and felt. Without that frame, Ford the novelist would not have benefited from this sight out of a moving train:

> I looked down upon the black and tiny yards that were like the cells in an electric battery. In one, three children were waving their hands and turning up their faces to the train; in the next, white clothes were drying. A little further on a woman ran suddenly out of a door; she had a white apron and her sleeves were tucked up. A man followed her hastily, he had red hair, and in his hand a long stick. (*SL* 61)

Granted the vision, and the distance, Ford paints an impressionist's picture. Friedrich Engels declared in 1844 that the visitor to any industrial town need never see sights like these, but the later Ford, using *all* the tools with which the time provided him, gives us an arguably complete, dramatically stark vision. It is stripped to its effective essentials by its containment, and larger than the frame is its claim upon our imagination. The train thus becomes a novelistic accoutrement, necessary to the just treatment of Ford's changing material. It is part of his recognition that the 'rules of life must of necessity be profoundly modified and destandardized' as the times demand.[26] Indeed, much of the modification seems to have taken place on, or as a result of, the totemic train.

As Nordau splutters to his climax in *Degeneration*, he regales us with the 'embodiments of degeneration and hysteria in the arts, poetry, and philosophy'. Ranged against this is his image of the end of the twentieth century in which 'art and poetry will only be cultivated by the most emotional portion of humanity: women, the young, and children'. With this emotional segregation, with those inclined to hysteria safely occupied, he predicts a generation for whom it will not be injurious 'to live half their time in a railway carriage'.[27] Ford, in more muted fashion, in 1907, fantasizes about the qualities of a still moral 'Englishman'. He will 'play the game' according to inwardly acknowledged rules without pandering to imposed behaviour. This would be, Ford says, like preserving a 'sort of virginity in a fine wrong-headedness'. It is about as likely, he concedes, as finding a 'countryman of great age' cherishing an 'invincible pride in never having been in a railway carriage' (*SP* 165). Trains attend modernity, they both unleash and contain its forces. Among the ranks of the writers who have appropriated this power, it would be hard to find a case of the railway virgin of the kind Ford describes.

NOTES

1. Ford Madox Ford, *Joseph Conrad: A Personal Remembrance* (New York: The Ecco Press, 1989), p. 166.

2. Max Saunders, *Ford Madox Ford: A Dual Life*, vol. 1 (Oxford: Oxford University Press, 1996), p. 195.

3. Ford Madox Ford, *Return to Yesterday: Reminiscences 1894-1914* (London: Victor Gollancz Ltd., 1931), p. 4.

4. Sir Llewellyn Woodward, *The Age of Reform 1815-1870* (Oxford: Oxford University Press, 1962), pp. 41-2. Eric Hobsbawm states that, although the initially explosive train revolution had passed by 1880, as many miles of railroad were constructed in the years from 1880-1913 as in the original 'railway age', *The Age of Empire 1875-1914* (London: Weidenfeld & Nicolson, 1995), p. 52.

5. Ford Madox Ford, *The English Novel: From the Earliest Days to the Death of Joseph Conrad* (London: Constable & Co. Ltd., 1930), p. 9.

6. Ford Madox Ford, *Ladies Whose Bright Eyes* (London: Constable, 1931), p. 26.

7. Ford, *The Soul of London* (London: Alston Rivers, 1905) – henceforth *SL*; p. 57.

8. Ford Madox Ford, *The Good Soldier*, ed. Martin Stannard (New York and London: W. W. Norton & Company, 1995) – henceforth *GS*; pp. 38-9.

9. In *The Spirit of the People: An Analysis of the English Mind* (London: Alston Rivers, 1907) – henceforth *SP*; pp. 141-4, Ford writes that: 'were the national spirit at all easy to raise, we should insist that our railway officials should search among the inventors until some system were devised by which all trains at all times could be worked by blindfolded men. Yet we suffer our bodies to be wearied, our trade to be harassed, our time to be lost [. . .] at hurried seasons of the year. [. . .] I have suffered much, and shall probably continue to suffer much, from the erratic train services of several lines without attempting to cure them with my pen'. Perhaps Ford means that he has not attempted to cure these ills in the direct fashion of Dowell, though Dowell has had very obviously limited success in regulating international train travel.

10. Ford Madox Ford, *The Marsden Case: A Romance* (London: Duckworth & Co., 1923), pp. 302-4.

11. Sigmund Freud, *The Origins of Psycho-Analysis: Letters to Wilhelm Fliess, Drafts and Notes, 1887-1902*, ed. Bonaparte *et al.* (London: Imago, 1954); letter from 18 August, 1897. The anxiety was not groundless: there were very serious rail accidents all over Europe and parts of America in the preceeding years. In 1885, smaller, domestic accidents increased with the introduction of continuous brakes, as drivers tended to over-rely on power braking and leave it too late. See Charles Meacher, *Quite By Accident* (Worcestershire: Square One Publications, 1994), pp. 23, 108.

12. Letter from 3 October, 1897.

13. John Erichsen, *On Railway and Other Injuries of the Nervous System* (London: Walton & Maberly, 1866), p. 126 (my emphasis).

14. This edition contained the original 6 lectures included in 1866, as well as 8 others. It was re-titled, *On Concussion of the Spine, Nervous Shock, and Other Obscure Injuries of the Nervous System* (London: Longmans, Green and Co., 1875), p. 196.

15. Sigmund Freud, *Standard Edition of the Complete Psychological Works*, ed. Strachey *et al.* (London: The Hogarth Press, 1953-74); report from Salpêtrière and work with Charcot in 1886: vol. 1, p. 12. In the discussion of the case of Little Hans, much of the patient's phobia is seen to relate to the railway: vol. 10, pp. 84 ff.

16. This is asserted by Erichsen (1875), p. 4.

17. Nordau writes that: 'in 1840 there were in Europe three thousand kilometers of railway; in 1891 there were two hundred and eighteen thousand. The number of travellers in 1840, in Germany, France and England, amounted to two and a half

SARA HASLAM

millions; in 1891 it was six hundred and fourteen millions. In Germany every inhabitant received, in 1840, eighty five letters; in 1888, two hundred letters [. . .]. All these activities [. . .] involve an effort of the nervous system and a wearing of tissue': *Degeneration* (London: Heinemann, 1895), pp. 38-41.

18. Ford's friend, the liberal politician, C. F. G. Masterman, observed in 1909 in relation to the new 'speed', that: 'We are compelled [. . .] to avail ourselves of the telegraph and the telephone; we are driven to the express train, the motor omnibus, the various expedients which are adapted to acceleration, rather than to happiness. If we do not adapt our lives to such accelerations, we are swept aside or trodden under by the crowds which press behind; like those who fail in the daily leap for the Brooklyn cars at New York, and are swept aside or trodden under almost unheeded': *The Condition of England* (London: Methuen & Co., 1909), p. 218. He suggests here another cause of the anxiety bound up with the revolutions in transport and technology: one will be buried if one does not keep up.

19. Peter Gay, *The Bourgeois Experience. Victoria to Freud*, Vol. 1, *Education of the Senses* (Oxford: Oxford University Press, 1984), p. 10.

20. H. G. Wells, *Tono-Bungay* (London: Macmillan & Co., 1909), p. 148.

21. Gustave Flaubert, *Madame Bovary,* tr. Eleanor Marx-Aveling, (London: Vizetelly & Co., 1886), p. 269. Erichsen cites an example of 'railway spine', though the result of a carriage accident, in 1766 (1875, p. 8).

22. Ford, *Parade's End* (Harmondsworth, Middlesex: Penguin, 1982), pp. 3-4, 12-18.

23. Ford discusses this genesis, placing great significance on the surroundings, in *It Was the Nightingale* (London: William Heinemann Ltd., 1934), pp. 187-207.

24. John Stallworthy, *Wilfred Owen: A Biography* (Oxford: Oxford University Press, 1977), p. 141.

25. Mrs. Humphry Ward, *A Writer's Recollections* (London: Collins, 1918), p. 12.

26. Ford, *The English Novel*, p. 16.

27. Nordau, *Degeneration*, pp. 541-3.

THREE MEMORIES OF A NIGHT: FORD'S IMPRESSIONISM IN THE GREAT LONDON VORTEX

Giovanni Cianci

Much has been written about Ford's literary impressionism, but, surprisingly enough, the connection and interaction with painting has been overlooked, or not properly focused, or not considered in all its importance.

Even in recent, well-informed and perceptive studies, for instance the chapter which Michael Levenson devotes to *The Good Soldier* in his volume *Modernism and the Fate of Individuality*,[1] the emphasis is still on Nineteenth Century French impressionism – on Monet – or on recent epistemology: and there is no mention of Post-impressionist painting which had displaced Impressionism and was contemporaneous with the composition of *The Good Soldier*. And this despite the fact that Ford was constantly in dialogue with the most daring experimental movements of his time.

Of course the reference to the French Impressionist painters is relevant: they were the first moderns, and they played a decisive role all over Europe in subverting the realistic conventions, paving the way for subsequent developments. But crucial in the maturation of Ford's formal experiments were the radical innovations brought about by Cubism and Futurism in the years between 1909 and 1915, which were to exert a great influence on the English scene before the war. So it is to them that we must revert if we want to define more properly the context in which Ford's impressionism developed, and at the same time to understand a salient component which characterizes Ford's literary impressionism and which put, at least in a specific passage, as we shall see, a distinctive stamp on his most experimental novel, *The Good Soldier*.

To this effect it is essential to remember that in those crucial years it was the arts which were the most innovative, and that painting in particular was the leading model for all experiments. 'Those were the passionate days', wrote Ford, 'of the literary Cubists, Vorticists, *Imagistes* and the rest of the *tapageux* and riotous *Jeunes* of that young decade'.[2] When in 1914 he described the impressionist as being the one who 'must always exaggerate',[3] he was thinking above all of the distortions, the deformations, used by the early avant-garde painting.

Let us recall a few declarations in order to confirm the primacy of the arts at that time. About his famous poem 'In a Station of the Metro' of 1913, Pound wrote that not finding the right words for his emotions, he finally found: 'an equation [. . .] not in speech, but in little splotches of colour [. . .] it was [. . .] the beginning, for me, of a language in colour'.[4] When D. H. Lawrence (he was then writing 'The Sisters', which would then be split up into *The Rainbow* and *Women in Love*) explained to Edward Garnett in a famous letter of 1914 that in his new way of narrating: 'you mustn't look for the old stable ego of the character,'[5] Lawrence had above all in mind not only 'the destruction of the I in literature' proclaimed by the 'Technical manifesto of Futurist literature' launched by Marinetti in 1912, but also the break up of the mimetic conventions pursued on the canvas by Futurist painters, with their emphasis on dynamism, power, flux and speed. And we all remember that in *The Good Soldier* Dowell says: 'the whole world for me is like spots of colour on an immense canvas' (*GS* 17) and that Nancy's final appearance in the same novel is described as 'a picture without a meaning' (*GS* 161).

Now, it is important to point out that Ford, in his declarations of poetics entitled 'On Impressionism' (especially in the one dated June 1914), among the new movements in painting refers us back specifically to Futurism ('On Impressionism' 175). My point is that Ford had the Futurists in mind not only because the Futurists were – and had been in London at that time – the most vociferous, but because in their manifestos concerning both painting and literature Ford could find – updated – the necessary link between modernity and urban experience which he had previously reflected upon and written about, mainly in his volume *The Soul of London* (1905), a volume which has been wrongly neglected by the commentators on Ford's impressionist technique.

Yet it is there that we can find a basic assumption underlying Ford's 'impressionism': that is to say the inescapable connection between living in a metropolis and the loss of totality, objectivity, permanence. It is in an urban environment where, to quote Marx (quoted by Marshal Berman) 'all that is solid melts into air,'[6] or in Ford's terms, where reality – in a never-ending process – is reduced to 'instability', 'tenuousness, 'haziness', 'evanescence'. It is when Ford confronts the reality of living in the modern city that he begins to lose the sense of stability, the coherence and intelligibility of what goes on, and realizes that the only felt experience which emerges is the continuous mobility, discontinuity and fragmentation of everything. As he wrote later in *The Critical Attitude* (1911), the 'impressions' one feels in the city:

> are so fragile, so temporary, so evanescent that the whole stream of life appears to be a procession of very little things, as if indeed all our modern life were a dance of midges. And indeed all our modern life is a dance of midges. We know no one very well, but we come into contact with an infinite number of people, we stay nowhere very long, but we see many, many places. We have hardly ever time to think long thoughts, but an infinite number of small things are presented for our cursory reflections.[7]

Ford was certainly exaggerating when, after listening to the leader of Futurism then in London, he said in 1914 that: 'there is not a single word of Marinetti's doctrines that I have not been preaching since I was fifteen'.[8] But, if we take into consideration *The Soul of London* and realize how important in that volume is the awareness of the centrality of urban experience, we can understand why Ford was

GIOVANNI CIANCI

bound to be attracted by what the Futurists said about the exceptional novelty of the *Erlebnis* of the city and the consequent absolute necessity of creating new codes and structures: the necessity of forging a new formal language in order to render the extraordinary experience of living in a metropolis, which, as Ford was often to repeat, constituted the essence of the modern spirit.

It is above all here, in *The Soul of London*, when Ford meditates on the phenomenon of metropolitan life, that we can get to the root of his 'impressionism' and discover that it was deeply connected with the crisis of representation brought about by the major changes which had enormously affected the urban life of the early twentieth century. To Ford, London is 'the apotheosis of modern life'.[9] London is the universe of transience, of dislocation, of impermanence, where one grows bewildered to the point of losing hold of one's identity. London's 'enormous increased size' has almost totally undermined the possibility for us of getting a familiar, univocal image of it: 'The City itself has no longer any visible bounds, walls, or demarcations' (*SL* 104). London is characterized by 'its utter lack of unity, of plan' (*SL* 13). It has lost its form. You can't see the whole of it, but only fragments: 'London is a thing of [. . .] "bits"' (*SL* 23). There is no longer any centre. The Londoner feels that: 'Connected thinking has become nearly impossible, because it *is* nearly impossible to find any general idea that will connect into one train of thought' (*SL* 88). 'History' (or, for that matter, we can say the plot, the causal or linear progression in fiction) 'becomes impossible' (*SL* 103). Hence the crisis of representation. If totality in all its complexity is no longer representable, its place will be taken by the fragment, the accidental. If we can't see the whole, because it is for ever eluding us, we should at least try to be faithful to 'the received impression', sensation, emotion, by rendering its original immediacy, 'not' – writes Ford, 'a sort of rounded, annotated record of a set of circumstances [. . .] not the corrected chronicle,' but 'the record of the impression of a moment' in all its chaos, vibration and blurring complexity ('On Impressionism' 174).

Michael Levenson has argued that:

> The momentary impression [. . .] displays itself only in rare conditions; generally speaking, it is only at times of perceptual or psychological stress that familiar images decompose into the sensations of which they are made.[10]

I would historicize this reflection and suggest that the times 'of perceptual and psychological stress' were precisely the ones which characterized the tumultuous pre-war years, and which, already in *The Soul of London,* Ford connected with the enormous transformations which life had undergone, particularly in the city setting. If we had more space, it would be of help here to bring into the picture a philosopher, to whom Benjamin himself was indebted, George Simmel, who in a famous essay (*'Die Grossstadte und das Geistesleben'* ('The Metropolis and Mental Life') which precedes Ford's volume by two years) correlated that stress to the *Erlebnis* in a big city. But more to the point, since they are constantly recalled by Ford himself in his theoretical pieces on impressionism and elsewhere, are the Futurist painters who were all the rage in those years, and who would bring to the extreme on canvas those dislocating effects which originated from the multiplicity of urban stimuli, the disturbing novelty of which had already drawn Ford's attention.[11]

To confirm Ford's interest in the new sensibility induced by modern urban life, let us consider some of the paragraphs in the second chapter of *The Soul of London,* the ones entitled for instance 'The new carriages', 'Entering on a motorcar – Its effects on the mind', 'The London landscape from a train window'; 'The electric tram at night' and so on. A few years later the Futurists would radicalize and dramatize in their manifestos and on canvas the

GIOVANNI CIANCI

bewildering effects, the revolution in the categories of space and time, caused by the new urban and industrial environment. In their 'Technical Manifesto of Painting' of 1910 the Futurists had written:

> The sixteen people around you in a rolling motor 'bus are in turn and at the same time one, ten, four, three; they are motionless and they change places; they come and go, bound into the street, are suddenly swallowed up by the sunshine, then come back and sit before you, like persistent symbols of universal vibration.
>
> How often have we not seen upon the cheek of the person with whom we were talking the horse which passes at the end of the street.[12]

This seems to me to stand in a remarkable relationship with what Ford would declare in 1914:

> Impressionism exists to render those queer effects of real life that are like so many views seen through bright glass – through glass so bright that whilst you perceive through it a landscape or a backyard, you are aware that, on its surface, it reflects a face behind you [. . .] And it is, I think, only Impressionism that can render that peculiar effect. ('On Impressionism' 174)

Again, when Ford says in the same piece that:

> It is [. . .] perfectly possible that a piece of Impressionism should give a sense of two, three, of as many as you will, places, persons, emotions, all going on simultaneously in the emotions of the writer. ('On Impressionism' 173)

he is echoing one of the basic canons of the pre-war avant-garde, the practice of 'simultaneity' advocated by some French artists of the early Modernism (from Cendrars to Delaunay) and particularly by the Futurists.[13]

By 1913-1914 the term Futurism is no longer a general indication of modernity, but a specific art movement and technique which had, after the declamations of Marinetti, the exhibitions of Futurist paintings and other events, monopolized the London scene. See for instance how Ford is careful, in the following passages (which come from his piece 'On Impressionism' of June 1914) to distinguish Futurism from Cubism. He is saying that – having discarded a conventional rendering of the scene, and having instead tried to record your impression:

> you would attain to the sort of odd vibration that scenes in real life really have; you would give your reader the impression that he was witnessing something real, that he was passing through an experience. ('On Impressionism' 175)

The parallel here is with one of the central tenets of Futurist technique, in which the spectator '*must [. . .] be placed in the centre of the picture*' so that 'He shall not be present at, but participate in the action'.[14] Let us remember that Dowell explicitly requires an active participation of the reader when, more than once, he says: 'I leave it to you' to decide – that is to say, I leave it to you to speculate about the meaning (or meanings) out of the 'maze' – 'the intricate tangle' – in which the complex situation has developed (*GS* 136, 156). And Ford goes on to say in the essay:

> You will observe [. . .] that you will have produced something that is very like a Futurist picture – not a Cubist picture, but one of those canvases that show you in one corner a pair of stays, in another a bit of the foyer of a music hall, in another a fragment of early morning landscape, and in the middle a pair of eyes, the whole bearing the title of 'A Night Out'. ('On Impressionism' 175)

I have gone through the catalogue (published in English) to the Exhibition of Works by the Italian Futurist Painters held in London at the Sackville Gallery in 1912.[15] And I have found that Ford's description of a Futurist canvas (which I have just quoted) seems to be reminiscent of a painting by the Futurist Luigi Russolo, entitled 'The Memory of a Night', composed in 1911, and on show at the Sackville. Russolo's canvas (the title in the original is '*I ricordi di una notte*') was an example of the so called 'painting of states of mind' in which, abandoning anecdotal narration, the painter aimed at rendering Bergson's 'psychic duration' (*la durée*) by painting the fluctuating processes of memory itself and by making use of the technique of simultaneity, which allowed for multiple experiences to come together (see the cover illustration).

In the emotive ambience of 'The Memory of a Night', the dynamic irruption of memory brings to the surface superimposed and heterogeneous images, fragmenting them in the space of the canvas: on the left, the full face of a woman (with the reflection of light on her hair); on the right, her profile (with the reflection on her hair of the horse above, but upside-down); above the rising sun; underneath, electric lights; in the corner on the left, a pair of gloves perhaps (or, better, a waving hand playing an invisible piano) then the silhouette of a passer-by with a multiplication of the outlines to suggest dynamism; on the right, a galloping horse (with the triangulation of his legs to convey the impression of movement), then a group of tottering houses, and a fragment of a concert hall (an admiring male audience).[16] Apollinaire would have said that Russolo attempted to render no longer the successive but the simultaneous. Breaking away from representational art, from the fixed event, from the connections of the plot, from 'history', Russolo had tried to render the epiphany of a mobile, dynamic memory. His aim was to render impressions, fragments of memory, before they become stabilized, articulated; 'corrected', Ford would say. In other words, paraphrasing Ford, this Futurist canvas did not narrate, but made impressions of 'A Night Out'

Of course Ford did not share the Futurists' enthusiastic acceptance of urban life and machinery. Basically he was hostile to modern industrialized society. Yet he felt the need, as an artist, 'to register my own times in terms of my own time',[17] and it is well known that in 1912, for instance, he pointed out: 'That is the matter with all the verse of today; it is too much practised in temples and too little in motor buses'.[18] In 1914 Ford wrote that: 'we of 1913 are a fairly washed-out lot and we do desperately need a new formula'.[19] He could even sound a bit Futuristic when he rejected 'the mawkish flap-doodle of culture, Fabianism, peace and good will'[20] and iconoclastically advocated 'Real good religion, a violent thing full of hatreds and exclusions'.[21]

In a famous dialogue reported by Ford himself, Wyndham Lewis the vorticist painter and writer accused him of being passé, 'finished', of being still the slave to a traditional technique.[22] Yet even while Ford was describing himself as an 'Impressionist', his writing was registering the impact of modernist painting. Let us take other 'memories of a night': the ones evoked by Dowell in connection with his wife's death in *The Good Soldier*. It is one of the many occasions on which Dowell wants to make his listeners 'see'. The passage strikes me as being experimental along the lines suggested by the Futurist prescription of 'dislocating and dismembering the objects',[23] conveying emotion, light, colours and sounds, although the Futurist exhilaration and exuberance is totally absent from Ford's universe:

[. . .] my recollection of that night is only the sort of pinkish effulgence from the electric lamps in the hotel lounge. There seemed to bob into my consciousness, like floating globes, the faces of those three. Now it would be the bearded, monarchical , benevolent head of the grand duke; then the sharp-featured, brown, cavalry-moustached features of the chief of police; then the globular, polished, and high-collared vacuousness that represented Monsieur Schontz, the proprietor of the hotel. At times one head would be there alone, at another the spiked helmet of the official would be close to the healthy baldness of the prince; then Schontz's oiled locks would push in between the two. The sovereign's soft, exquisitely trained voice would say 'Ja, ja, ja!' each word dropping out like so many pellets of suet; the subdued rasp of the official would come: 'Zum Befehl, Durchlaucht', like five revolver-shots; the voice of M. Schontz would go on and on under its breath like that of an unclean priest reciting from his breviary in the corner of a railway-carriage. That was how it presented itself to me. (*GS* 75)

If, as Paul Skinner argues in this volume, the style does not announce itself 'in tones of thunder' in this passage, it certainly does announce itself in terms of disruption very close to the new experimental 'impressionism' of the high modernist practice.[24]

NOTES

1. Michael Levenson, *Modernism and the Fate of Individuality* (Cambridge: Cambridge University Press, 1991), pp. 102-20.

2. 'Dedicatory Letter to Stella Ford' in Ford Madox Ford, *The Good Soldier*, ed. Martin Stannard (New York and London: W. W. Norton & Company, 1995), p. 4. Subsequent quotations from *The Good Soldier* (*GS*) are taken from this edition and referenced parenthetically within the text.

3. Ford Madox Hueffer, 'On Impressionism', *Poetry and Drama,* 2 (June 1914), 169. Subsequent references to this essay appear parenthetically within the text.

4. Ezra Pound, 'Vorticism' (1914) reprinted in *Ezra Pound and the Visual Arts,* ed. H. Zinnes (New York: New Direction Books, 1980), p. 203.

5. *The Letters of D. H. Lawrence*, ed. G. J. Zytaruck and J. Boulton, (Cambridge: Cambridge University Press, 1981), vol. 2, pp. 282-3.

6. M. Berman, *All That is Solid Melts into Air -- The Experience of Modernity*, (New York, Simon & Schuster, 1982).

7. Ford Madox Hueffer, *The Critical Attitude*, (London: Duckworth, 1911), p. 186.

8. Ford Madox Hueffer, 'Literary Portraits – XLIV: Signor Marinetti, Mr Lloyd George, St Katharine and Others', *The Outlook*, 34 (11 July 1914), 46; and compare: 'those Futurists are only trying to render on canvas what Impressionists *tel que moi* have been trying to render for many years' ('On Impressionism', 175). Ford had heard Marinetti lecture at the Doré Gallery in May 1914.

9. Ford Madox Ford, *The Soul of London* (1905) – henceforth *SL*, ed. Alan. G. Hill (London: J. M. Dent, 1995), p. 111. Subsequent quotations from this edition are referenced parenthetically within the text.

10. M. Levenson, *Modernism*, p. 113.

11. Most of the Futurist manifestos were available in English in London by 1913-1914. For a full bibliography of Futurist documents, exhibitions, events etc. on the London scene, see: V. Gioé, 'Futurism in England. A Bibliography (1910-1915)', *Bulletin of Bibliography*, 44:3 (September 1987), 172-88. I have dealt with the Futurists' campaign in England in 'Futurism and its Impact on Vorticism', *I. C. S. A. Cahier* No. 8/9, Bruxelles, 1988, 83-101. Another confirmation of the crucial Futurist presence in London comes from Lawrence Rainey, who has drawn attention to its impact on Pound in 'The Creation of the Avant-Garde: F. T. Marinetti and Ezra Pound', *Modernism/modernity*, 1:3 (September 1994), 195-219. See also his *Institutions of Modernism* (New Haven and London: Yale University Press, 1998).

12. From the 'Manifesto of the Futurist Painters' included in the Catalogue of the 'Exhibition of the Works by the Italian Futurist Painters' held at the Sackville Gallery, March 1912, p. 30.

13. For a full picture see Par Bergman, '*Modernolatria' et 'Simultaneità' - Recherches sur deux tendences dans l'avantgarde littéraire en Italie et en France à la veille de la première guerre mondiale* (Stockholm: Bonniers, 1962). To the point is also the excellent book by Marjorie Perloff, *The Futurist Moment -- Avant-garde, Avant-guerre, and the Language of Rapture*, (Chicago and London: The University of Chicago Press 1986).

14. 'Exhibition of the Works by the Italian Futurist Painters', p. 14.

15. See note 12.

16. Compare M. W. Martin, *Futurist Art and Theory 1909-1915* (1968), (New York: Hacker Art Books, 1978), pp. 89-90 and F. Roche-Pézard, *L'Aventure Futuriste 1909/1916* (Rome: Ecole française de Rome, 1983), pp. 316-17.

17. Ford Madox Hueffer, 'Impressionism – Some Speculations', *Poetry*, 2:5 (August 1913), 179.

18. Quoted by Frank MacShane, *The Life and Work of Ford Madox Ford* (New York: Horizon Press, 1966), p. 97.

19. Ford Madox Hueffer, 'Literary Portraits XVIII – Nineteen-Thirteen and the Futurists', *Outlook*, 33 (3 January 1914), 14-15.

20. *Ibid.*

21. *Ibid.*

22. Ford Madox Ford, *Return to Yesterday* (London: Victor Gollancz, 1931), pp. 417-19.

23. See 'The Exhibitor to the Public' (p. 9) in the Sackville Gallery Catalogue cited in note 14.

24. For a fuller analysis of this passage and other aspects dealt with in this article, see G. Cianci, '1905-1914: Ford "Metropolitano" tra Impressionismo e Futurismo', in Rafaella Baccolini and Vita Fortunati, eds, *Scrittura e Sperimentazione in Ford Madox Ford* (Firenze: Alinea Editrice, 1994), pp. 91-110. Skinner, p. 296 below.

FORD AND THE SIMPLE LIFE:
GENDER, SUBJECTIVITY AND CLASS
IN A SATIRIZED UTOPIA

Robin Peel

The first part of this title is likely to raise eyebrows. One reader pointed out that pairing 'Ford and the Simple Life' was a bit like bracketing Cromwell and Theatre Attendance or Casanova and Domesticity – concepts that would seem to suggest binary oppositions rather than ideas with a significant inter-relationship. One answer to that, of course, is the argument that we define ourselves through difference, by deciding what we are not, and that Ford's repeated quest for self-definition is in itself an adequate reason for discussing a set of practices and beliefs which Ford ultimately rejected and satirised in the book that he wrote under the pseudonym Daniel Chaucer, *The Simple Life Limited,* published in 1911. But in the space available I would like to take a different tack and argue that the identification of Ford as urban cosmopolitan modernist and urbane radical Tory does not do full justice to the unformed younger Ford, and overlooks his attraction to subversive questions about class and gender identity that drew him to live briefly among a Fabian and Simple Life community. I would also like to ask some questions about the way that the past is reconstructed and recast in the act of writing, and how imaginative texts written at some distance from an experience may reveal more about shifts in perceptions than they do about the actual formative experiences themselves. Finally I would like to consider the extent to which in 1911, Ford's thinking about gender, as expressed in the unfinished *Women & Men,* with its questions about the social construction of gender and the way that men learn about sexual difference through literature anticipates by eighty years Judith Butler's description of compulsory heterosexuality as a regulatory practice and gender as a performative act.[1]

Among many other things, Ford's most praised work, *The Good Soldier* (1915), which he wrote in the years immediately following the publication of *The Simple Life Limited*, presents the reader with ample evidence of the crisis in masculinity that continued in the post-Edwardian period up and into the First World War. Edward Ashburnham, the good soldier, is good only to the uncritical eye of the narrator Dowell, who sees only the surface Englishman and not the fragile and ultimately suicidal man that this veneer conceals. Dowell is even more wretched: not only passionless and unobservant, but an American who spends his time counting the steps from the health baths to his hotel room, not realising that his wife is having a sexual relationship with the man he so admires. Yet Dowell is one of the more attractive characters: his gullibility is based on trust, and his simplicity is combined with genuine affection. Quite early on it is made clear that he is descended from a Pennsylvania Dutch family, and his identity is rooted in a tradition that continues to practise the simple life to this day, eschewing cars, electricity and twentieth-century clothing.

Ford Madox Ford's roots are complex. What tends to be remembered is that he was related to the painter Ford Madox Brown, and that his father was German. Both elements haunted him: the link with the Pre-Raphaelite movement was a heritage that was a generation away, but one that interested him enough for him to undertake a biography of his grandfather. As a young man of 21 Ford found himself in the family house full of Ford Madox Brown's furniture, in Hammersmith a short distance from William Morris. He was aware of the attractiveness of a Brotherhood, and grew up in an environment receptive to the exciting debates between Socialism and Anarchism. When he and his new bride Elsie Martindale took flight to the countryside, it was as much to recover from the trauma of family bereavement and the scandal of their unsanctioned marriage as it was anything else. Then, after a period of recovery in which they did indeed live out the Simple Life in the rather too rurally isolated Pent Farm in Sussex, they packed up their smocks and decided to move.

The Limpsfield community, which Ford and Elsie joined in 1898, was not really an artists colony, nor was it a utopian experiment in the way that Brook Farm in America had been, although Ford's retrospective representation of Limpsfield bears comparison with the circumstances in which Hawthorne came to satirise the Brook Farm experiment in *The Blithedale Romance* (1852). Limpsfield, if it was a colony at all, was a colony without any official structure or central organisation, for while some of its members lived the simple life full time, others were commuters on the recently completed Croydon, Oxted and East Grinstead Railway. Its modern equivalent would be somewhere like Totnes and Dartington in Devon, where people who believe in a particular lifestyle live among others who do not. But the group that believed in certain aspects of an alternative lifestyle was sufficiently dominant to give the area around the common known as the Chart a particular character, expressed in social practices, dress and ideals.

The late nineteenth century philosophy of the Simple Life was partly a by-product of the Arts and Crafts movement, and many of those who practised the Simple Life wore the kind of working smocks favoured by Morris. But equally it found inspiration in the writing and lifestyle of Edward Carpenter, who grew his own food and lived among the working men and women of the Derbyshire Dales. In turn, Carpenter and other middle-class Englishmen such as C. R. Ashbee, a friend of Carpenter's at Cambridge who took the Guild of Handicraft from Whitechapel to Chipping Campden in the Cotswolds, were inspired by a combination of socialism and temperament to retreat from the busy city to the 'simple rural idyll of craftsmanship and husbandry'.[2] This idyll itself drew on other models. In New England in the 1840's Transcendentalist and communitarian thinking inspired rural utopian experiments such as Bronson Alcott's community at Fruitlands and the Fourierist community at Brook Farm. Somehow the emphasis on community, which attracted both men and women in America, was transmuted into an emphasis on male Brotherhood when utopianism was practised in England. As Fiona MacCarthy observes in her study of C. R. Ashbee's Cotswold community: 'Women of the Simple Life were almost always in the background'.[3] Ashbee and Carpenter surrounded themselves with young men because they were sexually attracted to them, but it was precisely these 'Uranian' men, to use the term favoured by Carpenter, who argued for a redefinition of the roles between the sexes.

Carpenter's lifestyle, working his three fields at Millthorpe, had impressed Morris who 'was almost envious of the little village house in Derbyshire with seven acres where Carpenter lived in close community, social and sexual, with labourers from Sheffield'.[4] Here was a man, not afraid of hard manual labour, who also found time to throw himself into nearly all the reforming movements of the period. Carpenter, like the majority of the reformers of the time, came from a privileged background, and had been influenced by William Godwin, Thoreau's *Walden* (1854), and Whitman's *Leaves of Grass* (1855). But, more than anything, he had been inspired by Henry Mayers Hyndman's *England for All*, a booklet published in 1881, that interpreted Marx in a way that was extremely influential on the early character of English Socialism.

It is the analysis of sexual politics rather than the economics that makes Carpenter's version of the Simple Life interesting, though Carpenter himself explained how the two were linked and how women's freedom required a form of communism. In 1896 the little Labour Press in Manchester published *Love's Coming of Age*, the book having been dropped by Fisher Unwin in the wake of the Wilde trial. The book, which described the relationship between sexual and economic reform, anticipating the argument in *Homogenic Love* (1896) that heterosexuality was responsible for the growth of Western materialism, took time to become well known outside the socialist network in England, but by 1902 it was being translated into German and, if we can trust Carpenter's own version of history, was taken as a text book by the more radical elements at the first German Women's Congress in 1912. In advocating sexual relationships other than those within monogamous marriage, Carpenter was proposing an agenda which, as he had readily understood, had wider implications than for what he called 'homogenics':

> I realized in my own person some of the sufferings which are endured by an immense number of modern women, especially of the well to do classes [. . .] as well as by that large class of men [. . .] to whom the name of Uranians is often given.[5]

By the time that Ford came to write *The Simple Life Limited* and *Women & Men* – the latter started in 1911 but not published until 1923 – Havelock Ellis's influential *Studies in the Psychology of Sex* (1901) had been published in America, and women such as Frances Swiney (1906), the Pankhursts and Olive Schreiner had challenged contemporary preconceptions about female sexuality and behaviour. But, although women such as Kate Chopin in America and Ellen Key in Sweden were raising similar questions, Carpenter expressed unease that it had fallen to a man to open the debate in print in England in the 1890's:

> *Love's Coming of Age* ought, of course, (like some parts of *England's Ideal*) to have been written by a woman; but although I tried, I could not get any of my women friends to take the subject up, and so had to deal with it myself. Ellen Key, in Sweden, began – I fancy about the same period – writing that fine series of books on *Love, Marriage, Childhood* and so forth, which have done so much to illuminate the Western World; but at that time I knew nothing of her and her work.[6]

What Ford saw practised at Limpsfield bore little relation to the radicalism of socialist theory and these new ideas about the relations between the sexes. It was the faddishness loathed by Carpenter that struck Ford – the faddishness that made Carpenter more famous for the sandals he sewed than for his ideas (though that didn't stop Carpenter advertising his sandals in the journal of the New Fellowship, *Seed Time)*. Such inconsistencies appeared to turn utopianism into no more than a fashionable lifestyle in which the required vegetarianism and rural clothing was practised at home by some middle class Fabians who travelled to their London offices everyday. In his biography of Stephen Crane, who lived near the Chart in a house the commuters would all pass on their way to the station at Oxted, R. W. Stallman speaks of beards and homespun clothes in medieval style, and the drinking of mead from bullocks horn cups.[7] It was a version of the simple life that disgusted Tolstoi, who in the 1880s and 1890s at Yasnaya Polyana adopted a simple life himself, becoming a vegetarian and wearing peasant dress. Tolstoi was against colonies precisely because they led to organisational structures, however loose. Like Thoreau Tolstoi believed that change had to occur within individuals, and this powerful individualistic ethic was shared by Ford, who throughout his life seemed to be most happy when distancing himself from groups that had initially attracted him, or when coming into contact with those whose world view and temperament he did not share.

Ford and Elsie moved into Gracie's Cottage, Limpsfied in March 1898 having been invited there by Edward and Constance Garnett, Ford's childhood friends from London. The Garnetts had gone to live in the Chart woods to be remote and to avoid society. The woods at the edge of the Weald satisfied these requirements, but they were not completely isolated there. The railway line from London to nearby Oxted had opened in 1884, and this access had attracted Henry Salt who had resigned his postion as schoolmaster at Eton to live the Simple Life on one hundred pounds a year. The Salts were Fabians, and other Fabians soon followed: Sydney and Margaret Olivier in 1891 and Edward and Marjorie Pease. The Garnetts moved to Limpsfield Chart to be close to the Oliviers, whose four daughters would, in theory, provide companionship for their son David.

Ford and Elsie stayed in Gracie's Cottage for only one year and moved when their lease expired in March 1899. Yet during that year Ford met Stephen Crane and Joseph Conrad, both of whom came to Gracie's Cottage. Crane was younger than Ford, but had already been published. His chameleon-like character was not unlike Ford's own, and, when Ford came to write about the Limpsfield period in *Return to Yesterday* (1931), he did so in a mood of fond reminiscence, quite unlike the mood of *The Simple Life Limited*. Joseph Conrad was a much more stolid, older man in his forties when Garnett introduced him, and their initial conversation, as recalled by Ford, was on the subject of work. Ford was in his gardening clothes, which may have been his simple life clothes, and Conrad took him for a gardener. When he understood him to be Hueffer, he commented on how good a setting the cottage was for work. Work was Conrad's obsession, and it is interesting that Ford, who had become a Roman Catholic in 1892 when he was 19, and who regarded Puritanism as unrealistically idealistic, was moved to collaborate with a man who temperamentally was so different. It is tempting, perhaps too tempting, to psycho-analyse this meeting as an encounter with a figure who would serve to replace the authority of the grandfather, who in turn had assumed a significance following the death of Ford's father when Ford was only 16. His grandfather had famously painted a picture called 'Work', and Ford had perhaps inherited this tendency to romanticise the practical and the virtues of industry. Again like Nathaniel Hawthorne, he was appreciative of the energy of Puritanism: in England, as in America, the Puritans had been responsible for moves towards democracy. Richard Heath, who with his family moved into Gracie's cottage after Ford and Elsie had left, had published 'The Puritan Ideal' in *Seed Time* (April 1891) looking forward to the day when the Social Commonwealth would be reborn. But Ford was not a Puritan, and this may help to explain why, in novels such as *The Good Soldier,* he is so understanding of, and sympathetic towards, characters who are strikingly various and different.

The *Simple Life Limited* shows much less understanding. Although extremely witty at times, overall the novel seems less of a satire and more an act of personal exorcism. In revisiting his past Ford seems intent on an act of Peter-like renunciation, almost as if this former self that was the very young Ford is an embarrassment to the 1911 Ford, who has just completed an exciting period at the centre of

London literary society as the editor of the *English Review*. The Simple Life community is full of cranks, but Ford was tolerant of cranks, especially if their crankiness was accompanied by a sense of humour. The 1907 periodical *Ye Crank* claimed to take its name from the idea of a crank handle starting 'a revolution', but there was a sense of self irony there. Ford and Elsie had been willing enough to appear 'cranky' themselves. No, it was the hypocrisy and fraudulence that Ford attacks in this novel.

'We object [. . .] to all such things as individual property, marriage, revealed religion, the unequal distribution of wealth',[8] says Ophelia Bransdon, but, like Zenobia in *The Blithedale Romance,* she abandons her beliefs very easily when the attractions of the outer world present themselves. The misanthropy that runs through Ford's novel includes a persistent strain of misogyny. Of the two newlyweds – they have married as an act of rebellion, not conformity – it is Ophelia, and not Hamnet, who is the priggish one, and the main target for the satire: 'We have neither of us tasted flesh meat or alcohol in our lives and we are compiling a book called "Health Resides in Sandals"' (*SLL* 17). Miss Egmont, who is attracted to the colony's moving spirit, Horatio Gubb, is 'a hard lady of may be fifty, with a hooked nose, a light skin, greyish curly hair, and prominent spectacles that hardened already grey eyes' (*SLL* 85). Even Miss Stobhall, sincere and genuine socialist, is a crank who bores Hamnet with her readings from Marx. The four daughters that Mrs Lee hauls around in her donkey cart wish they were men in a way that at first suggests genuine frustration at the limitations of being young women (dressed, moreover, to look like men). But two of them want to be young men to help their father in the city while the other two wish they were men to help mother with the Simple Life – two activities which Ford presents as totally unsound. Against this it is possible to point only to women as victims, to the women, notably Mrs Bransdon and Mrs Gubb, who fall prey to the men's obsessions and are literally destroyed by them. Gubb's treatment of women is shown to be particularly callous and self centred. Even so, there is little here to indicate a writer who was able to question contemporary assumptions about gender. The dominant voice is that of the sceptical satirist, and gender equality is ridiculed because the Simple Lifers, who profess to believe in it, are fraudulent and ridiculous themselves. Ford is so eager to take revenge on his past, he includes a mocking self-reference to the person he had once been perceived as. Pomeroy Roden, a disciple of the Simple Life, is making a hopeless job of pummeling leaves of tobacco:

> He had read of this proceeding in one of the work of Mr Ford Madox Hueffer, an author esteemed by the Lifers as an authority upon the habits of the Middle Age and the Renaissance. (*SLL* 55)

Yet the record suggests that Ford, even as he was writing this novel, was in the process of resituating himself. In the same year that *The Simple Life Limited* was published, Ford began writing *Women & Men*, his study of the differences between the sexes, that was eventually published by Ezra Pound in 1923. In *Women & Men* Ford touches on the possibility that the way that men in a patriarchal society learn to construct the difference between men and women is through reading literature, an idea he had explored a year before in 'The Woman of the Novelists'.[9] He demonstrates this by satirising the relief with which the advanced Young Liberals discover Otto Weininger's *Sex and Character* (1903), which had 'proved' scientifically that women were inferior animals, and by providing impressionistic sketches of strong working countrywomen from his Sussex days (the days prior to his year in Limpsfield), women whose independence of mind and body refuse to conform to the stereotypes that were then the cultural norm.

Perhaps the apparent contrast between the perspective of these two works is best explained not simply in terms of Ford's contact with, and support for, the suffragette movement that his relationship with Violet Hunt brought about – he had joined a suffragist procession in 1907 and in 1913 was to write a suffragette pamphlet,

This Monstrous Regiment of Women, for the Women's Freedom League. The connection is possibly more complex, in that what Ford is attacking in the Simple Life is the artificiality of role playing, and what he is considering in *Women & Men* – and what he explores further in *A Call* and *The Good Soldier* – is the possibility that gender roles are themselves a performance. In questioning an essentialist difference between women and men, he was running counter to much suffragist rhetoric which argued that there *is* such an essential difference, and, as slogans and letters to the *Times* showed, that life and God are feminine.

In so doing, Ford was tentatively exploring ideas extended and elaborated more recently, ideas about the performative nature of gender. Judith Butler, drawing partly on Foucault, has described gender as a regulatory practice that institutionalises difference and privileges heterosexuality by emphasising difference, leading to the hegemonic belief in sexual duality. Sex itself is the prediscursive domain which assumes an essentialist duality and precludes the possibility that gender is performatively constituted. Ford does not quite make that leap, but, in his understanding that gender roles are enacted and that sexual duality needs to be questioned, he contributed to a strand in modernism which was developed by a succession of modernist women writers, including Charlotte Mew, May Sinclair, Dorothy Richardson, Natalie Barney and Djuna Barnes, and which in some senses can be seen to have had greater long term consequences for the development of narrative fiction than the experimental forms of writing which we associate with Pound, Joyce and Eliot. In writing *The Simple Life Limited,* Ford had exorcised the past and paved the way for the reinvention of himself as a writer engaging thoughtfully with the relationship between literature and gender, as explored in *Women & Men,* and with selective practices of the modernism he had championed in *The English Review,* as explored in *The Good Soldier.* Ford may have remained a radical Tory by temperament, and, like many of the early modernists, suspicious of democracy, modernity and popular culture, but by asking questions about the ways that at our most fundamental level we perform roles constructed for us by our culture, he can now be seen to be in advance of many of his male contemporaries.

Further Bibliography

Edward Carpenter, 'Simplification of Life' in *England's Ideal and Other Papers on Social Subjects* (London: George Allen and Unwin Ltd, 1887)

Edward Carpenter, *Love's Coming of Age* (Manchester: Labour Press, 1896)

Wendy Cumming and Elizabeth Kaplan, *The Arts and Crafts Movement* (London: Thames and Hudson, 1991)

Ford Madox Ford, *Women & Men* (Paris: Three Mountain Press, 1923)

Ford Madox Ford, *The Good Soldier* (New York and London: W. W. Norton & Company 1995)

Michael Jacobs, *The Good and Simple Life: Artist Colonies in Europe and America* (Oxford: Phaidon, 1985)

Alan Judd, *Ford Madox Ford* (London: William Collins and Sons, 1990)

Max Saunders, *Ford Madox Ford : A Dual Life*, 2 vols (Oxford: Oxford University Press, 1996)

Frances Swiney, *The Cosmic Procession, or the Feminine Principle in Evolution* (London: Ernest Bell, 1906)

NOTES

1. Judith Butler, *Gender Trouble: Feminism and the Subversion of Identity* (London: Routledge, 1990).

2. Fiona MacCarthy, *The Simple Life: C. R. Ashbee in the Cotswolds* (London: Lund Humphries Publishers Ltd, 1981), endpaper.

3. MacCarthy, *The Simple Life*, p. 132.

4. Fiona MacCarthy, *William Morris: A Life for Our Time* (London: Faber and Faber, 1994), p. 456.

5. Edward Carpenter, *My Days and Dreams* (London: George Allen and Unwin Ltd, 1916), p. 97.

6. *Ibid.*, p. 197.

7. R. W. Stallman, *Stephen Crane: A Biography* (New York: George Braziller, 1965).

8. Ford, under the pseudonym 'Daniel Chaucer', *The Simple Life Limited* (London: The Bodley Head, 1911), p. 7. Subsequent references appear in parentheses in the text, using the abbreviation *SLL*.

9. 'The Woman of the Novelists' was first published in *Vote*, 2 (27, August, 3, 10, and 17 September 1910), and included as Chapter VII in *The Critical Attitude* (London: Duckworth, 1911), pp. 145-69. Speaking of 'the woman of the novelists' Ford explains: 'For you, who are women, this creature is not of vast importance as an object lesson. For us men she is of the utmost. We fancy that, for most of us she is the only woman we know': *The Critical Attitude*, p. 148.

II

THE GOOD SOLDIER:
DESIRE, TEXT, AND HISTORY

IRONY AND THE MARRIAGE PLOT
IN *THE GOOD SOLDIER*

Davida Pines

In modernism, marriage generates, rather than inhibits, narrative. Whereas in traditional courtship novels of the nineteenth century marriage coincides with the satisfaction of desire, and consequently with the novel's end, in modernism marriage is represented as inherently flawed or incomplete, and therefore, in D. A. Miller's terms, 'narratable'. For Miller, novelistic production is motivated by 'insufficiencies, defaults, [and] deferrals', while novelistic closure assumes the achievement of a whole, and correspondingly, of a 'state of quiescence' or stasis: the 'state of lack', Miller notes, '. . . can only be liquidated along with the narrative itself'.[1] In Ford Madox Ford's *The Good Soldier* (1915), marriage is the subject rather than the object of the novel; it drives the narrative rather than simply signalling and signifying its end. The notion of a perfect union is treated ironically, and by the novel's conclusion it is marriage itself, rather than a particular hero or heroine, whose wayward energies and desires have been tempered and disciplined. Those elements of the novel which appear to disrupt the traditional 'marriage plot' structure are ultimately incorporated within its confines. Evacuated, however ironically, of meaning, marriage, in *The Good Soldier*, emerges as an empty but intact shell; the 'perfect union' emerges undercut but nonetheless very nearly unscathed.

In a traditional 'marriage plot', or courtship novel, marriage is the centre of a stable system of meaning. Jane Austen's fiction, for example, 'is rigorously designed in terms of a resolution that leaves no residue or excess remaining to be told' (Miller 19). 'The perfect union of Emma and Mr. Knightly virtually must end the novel; otherwise it would not be a perfect union"' (Miller 5). In *The Good*

Soldier, marriage no longer presupposes traditional, or sacramental, meanings. Nancy's awakening to the meaninglessness of the marriage bond underscores this. In contrast to Leonora's unblinking response to a newspaper's report of an adultery and the ensuing divorce, Nancy registers shock. A rigorously taught Catholic, Nancy has, until this particular moment in the novel, never thought of marriage as other than a foundational truth. Faced with the reality of divorce, Nancy 'felt a sickness – a sickness that grew as she read. Her heart beat painfully; she began to cry'.[2] As the new information begins to penetrate Nancy's consciousness, the world around her seems to empty of its previous significance:

> In her eyes the whole of that familiar, great hall had a changed aspect. The andirons with the brass flowers at the ends appeared unreal; the burning logs were just logs that were burning and not the comfortable symbols of an indestructible mode of life. (*GS* 141)

The 'law of the [Catholic] church', which, as Carol Jacobs notes, 'insists on the indissoluble one-to-one relationship between man and wife and implicitly between sacramental text and meaning', is here disrupted for Nancy.[3] 'Aren't marriages sacraments?' she sobs. 'Aren't they indissoluble? . . . . I thought you were married or not married as you are alive or dead' (*GS* 141). No longer a defining or essential aspect of identity, marriage becomes for Nancy, as it has already become, in varying degrees, for the other characters in the novel, a sign no longer linked to its referent, a structure whose meaning is constantly deferred.

The traditional courtship novel, then, in which marriage equals the satisfaction of desire and the end of experience, gives way in *The Good Soldier* to a representation of marriage as that which encourages and enables the proliferation of possible relations and significations. When Florence decides to marry, for example, she does so in order to escape the circumscribed world inhabited by her prudish aunts and to gain access to the world at large; her marriage signals the beginning rather than the end of her sexual freedom. Allowing the strictures of marriage (and the well-crafted fiction of her susceptible 'heart') to cloak her with unearned respectability, Florence successfully delivers herself first to Europe and then into the arms of her former lover. Far from presupposing the existence of sexual desire for her intended husband, marriage for Florence seems specifically to defend against such desire; it enables rather than curtails the pursuit of other men. As Dowell reports, Florence herself is unflinching in the requirements she makes of her intended husband and, in effect, of marriage:

> She wanted to marry a gentleman of leisure; she wanted a European establishment. She wanted her husband to have an English accent, an income of fifty thousand dollars a year from real estate and no ambitions to increase that income. And – she faintly hinted – she did not want much physical passion in the affair. (*GS* 58)

Florence's only remaining stipulation is a bedroom of her own and the guarantee of uncompromised privacy. Her marriage to Dowell is an empty structure dependent on Dowell's blindness and the absence of mutual desire: 'I determined', Dowell archly assures the reader, 'with all the obstinacy of a possibly weak nature, if not to make her mine, at least to marry her' (*GS* 57). Like Florence, he is interested in achieving the form, if not the content, of marital relations.

Florence's wholly unsentimental conception of marriage permits her to incorporate adultery within its structures. Edward Ashburnham differs from Florence in the way he justifies such an arrangement. Ashburnham exists in a world buffered by romantic – that is, novelistic – notions of a perfect union. It is his conveniently sentimental belief in the existence and possibility of a perfect union that provides the rationale for his multiple adulteries. While the novel questions the existence of a final, all-consuming love, Edward clings valiantly to what Dowell describes as an 'intense, optimistic belief that the woman he was making love to at the moment was the one he was destined, at last, to be eternally constant to. . . .' (*GS* 25). Fidelity, Ashburnham reasons, is owed to 'true love', not to an empty marriage contract. Thus, Edward commits adultery in the name of a displaced perfect union. His sentimentality rationalizes what Florence's pragmatism readily admits, namely that marriage does not eliminate the desire for, but in fact seems to engender, extra-marital relations. While Florence's relations depend on Dowell's possibly witting blindness to them, Ashburnham's depend on a similar blindness: sentimentality blankets the failure of his marriage.

Edward's devotion to 'perfect union' rather than 'perfect marriage' allows him to justify behavior that would otherwise prove incompatible with his image of himself as high romantic hero. Leonora, on the other hand, still believes that perfect happiness ought necessarily to coincide with marriage. What matters most to her, however, is the structure rather than the content of the marital relation: regardless of whether marriage does equal happiness, it should, in Leonora's view, equal stability. As in traditional courtship novels, marriage, again from Leonora's perspective, ought to enact 'a resolution that leaves no residue or excess remaining to be told' (Miller 19).

Thus, Leonora's goal is to achieve equilibrium within her marriage despite her husband's excesses. Edward's affairs have inevitably led him into financial, if not moral, debt, and Leonora sets herself the task of managing his accounts and limiting his (as well as her own) expenditures. 'So she went at it', Dowell notes.

> They were eight years in India and during the whole of that time she insisted that they must be self-supporting [. . .] She gave him [. . .] five hundred a year for 'Ashburnham frills' as she called it to herself – and she considered she was doing him very well. (*GS* 111)

Similarly, Leonora attempts to manage Edward's love affairs. By way of compensating Edward for the return of Mrs. Basil to Major Basil, the blackmailing husband, for example, Leonora arranges and funds the passage from India to Europe of Edward's newest love interest, Maisie Maidan, in order that Edward might have company and distraction at Nauheim. Dowell explains, '[Leonora] thought that if [Edward] could smile again through her agency he might return, through gratitude and satisfied love – to her. . . [Indeed], [s]he had the vague, passionate idea that, when Edward had exhausted a number of other types of women he must turn to her' (*GS* 119). While Leonora maintains the hope that proper management of Edward's passions might eventually result in these passions taking her as their object, she is nonetheless willing to accept that Edward's 'true love' might in fact be someone other than herself. In fact, given the exhausting nature of managing Edward, it is not surprising that, as Dowell remarks, 'she would really have welcomed it if [Edward] could have come across the love of his life [since] [i]t would have given her a rest' (*GS* 49). Leonora is willing to accept closure in whatever form it is offered.

Despite Leonora's best efforts to contain Ashburnham's passions, he turns from Maisie to Florence, and after Florence to Nancy. While Florence's vulgarity disgusts Leonora, it is Ashburnham's interest in Nancy that proves the most debilitating. What is different about Edward's passion for Nancy is his determination not to give in to it. It seems that Edward has begun to understand the nature of his own desires, namely, that the only way for him 'to be eternally constant to' anyone is simply to refuse to satisfy his desire. Nancy will be 'the final passion of [Edward's] life', not because she is his 'perfect match', as Leonora jealously suspects, but because Edward has chosen to withhold his passion for her. It is this decision which causes Leonora's breakdown. She has learned to manage and compensate for excess; she finds herself incapable of coping with unending lack: 'Upon her return from Nauheim Leonora had completely broken down – because she knew [that] she could trust Edward' (*GS* 130). Trust, in this case, signifies unsatisfied desire. In Miller's terms, the Ashburnhams' marriage has been 'narratable' up until this point in that it has produced, rather than resolved, or satisfied, desire. Leonora has worked to create resolution, if not by achieving her own perfect union with Edward, at least by aiding Edward in finding the 'true' or 'final' object of his passions. She is willing to live within a triangular relation, as long as the third member of the trio is a known and stable entity. While Nancy will remain a stable figure within the triad, Edward's unconsummated passion for her resists closure. Thus, Edward thwarts Leonora's attempts to achieve a state of 'non-narratability', for the state of lack introduced by Nancy will not be liquidated. It is, in fact, Edward's dearest hope, that 'the girl, [Nancy] being five thousand miles away, would continue [indefinitely] to love him' (*GS* 153).

'If you think', Leonora tells Ashburnham, determined at last to break the silence surrounding his passion for Nancy, 'that I do not know that you are in love with the girl. . . ', but she trails off, parrying her own blow. 'She [had begun] spiritedly', Dowell reports, 'but she could not find any ending for the sentence' (*GS* 136). In fact, the marriage sentence that Leonora serves and in which she is trapped is one of open-endedness. Her world is restricted not by closure, but by its lack. 'If you want me to divorce you', Leonora finally offers by way of finishing her (marriage) sentence, however drastically, 'I will. You can marry her then. She's in love with you' (*GS* 136).

In the end, drastic measures, at least on Leonora's part, are unnecessary. Ashburnham's suicide in the name of unending passion and sentimentalism frees Leonora to embark on another marriage union, this time with Rodney Bayham of Bayham, with whom she had tried, three years previously, to have 'her abortive love-affair' (*GS* 132). It seems particularly appropriate that Leonora's marriage to Bayham has its roots in adultery, for the marriage, notwithstanding its trumpeted 'normalcy', incorporates and accomodates a triangular marital structure. 'I mean to say', Dowell begins his ironic paean to the 'normal',

> that in normal circumstances [Leonora's] desires were those of the woman who is needed by society. She desired children, decorum, an establishment; she desired to avoid waste, she desired to keep up appearances . . . . It was like that for Leonora. She was made for normal circumstances – for Mr. Rodney Bayham, who will keep a separate establishment, secretly, in Portsmouth, and make occasional trips to Paris and to Buda-Pesth. (*GS* 153)

The 'normal' marriage, then, means adultery; it presupposes a separate establishment, kept secretly, in the midst of the marriage union. Thus, the complex interaction of twos against threes that has been woven throughout the novel has here become institutionalized. Just as Florence and Dowell travelled each year from Paris to Nice to Nauheim, thereby inscribing a triangular route which imitated the erotic structure of their marriage, so too will Bayham travel from Paris to Portsmouth to Buda-Pesth, thus inscribing a similar triangular pattern. The 'minuet de la cour' (*GS* 11), the pair dance done to triple meter, which Dowell invokes nostalgically through the novel, is here normalized. Leonora has what she missed in her relationship with Ashburnham: a stable triad. Morever, the triangular structure will be reproduced, for Leonora has a child.

That Dowell takes an ironic stance towards the 'normal' circumstances of Leonora's marriage is clear. 'Well, that is the end of the story', he begins his peroration:

> And, when I come to look at it I see that it is a happy ending with wedding bells and all. The villains – for obviously Edward and the girl were villains – have been punished by suicide and madness. The heroine – the perfectly normal, virtuous and slightly deceitful heroine – has become the happy wife of a perfectly normal, virtuous and slightly-deceitful husband. She will

shortly become a mother of a perfectly normal, virtuous, slightly deceitful son or daughter.

'A happy ending', he finishes, 'that is what it works out at' (*GS* 160). As much as Dowell's irony undercuts the marriage plot and its accompanying happy ending, however, it does not explode this structure. An ironic formulation of a 'perfect union' is fundamentally conservative of it, for it not only relies on the 'original' or 'traditional' meanings in order to parody them, but insists that the reader or listener remember the earlier forms. It keeps the original meanings in circulation.

In a similar vein, Dowell might, with Florence and Edward dead, and Leonora remarried, have severed his relations with the past. He has no obligation to Nancy, and little hope that 'her reason will ever be sufficiently restored to let her appreciate the meaning of the Anglican marriage service' (*GS* 151). Nonetheless, he stays with her. She is '[e]nigmatic, silent, utterly well-behaved as far as her knife and fork go', yet he prefers to remain attached to an empty structure, 'a picture without meaning', than to break away entirely from the dream of the perfect union (*GS* 161). Nancy is a reminder of the marriage he had imagined himself to have been living; she is a link to the 'perfect foursome' to which he had believed himself connected. 'They were three to one', Dowell relates near the beginning of the novel, '– and they made my happy. Oh God', he moans, 'they made me so happy that I doubt if even paradise, that shall smooth out all temporal wrongs, shall ever give me the like. And what could they have done better', he asks, invoking a version of the marriage vow, 'or what could they have done that could have been worse?' (*GS* 52). Dowell bears a nostalgic relation to the past that is enacted through irony: in undercutting his 'three-to-one' marriage, he remembers and savours it.

The function of irony, then, in relation to the marriage plot is a conservative one. On the other hand, the triangular structure of irony (that is, the use of language with one meaning for a privileged audience and another meaning for those addressed) imitates the triangular structure of adultery – a structure that has been incorporated within the institution of marriage by the end of the novel. Thus, irony works in this case to articulate the simultaneous conservation and disruption of the marriage tradition. It encourages a critical assessment of marriage, while at the same time enabling the persistence of its attendant illusions.

NOTES

1. D. A. Miller, *Narrative and Its Discontents: Problems of Closure in the Traditional Novel* (Princeton: Princeton University Press, 1981) – henceforth 'Miller'; p. 3. Subsequent page references will appear in the text.

2. Ford Madox Ford, *The Good Soldier*, ed. Martin Stannard (New York and London: W. W. Norton & Company, 1995), p. 14. Subsequent page references will appear in the text, with the title abbreviated to *GS*.

3. Carol Jacobs, *Telling Time: Levi-Strauss, Ford, Lessing, Benjamin, de Man, Wordsworth, Rilke* (Baltimore: The Johns Hopkins University Press, 1992), p. 86.

EMPIRE, ETHNOLOGY AND *THE GOOD SOLDIER*

Caroline Patey

Dark at Heart

If ever it had been innocent and unobtrusively referential, the word 'heart' ceased to be so in the very early years of the twentieth century. *The Heart of the Empire* – edited by C. F. G. Masterman – and *Heart of Darkness*, both published in close succession, are unequivocal indications that hearts have left the lexical area of individual emotions and conflicts only to be reborn in the semantic field of imperial discourse, even if with divergent and unstable meanings. Where to locate a heart of darkness which hovers uneasily between Africa and Europe is still an object of debate. If Masterman's heart is unambig-uously set in London, it is equally wrapped in obscurity. Deprived urban areas are phrased as 'unknown regions' and 'terra incognita', and there is undoubtedly a strong 'cartographic' affinity between the explorers of the abysmal city and the Congo travellers: Marlow's childhood map with its many colours echoes London's 'poverty map' with its 'blotches of black and dark blue that arise now in the midst of the red artisans' quarters instead of in the yellow area of riches'.[1] Darkest Africa competes with, or doubles or intersects, darkest London.[2] Wherever they may be, hearts are shrouded in shadows and 'unknowability' and testify to a growing anxiety about space, an uneasiness which also finds expression in the recurring obsession with maps and mapping.

Though it becomes a commonplace cliché, the heart/darkness trope is nonetheless revealing in virtue of its conflicting denotations, and alerts us to a growing disturbance in traditional ethnocentric assumptions. In the light of a metaphorical cluster so ubiquitous in the English culture of the time, and given Ford's friendship with both Masterman and Conrad, the cardiological obsession of *The Good Soldier* appears no naive or random motive; indeed, all Ford's hearts are discovered to have, for one reason or the other, constant associations with darkness and gloom. More than anything else, perhaps, the idea of 'Florence clearing up one of the dark places of the earth, leaving the world a little lighter than she had found it'[3] reads as a caustic reminder of the fuzzy wilderness/civilisation (or darkness/light) dialectic and of its spatial and ideological implications.

Misreading *Heart of Darkness*

No surprise, therefore, if *Heart of Darkness* appears as one of Ford's subtexts; it is certainly no coincidence that numerous Conradian clues should be disseminated throughout *The Good Soldier*. One of the most intriguing and disruptive has to do with a long unexpected digression by the narrator about Brussels – the unnamed starting point of Marlow's journey to Africa. Incongruously and at great length, Dowell goes into the details of unsynchronised railway timetables and laments the difficulty for anyone arriving at Calais with the boat train to catch the Brussels connection, thereby implying that he and Florence had often undergone the experience of 'running!–along the unfamiliar ways of the Brussels station'; an experience felt to be greatly dangerous for Florence's health: 'My wife used to run [. . .] But once in the German express, she would lean back with one hand to her side and her eyes closed' (*GS* 39-40). Since Florence is 'medically' not fit to cross the Channel, why is she catching the Calais boat-train, and why should she have to rush from one train to another pretending to play havoc with her fragile heart? This narrative contradiction is indeed enhanced a few pages later, when Dowell ponders on the fact that 'even on the fairest day of blue sky, with the cliffs of England shining like mother of pearl in full view of Calais, [he] would not have let her cross the steamer gangway to save her life' (*GS* 64-5). Unaware of the realistic tyranny of cause and effect or, much likelier, more than willing to subvert it, Ford rewrites the Brussels-Congo journey into a Brussels-Nauheim parody.

In more general terms, there is a consistent narrative and semantic osmosis from Conrad to Ford. The brief mention of an 'Italian baron who had much to do with the Belgian Congo' (*GS* 88) winks at yet another colonizer: 'All Europe contributed to the making of Kurtz'. [4] The question of brutishness – a major problem in *Heart of Darkness* – is often debated: is Ashburnham a brute? A recurring problem which is given divergent answers; and Nancy's father is feared for his 'brutalities'. While no unspeakable rites are to be found in *The Good Soldier*, a lot appears to be beyond the possibility of linguistic formulation: Leonora, for instance, often deems her husband's behaviour 'unspeakable'. Like the African jungle, Mitteleuropa has its terrors, more and more 'horrors' plague the world of the Ashburnhams as well as Dowell's. In such a context, the surfacing of violence – in Maisie's 'murder', for example – or the open expression of contempt for the natives of Africa – 'hang humanity' – may remind the reader of more explicit exterminations (*GS* 88). Conrad's shadow even reaches beyond Congo reminiscences: Ashburnham jumping into the Red Sea to rescue a Tommy contrasts with Jim's cowardice, and Leonora's father confessing to being at the end of his tether evokes yet another of Conrad's stories and yet another father-daughter relationship.

This self-conscious embedding of Conrad's voices in *The Good Soldier* has been explored by Thomas C. Moser, who stresses the many Dowell-Marlow parallelisms:

> Dowell is as close to Marlow as Ford could ever get [. . .his] choice of hero is Marlowian as well. Like Jim, Edward is a big, blond, handsome, inarticulate Englishman [. . .] Dowell, again, like Marlow, handles masterfully the meaningful, illustrative digression. [5]

However, beyond the consummate craft, the homage to the much admired master is also a deliberate misreading: Conrad's world is manipulated, turned upside down and inside out, scattered as if by the wind of a different syntax and divergent meanings. However blurred and unstable, for instance, the geography of *Heart of Darkness* retains some sort of distinction between here and there, Africa and Europe. Ford, on the other hand, ignores this shadow line so entirely that the civilized minuet of the pre-war European spa-society continuously dissolves into the tropes and vocabulary of the wilderness: 'perils for young American girlhood' are supposed to be lurking 'in the European jungle' and Paris is 'full of snakes in the grass'. In a ludicrous mimicry of tropical adventures, Maisie Maidan's dead body appears to be 'closed between the jaws of a gigantic alligator', and, when Ashburnham appears in the hotel dining room, his gait is such that he 'might have been walking in a jungle'. Not surprisingly, then, the articulate drawing-room conversation shifts to 'screaming hysterics', and love-making is considered an activity akin to exploration and the 'acquiring of a new territory' (*GS* 62, 56, 24, 12, 79).

Colonial Plots

Beyond the subtle filiations of intertextuality, however, the trace of Conrad's dislocated and relocated imperial geography suggests that closer attention should be dedicated to the colonial plots which frame and criss-cross the narrative of *The Good Soldier*. The much-glossed title offers the first of many indications, apparently pointing to Ashburnham's 'imperial' soldiership and anticipating the deployment of the implicit virtues of a faithful British subject: Ashburnham is, after all, 'an excellent magistrate, a first rate soldier, one of the best landlords in Hampshire, England' as well as 'upright, honest, fair dealing, fair thinking' (*GS* 14, 79). Edward embodies and, at the same time, deflates the official discourse of nationality and the manly and ethnocentric mystique associated with it: 'Imperial consciousness opened out before you in vistas as dazzling as they were unexplored. You were furnished, without effort on your own part, with traditions of valour and physical perfection: you stood, a scion of the sole white race, on the pinnacle of a world occupied solely otherwise by the parti-coloured'.[6]

Ineluctably, the good English soldier leads us to his battlefields – in Ashburnham's case more amorous and exotic than warlike. Ashburnham's military career, however, provides Ford with an occasion to take his readers on a sardonic colonial grand tour. India, where the characters are lured for sordid financial reasons, proves little more than a dream of oriental clichés, sensual gardens and sentimental moonlights. The South African war is briefly hinted at through the grotesque comedy of British soldiers leaving 'hundred bottle cases of champagne at five guineas a bottle on the veldt' (*GS* 113). Less remotely, imperial policy is also seen through the lenses of the Irish settlers, harassed by endemic troubles and poverty. Leonora's birth in a family of Irish landlords unveils the drama of the 'small beleaguered garrison in a hostile country'; there are various allusions to the then growing violence between Gaelic-Irish and Anglo-Irish; and, in such a context, the bitter religious conflict between Edward and Leonora acquires clear colonial undertones: 'Those were troublesome times in Ireland, I understand. At any rate Colonel Powys had tenants on the brain–his own tenants having shot at him with shotguns' (*GS* 47, 97).

The relevance of the Irish plot is of course enhanced by the passionate interest Ford had in the emancipation process in Ireland, 'The oldest colony of all'.[7] Even the United States is viewed as an ex-colony rather than as the world-power it was about to become at the beginning of the twentieth century. The very name of the ship 'Pocahontas' is a clue to the past 'glories' of exploration; the Hulbirds left England in 1688; and repeated mentions of General Braddock recall the revolution – obviously a trauma for Florence's aunts who had 'backed the losing side in the war of independence and had been seriously impoverished and quite efficiently oppressed for that reason' (*GS* 59). The whole chain of colonial history – exploration, emigration, settlement, independence, through to the post-colonial era – is thus represented in miniature. It is difficult to be blind to the fact that private hearts have a lot to do with the public history of the Empire.

Deeply inscribed in the narrative of *The Good Soldier*, this shifting colonial map is, first of all, an invitation to place the novel where it also belongs, namely at the heart of the raging debate on nationality and empire, in full flow at the beginning of the century. It is also a good occasion to assess the political dimension of Ford's modernism and modernity. While remembering that the pre-war years were crucial for the ideological construction of Englishness, let us also not overlook the fact that Ford and many of his closer friends were actively involved in puncturing the balloons of national and imperial rhetoric. Quite a few indeed reacted strongly against the 'new spirit which had been fostered by Mr Chamberlain, Mr Rhodes [. . .] and had become articulate in the vigorous doggerel of Rudyard Kipling', and resented 'the hypnotisation by the pomp and pageantry of war'.[8] For all his sentimental Toryism, Ford definitely did his part to undermine, unfalteringly if humorously, the imperialist fallacy: 'Being profoundly impressed by the uselessness to England of the British Empire [. . .] and wishing solely that South Africa might be returned to its real owners, the natives, and Kruger and Mr. Chamberlain hung on the same gallows, I was once chased for three quarters of a mile along Oxford St. by a howling mob of patriots. That was during the South African wars'.[9] However, while Masterman and Ford, among others, thundered against the 'callous scoundrels' in Africa[10] and welcomed the idea of a nation without an empire, other voices were arising to promote a muscular and masculine sense of national cohesion and expansion.

Robert Baden-Powell's *Scouting for Boys. A Handbook for Instruction in Good Citizenship* (1908) launched a long-lasting process of shaping English minds and bodies and trying to convince younger generations that they 'belong to the British Empire, one of the greatest empires that has ever existed in the world'.[11] Between 1903 and 1910, *The Riddle of the Sands,* by R. Erskine Childers, went through three successive editions and established a grammar for the novel of invasion while mobilising paranoid fears of an enemy. More insidious was the Society for Pure English, founded in 1913, which aimed at preserving the language from the invasion of foreign and mongrel tongues.[12] The motif of a 'pure' language incidentally throws an interesting light on the polyglottism of *The Good Soldier*, a novel where local accents and verbal modes loom large in the narrative conflicts: American English ('Florence's nasty New York sayings') or Dowell's Pennsylvania Duitsch accent contrast with the southern English of Ashburnham – who 'talked like a good book' (*GS* 28, 26). *The Good Soldier* thus echoes important issues in the debate then current on language, but its narrator also approaches the problems from a curiously misplaced and unsettled point of view. Far from volunteering statements or asserting opinions, Dowell's voice of uncertainty – to use Ann Barr Snitow's words – expresses a decentered vision of the Empire and materializes the fragmentation of Standard English into a multiplicity of idioms. Precisely this helplessness exposes the cracks and flaws of imperial discourse and re-stages the dynamics of a faltering colonial and national identity.[13]

The imperial theme and Dowell's stuttering utterance may hopefully lead us a step further into the understanding of Ford's puzzling epistemology. In a text saturated with the language of ethnology (primitive marriage, capture, polygamy, sacrifice, sex battle, sex instinct . . .),[14] the interaction of an alien observer's stumbling prose with topical colonial allusions requires that *The Good Soldier* also be placed in the context of the young and energetic anthropological discussion then taking place in England. Ford – and Conrad, whose presence in the textual palimpsest is not to be forgotten – lived and worked in the years when British anthropology was striving to free itself from its colonial matrix and evolving quickly from the armchair method of the questionnaire to direct inquiry and field observation. The legitimation of anthropology as a scientific and academic discipline involved deep epistemological and

CAROLINE PATEY

ideological turmoil which no doubt reached the enlightened society then concentrated around Rye and Winchelsea.[15] True, there seems to be no record of Ford's knowledge of either armchair or field ethnology, but we know of strong affinities, not to say intertextualities, between Conrad, on the one hand, and Frazer and Malinowski, on the other.[16] Apart from Conrad – whose intellectual encounter with Frazer took place in a moment of intense collaboration with Ford – likely mediations between Ford and the world of ethnology might have involved most of his friends and protégés, from H. G. Wells and W. H. Hudson to D. H. Lawrence, Wyndham Lewis and John Galsworthy.[17]

No doubt, Ford's own curiosity and omnivorous reading must have acquainted him with the second edition of *The Golden Bough* (1900) and the discussion it lead to, which drew attention to Frazer's contradictions and sometimes doubtful reliability. It so happens, moreover, that Ford's 'The Mother, A Song-Drama' was published in the April issue of the *Fortnightly Review,* which also included a long, analytic and polemical review of 'Mr. Frazer's Theory of the Crucifixion', a section of the 1900 edition of *The Golden Bough* which was deleted from the subsequent reprints. Thanks to its author Andrew Lang's obvious wish to expose Frazer's many weaknesses, the review offers a wonderful insight into some aspects of ritual sacrifice and sacred harlotry.[18] Had Ford's curiosity been tickled, there was no shortage of ethnological literature to satisfy it: from Alfred C. Haddon's report of the Torres Straits expedition (1901) to Frazer's *Totemism and Exogamy* (1910) and Malinowski's *The Family among the Australian Aborigines* (1913).

This is unfortunately not conclusive data. It does, however, confirm that diffused anthropological moods, terminology and approaches to facts were then permeating much of English culture and that the data was easily available to Ford. When C. F. G. Masterman describes the 'life and manners and habits of the aborigines' as they may be observed 'in the other London beyond the water', and Grant

Allen investigates the comic possibilities of ethnological distance in *The British Barbarians,*[19] making light of ethnocentric axioms, they both draw freely from the recently discovered reservoir of anthropological tropes. Ford himself was trying his pen at ethnological writing of a kind in the trilogy *England and the English: An Interpretation.*[20] In spite of huge differences in depth and intention, Ford does share some methodological elements with field workers of a more academic stance: an objectifying tendency to classify, a questioning attitude in front of the customs of the tribe, a stress on observation from an external and displaced point of view. *The Good Soldier*'s debt to *The Spirit of the People* stands as evidence of the ideal continuity between 'ethnology' and narrative. Undoubtedly, the chapter entitled 'Conduct' – which starts with an unambiguous anti-colonial statement – has left a deep mark on some central motives of the novel: the 'things' that should not be mentioned in English culture (religious topics, relations of the sexes, poverty-stricken districts . . .), the repression of emotions, a sketch of the perfect Englishman as a mystical sportsman, the famous station episode which offers a first draft of Edward Ashburnham, all these motifs have migrated from essay to narrative with great ease (*SP* 143, 145, 146, 152). While in the process of defining its own scientific and academic status and discovering new modes of approaching otherness, anthropology was undoubtedly in the air, in the culture and in the language of England.

The Customs of the Tribe
Whether deliberately incorporated or absorbed in more surreptitious ways, anthropology seems, therefore, to have contributed to the making of *The Good Soldier*. A first inkling is to be found in an apparently discordant lexical choice. When the narrator recalls Edward's desire to be a 'polygamist' (*GS* 125), the conventional story of womanizing, adultery and unfaithfulness is set to a new tune and displaced into an entirely different semantic field. In this light,

'Edward carrying on intrigues with other women, with two at once, with three' (*GS* 117) invites the reader to rethink the conflicts of the novel in terms of social and cultural patterns rather than individual passions. Edward's 'polygamy' is echoed by Florence's 'polyandry' – a word not found in *The Good Soldier*, though the practice is: 'And, by the time she was sick of Jimmy [. . .] she had taken on Edward Ashburnham' (*GS* 65), while of course being married to Dowell. Dowell's 'capture' of Florence, thanks to the night and the help of a ladder, and his subsequent comment about 'how primitively these matters were arranged in those days [. . .]' (*GS* 60) reinforces these ethnological undertones. Marriages by capture or elopement, Malinowski explains, were common among the 'violent forms of obtaining wives'.[21] The same conviction is to be found in Frazer: 'There are signs to show that marriage by capture was once the rule'.[22]

Latent polyandry – together with explicit capture and polygamy – sketch the underlying pattern of the novel and confirm its affinity with the anthropological discussion. Indeed, the group formed by the Ashburnhams and Nancy, so often questioned for its elusive internal relations, may perhaps be best understood if approached in terms of kinship.[23] Malinowski – in a first book published a few months before Ford started writing *The Good Soldier* – gives us an initial insight into what was to become the ethnological question *par excellence*. After stating that 'the class of kinship ideas [. . .] must affirm an intimate bond of some kind between the parties involved', the ethnographer contends that kinship must not be confused with consanguinity, which it would be incorrect 'to treat as a constant and indispensable constituent of parental kinship'.[24] In Australia, as in the narrative country of *The Good Soldier*, blood-ties are simply not the relevant paradigm, whether they exist or not: Nancy is a ward, Edward a guardian, Leonora an aunt or a friend, all three of them implicated in the mysterious entanglements of primitive kinship. This suggestion is supported and further illuminated by the fact – generally acknowledged by most ethnographers, and originally pointed out by Malinowski – that 'the majority of Australian tribes are wholly ignorant of the physiological process of procreation'.[25] This comes as a strikingly appropriate clue to one of the much glossed enigmas of *The Good Soldier*: 'Edward Ashburnham [. . .] at the time of his marriage and for perhaps a couple of years after [. . .] did not really know how children are produced. Neither did Leonora' (*GS* 99).

In his perplexed appreciation of alien customs, the narrator even seems to follow Malinowski's warning not to generalise but to read cultural fact in the light of geographical difference: 'It is the law of the land' (*GS* 151) which forbids Dowell to marry Nancy. Indeed, this 'I cannot marry her' is only one of a string of vetoes linked to marriage, an obsession that runs through the novel and bears an uncanny resemblance to Frazer's thoughts on exogamy: 'A community was bisected into two exogamous and intermarrying groups, and all men and women were classified according to the generation and the group to which they belonged. The principle of classification was not "Whom am I descended from", but "Whom may I marry"'.[26] A haunting question to everyone in *The Good Soldier*, to be sure. Mad women cannot marry allegedly healthy men, and marriage, as Nancy discovers with horror, is no ontological or irreversible affair: 'I thought you were married or unmarried as you are alive or dead [. . .] That, Leonora said, is the law of the Church. It is not the law of the land' (*GS* 141). Customs change according to the local community which originates them or, indeed, according to the totemic group one belongs to: what is possible for the Anglican Brands – as it had been for Henry VIII – is forbidden to the worshippers of a Catholic God. Exogamy, writes Frazer, is stern, pitiless, and puritanical, as Dowell no doubt agrees: 'Not one of us had got what he really wanted' (*GS* 151). In his bemused way, Dowell is groping in the dark to grasp, formulate and perhaps interpret the intricate cultural patterns of the English tribe, its customary and religious rules, norms, vetoes and fetishes; and, to do so, he has to decipher a system of facial and verbal expressions as well as the technicalities of English life.

Frazer's voice, however, is not limited to matrimonial norms. A suspicious – and seemingly gratuitous – piece of mistletoe (*GS* 135) alerts us to the fact that *The Golden Bough* had become a widely shared cultural currency,[27] and that Nancy, a huntress repeatedly associated with horses, owes some aspects of her character to the Frazerian Diana, in whose ritual 'fire seems to have played a foremost part'.[28] Nancy's erotic fantasies are similarly ignited: 'Flame then really seemed to fill her body [. . .] he was kissing her on her face that burned and on her neck that was on fire' (*GS* 144). Or should we connect Diana to Leonora, since she also rides and hunts with Bayham, uses a riding whip and is worshipped by the would-be vestal Nancy as the Virgin Mary, who according to Frazer, is a Christian displacement of Diana: 'The Christian church appears to have sanctified this great festival of the Virgin goddess by adroitly converting it into the festival of the Assumption of the Blessed Virgin on the 15 of August'? (*GB* 14)

Other *personae*, however, gather around Nancy. She is also a likely candidate for sacred prostitution, an argument that fostered endless discussions after the second edition of *The Golden Bough*. To the girl, Edward is a godlike 'precious lamb', to whom she is ready to sacrifice her virginity – 'I am ready to belong to you, to save your life' (*GS* 154) – all this in a context where prostitution and harlotry are constantly evoked and alluded to. Enough, it would seem, to establish some kind of contiguity with the 'servants or slaves of the gods' who 'in common parlance are spoken of simply as harlots' (*GB* 320). Nancy's Frazerian affinities are moreover reinforced by her redundant and disconcerting involvement with Saturnalia (*GS* 85), a motif which reasserts the disturbing overlapping of so-called civilised order and pagan rituals as a time 'when the whole population give themselves up to extravagant mirth and jollity and when darker passions find a vent which would never be allowed them in a more staid and sober course of civilised life', in the form of 'wild orgies of lust and crime' (*GB* 630).

Finally, Edward's death, textualized as a sacrifice with strong ritual overtones, leads us to the Scapegoat theory. At first a Christ-like figure, Ashburnham is tortured by the two women: 'I seem to see him stand, naked to the waist [. . .] and flesh hanging from him in rags' (*GS* 152). Dowell's ever hesitating narrative then offers a more 'primitive' version of the same moment: 'They were like a couple of Sioux who had got hold of an Apache and had him well-tied to a stake' (*GS* 152). Whatever the mode of his violent death, Edward is implicitly sacrificed, because 'society can only exist if the normal, if the virtuous, and the slightly-deceitful flourish, and if the passionate, the headstrong and the too-truthful are condemned to suicide and to madness' (*GS* 160-61); 'Edward must die, the girl must lose her reason [. . .] in order that a third personality, more normal, should have, after a period of trouble, a quiet, comfortable good time' (*GS* 148-9). Ashburnham is the scapegoat upon whom the sins and evils of the people are laid, his death effecting a 'total clearance of all the ills that have been infesting the people' (*GB* 587, 589, 670).

The Ethnographer's Burden
Knitting together ethnology and fiction, *The Good Soldier* proves to be the fascinating – and in certain ways still not wholly explored – document of a close intellectual encounter between distinct cultural pursuits. The sole fact of using ethnological tools – traditionally employed in the context of 'primitive' societies – in a European plot creates much disturbance in the traditional geopolitical mapping of the globe. For it implies, of course, that Ford treats the European gentry that occupies the centre as he would the native people of the periphery. The novel literally shows us the English being ethnologized, a subversive affair, presumably, in 1915, though, we have seen, favoured by other writers. Moreover, Dowell's specific position as an American contributes to the further blurring of the

boundary between the anthropologist and the native object he is studying. The detached glance of the anthropologist is directed by the former colonial subject upon the European gentry. Dowell is an amphibious narrator who combines uneasily the status of the native with the detached glance of the would-be scientific observer, and in this sense interestingly anticipates Malinowski's prediction that the anthropologized would eventually appropriate the weapons of the ethnographer.

But the fact that different discursive modes are woven into the same narrative also raises the question of their relation. In other words, how does ethnology relate to fiction and fiction to ethnology? Post-modernity has alerted us to the problem of the heuristic status of history and the authority of scientific discourse. And authority, or the lack of it, is precisely the problem that Dowell's precarious ethnological fiction (or fictitious ethnology) obliges his readers to address. In this sense, his story shows an affinity with the preoccupations of contemporary ethnology, constantly assailed by the impossibility of self-legitimisation in its chase for cultural truth: 'In short, anthropological writings are themselves [. . .] fictions; fictions in the sense they are something made, something fashioned [. . .] not that they are false, unfactual, or merely "as if" thought experiments'.[29] Clifford Geertz's words are actually a welcome reminder that the truth/lie discussion around Dowell has lost whatever pertinence it had; as Ford, incidentally, well knew when he wrote that 'books aim at renderings rather than statements' (*SP* xvi). True to the constitutive ambiguity of fiction/ethnology, Dowell's narrative 'renders' the anxiety of a failing objectivity and the downfall of positivistic certitudes.

It also gives us a fresh insight into the famously confusing epistemology of a novel that stumbles from uncertainty to doubt 'in a very rambling way so that it may be difficult for anyone to find their path through what may be a sort of maze' (*GS* 119). Dowell finds himself in the awkward situation of the ethnologist who faces the alien other without knowing much of their language nor of their customs, and has to piece together raw data and fragmentary pieces of information. He has to depend on informants whose reliability is dubious, and to follow indeed the methodological advice Malinowski offers in the first chapter of *The Family among the Australian Aborigines*. Many pages are dedicated, often in the interrogative form, to the assessment of the informants as well as to the method of asking questions in the right way and of weighing the evidence at length; it is essential to hear many opinions on the same subject, and once this is done, to find one's way in the maze of heterogeneous statements. What emerges very clearly in these beautiful pages is the hermeneutic – Malinowski actually uses this word – fragility of the observer whose interpretation must be, as it were, suspended: 'Some of the statements may be regarded as untrustworthy. The correct interpretation of others may be determined; and thus the contradiction will vanish. Sometimes, it is impossible, the contradictions remain irreducible. Then they must be simply pointed out'.[30] Dowell, as an ethnologist, is trapped in a similar set of limitations. His informants are hardly dependable: 'I asked Mrs. Ashburnham whether she had told Florence that and what Florence had said and she answered [. . .]' (*GS* 14). He is forced into repetition (weighing his evidence?) and contradiction: is Ashburnham a brute or the 'painstaking guardian' (*GS* 14) to the whole world? Is Leonora the saint or the villain of the piece? That he reaches so few conclusions may prove that Dowell is bad at his job, but his approach to the European natives remains nonetheless close to the ethnological mode and doomed by the same epistemological frailties.

Much of this weakness is due to the double position of the observer, who is somehow part of the action he observes, as, with amazing perspicacity, Malinowski already knew in 1913.[31] In his unwittingly double role, Dowell also performs the last act of the ethnographer's part, confusing his identity with Ashburnham's and experiencing the impossible desire of the anthropologist, the passion that 'leaves his questions unanswered': 'I loved Edward Ashburnham [. . .] I love him because he was just myself' (*GS* 161).[32]

More than anything else, Dowell is caught in the painful process of translation – or, using Ford's terminology, 'rendering' – which is the lot of the ethnographer: 'Ethnography is thick description. What the ethnographer is in fact faced with [. . .] is a multiplicity of complex conceptual structures, many of them superimposed or knotted into one another, which are at once strange, irregular and inexplicit and which he must contrive first to grasp and then to render'.[33] Rendering therefore means synchronising chunks of data which have been given in no sequential order, a result Dowell tries hard to achieve, however unsuccessfully: 'One goes back, one goes forward. One remembers points that one has forgotten and one explains them all the more minutely since one recognises that one has forgotten to mention them in their proper places and that one may have given, by omitting them, a false impression' (*GS* 120). Dowell is thus, perhaps, given an *a posteriori* forgiveness for his illogical and disjointed narrative, since coherence, in ethnology or fiction, is not necessarily a positive value: 'Coherence cannot be the major test of validity for a cultural description [. . .] there is nothing so coherent as a paranoid's description or a swindler's story. Nothing has done more to discredit cultural analysis than the construction of impeccable depictions of formal ordering whose actual existence nobody can believe'.[34]

Translation also implies fixing the volatile data of oral communication and perception on the page and bridging the gap between the process of listening/speaking and writing. It is an uneasy voyage from one form to another and from field to page that Dowell invites us to, referring twice to his diaries and acknowledging he has been writing for months while addressing an ideal listener: 'The ethnographer "inscribes" social discourse; he writes it down. In so doing, he turns it from a passing event which exists solely in its own moment of occurrence, into an account which exists in its inscriptions and can be re-consulted'.[35] But this uneasiness – textualised into the tormented tropes of ethnological analysis – hypothesis, repetition, oxymoron, suspension – is precisely the stuff of *epistemic* density. Dowell's failure to understand may well be the ethnographer's burden: 'Cultural analysis is intrinsically incomplete. And worse than that, the more deeply its goes, the less complete it is. It is a strange science whose most telling assertions are its most tremulously based'.[36] Losing his way in translation, Dowell formulates and addresses the crucial questions of twentieth century epistemology and ethnology; and if he fails to answer them, it makes him, and Ford, all the closer to us.

NOTES

1. C. F. G. Masterman, 'Realities at Home', in C. F. G. Masterman, ed., *The Heart of the Empire: Discussions of Problems of Modern City Life in England, with an Essay on Imperialism* (London: T. Fisher Unwin, 1901), pp. 2-52 (p. 21).

2. The memory of Henry M. Stanley's *In Darkest Africa* was still fresh and clearly reverberated on everyone's darkest city, whether Masterman's, William Booth's, Jack London's or indeed Ford's, especially in *The Soul of London*. For a discussion of William Booth's *In Darkest England* (1890) as a response to Stanley's *In Darkest Africa*, see Robert Hampson, 'Conrad and the Idea of Empire', *L'Epoque Conradienne* (Limoges, 1989), pp. 9-22.

3. Ford Madox Ford, *The Good Soldier*, ed. Martin Stannard (New York, London: W. W. Norton & Company, 1995) – henceforth *GS*; p. 34. Subsequent references to this edition are given in the text.

4. Joseph Conrad, *Heart of Darkness* (Harmondsworth: Penguin Classics, 1988), p. 86.

5. Thomas C. Moser, *The Life in the Fiction of Ford Madox Ford* (Princeton: Princeton University Press, 1980), pp. 156-7.

6. Ford Madox Ford, *A History of our Own Times*, ed. Solon Beinfeld and Sondra J. Stang (Bloomington and Indianapolis: Indiana University Press, 1988), p. 118.

7. Ford, *A History of our Own Times*, p. 119.

8. G. P. Gooch, 'Imperialism', in C. F. G. Masterman, *The Heart of the Empire*, pp. 308-397 (p.310).

9. Ford Madox Ford, *Return to Yesterday: Reminiscences 1894-1914* (London: Victor Gollancz, 1932), p. 77.

10. Ford Madox Hueffer, *The Spirit of the People* (London: Alston Rivers, 1907) – henceforth *SP*; p. 143.

11. R. Baden-Powell, *Scouting for Boys, a Handbook for Instruction in Good Citizenship* (London: C. Arthur Pearson Ltd., 1908), p. 17.

12. The 'manifesto' of the S. P. E. was published in 1919. See *S. P. E. Tracts* 1 (Oxford: Clarendon Press, 1919). The stress of these first tracts is mostly on the importance of 'naturalizing' foreign words and of the preservation of the 'picturesque vocabularies of local vernaculars', p. 9.

13. Ann Barr Snitow, *Ford Madox Ford and the Voice of Uncertainty* (Baton Rouge: Louisiana State University Press, 1984).

14. Ford, *GS* 121, 125, 79, 152.

15. For an excellent approach to the history of British anthropology see George W. Stocking ed., *Observers Observed. Essays on Ethnographic Fieldwork* (Madison: University of Wisconsin Press, 1983); especially G. Stocking, 'The Ethnographer's Magic: Fieldwork in British Anthropology from Tylor to Malinowski', pp. 70-120.

16. Robert Hampson offers a detailed account of the Frazer-Conrad relation in 'Frazer, Conrad and "the Truth of Primitive Passion"' in R. Fraser, ed., *Sir James Frazer and the Literary Imagination* (London and Basingstoke: Macmillan, 1990), pp. 172-91. James Clifford, alternatively, focuses on the Malinowski-Conrad bond: 'On Ethnographic Self-fashioning: Conrad and Malinowski' in *The Predicament of*

Culture: Twentieth Century Ethnography, Literature and Art (Cambridge: Harvard University Press, 1988).

17. Nicholas Delbanco in *Group Portrait: Joseph Conrad, Ford Madox Ford, Henry James, H. G. Wells and Stephen Crane* (London: Faber and Faber, 1982), p. 32, quotes Ada Galsworthy's notebooks where she mentions the regular callers at their home: among others, Hudson, Ford, S. Colvin, E. Gosse and G. Murray, who was in touch with the Cambridge group of ethnologists.

18. *Fortnightly Review*, 69 (April 1901), includes Ford Madox Hueffer's 'The Mother: A Song-Drama', 741-6, as well as Andrew Lang's 'Mr. Frazer's Theory of the Crucifixion', 649-62.

19. C. F. G. Masterman, *From the Abyss, of its Inhabitants, by One of them* (London: J. M. Dent and Sons, 1911), reprinted from *The Speaker* and *The Commonwealth*, 1902/3, p. 23. Grant Allen, *The British Barbarians: A Hill-Top Novel* (London: John Lane, 1895).

20. Ford Madox Hueffer, *England and the English: An Interpretation* (New York: McClure, Phillips and Co., 1907). This edition includes *The Soul of London*, *The Heart of the Country* and *The Spirit of the People*, respectively 1905, 1906, 1907.

21. Bronislaw Malinowski, *The Family among the Australian Aborigines* (London: University of London Press, 1913), p. 53.

22. James G. Frazer, *Totemism and Exogamy: A Treatise on Certain Early Forms of Superstition and Society*, 4 vols (London: Macmillan, 1910), vol. 4, p. 300.

23. Is Nancy Edward's daughter? It is true, after all, that 'The girl with whom Ashburnham has become infatuated might be his own illegitimate daughter': Max Saunders, *Ford Madox Ford. A Dual Life*, 2 vols (Oxford-New York: Oxford University Press, 1996), vol. 1, p. 422.

24. Bronislaw Malinowski, *The Family among the Australian Aborigines*, p. 183. Malinowski adds: 'What is essential is to point out that our peculiarly European idea of kinship, which necessarily involves consanguinity, cannot be applied to other societies without discussion [. . .] It would seem convenient to reserve the word 'consanguinity' to relationships based upon community of blood and to use the word 'kinship' to denote the parental relationship in general'; p. 179.

CAROLINE PATEY

25. Bronislaw Malinowski, *The Family among the Australian Aborigines*, p. 232; see also pp. 179-81: 'the most noteworthy cases in regard to the present subject are those whose fatherhood in its social sense is not consanguineous owing to the ignorance of the physiological law of reproduction [. . .] This ignorance is of general sociological importance, because there are well-founded reasons for believing that it was once universal among primitive mankind.'

26. James G. Frazer, *Totemism and Exogamy*, p. xii.

27. For the impact of Frazer's work on English culture, see J. B. Vickery, *The Literary Impact of the Golden Bough* (Princeton: Princeton University Press, 1976); R. Fraser, *The Making of The Golden Bough. The Origins and Growth of an Argument* (London and Basingstoke: Macmillan, 1990); and R. Fraser, ed., *Sir J. G. Frazer and the Literary Imagination*.

28. James G. Frazer, *The Golden Bough. A Study in Magic and Religion*, edited by R. Fraser (Oxford: Oxford University Press, 1994), p. 13. Subsequent references to this edition, abbreviated to *GB*, are given parenthetically in the text.

29. Clifford Geertz, *The Interpretation of Culture. Selected Essays* (1973) (London: Fontana, 1993), p. 15.

30. Malinowski, *The Family among the Australian Aborigines*, pp. 14, 23.

31. When he states that in field-work, the method of observation affects the final statement; *The Family among the Australian Aborigines,* p. 23.

32. David Richards, *Masks of Difference. Cultural Representations in Literature, Anthropology and Art* (Cambridge: Cambridge University Press, 1994), p. 231.

33. Geertz, *The Interpretation of Culture*, p. 10.

34. Geertz, *The Interpretation of Culture*, p. 18.

35. Geertz, *ibid.*

36. Geertz, *The Interpretation of Culture*, p. 29.

'THE SEEING EYE': DETECTION, PERCEPTION AND EROTIC KNOWLEDGE IN *THE GOOD SOLDIER*

Sally Bachner

In one of Sir Arthur Conan Doyle's Sherlock Holmes stories, 'A Scandal in Bohemia,' Watson offers an explanatory aside about his illustrious friend. He says of Holmes:

> All emotions, and [love] particularly, were abhorrent to his cold, precise, but admirably balanced mind. He was, I take it, the most perfect reasoning and observing machine that the world has seen: but, as a lover, he would have placed himself in a false position [. . . For] the trained reasoner to admit such intrusions into his own delicate and finely adjusted temperament was to introduce a distracting factor which might throw a doubt upon all his mental results. Grit in a sensitive instrument, or a crack in one of his own high-power lenses, would not be more disturbing than a strong emotion in a nature such as his.[1]

Such a description in the context of a discussion of epistemology in *The Good Soldier* may appear slightly perverse. After all, the magnitude of Dowell's epistemological failure is matched only by the wild success of nearly all of Holmes' efforts. In fact, it is with Watson that the more productive comparison lies, particularly in their shared ideas about human epistemology. Watson's 'observing machine' finds its corollary in John Dowell's idea of 'the seeing eye': both represent an ideal of unchecked empirical power just beyond their grasp.

This paper places Ford's novel within the detective tradition of Conan Doyle's Sherlock Holmes stories in order to reconstruct a lost epistemology at the 'hidden heart' of Ford's novel. While the epistemological imperative in Sherlock Holmes is easily apprehended, it can appear only instrumentally important to Ford's novel. *The Good Soldier* engages us so obsessively in the puzzle of what it means that we have often failed to attend to the prior question of knowing how it came to be so vexed and so urgent in the first place. From the very first pages of the novel we are put on the scent of a mystery, alluded to in the narrator's four references to 'poor Florence' within the first four paragraphs.[2] Dowell describes the relationship between the two couples as a 'minuet de la cour' only to insist in the next paragraph that 'It wasn't a minuet [. . .] it was a prison full of screaming hysterics' which is followed by yet another paragraph in which Dowell says he can 'swear by the sacred name of my creator that it was true. It was true sunshine' (*GS* 11-12). The close of that same chapter with the lines 'It is all a darkness' sets up the novel as a process of suspenseful enlightenment whereby acts of deception and narrative dissimulations are stripped away (*GS* 15).

Although the Holmes stories and Ford's novel both foreground particular epistemological problems, they in turn suggest that human knowing is itself the puzzle to be solved. As textual puzzles these texts both construct crises of knowledge and offer compensatory strategies for hermeneutic and epistemological success. As a detective of barely visible traces, Sherlock Holmes holds out the hope that, if we only look with adequate attention, all will become visible. This fantasy of a visual empiricism without bounds is taken up by Dowell, who insists that his unflagging failure to know is an index only of his stunted observational powers. Yet in both these narratives, the eye finds itself unable to see well enough, a problem no regimen of emotional hygiene or increase in magnification can surmount. In this epistemological universe, where the eye stands in for sense perception and sense perception stands in for epistemology as a whole, the 'grit' in the machine represents a full blown epistemological crisis. The inaccessibility of the human heart – as both a symbol of inscrutable passion and a biological liability for the novel's 'heart patients' – is the central obstacle to epistemological success. The hidden heart is a rallying cry against the inability of scientific observation to penetrate interiority.

It is into this hesitation about detached observation that ident-ification enters as an unacknowledged solution to the problem of truth toward which *The Good Soldier*, and to a lesser extent Doyle's stories, strain. The strategies of identification, of aligning one's own point of view with that of another in an act of love and investiture, allows the 'detective', be she Holmes, Dowell or the reader, to overcome the limits of both objectivity and subjectivity in the production of truth. The eye begins as a vital means of objective observation, only to become the symbolic medium through which identification, and thus knowing, take place. *The Good Soldier*, following a strategy glimpsed in Sherlock Holmes, suggests that identification with another is the necessary precondition for revelation; it is necessary to go beyond the individual ego in order to know. Identification is the route through which the empirically untraversable space between subjects can be broached.

This identificatory solution to these narratives' epistemological problems retains the symbolic and practical centrality of the eye only now in the service of an eroticized, not objective, form of knowing. *The Good Soldier*, extending the logic of a strategy glimpsed in Sherlock Holmes, suggests that desire for and identification with another is the necessary precondition for revelation, not a threat to it. Identification in the Sherlock Holmes stories and in *The Good Soldier* thus deviates from the Freudian model in that it is accompanied by, if not inseparable from, sexual desire. Diana Fuss, in her *Identification Papers*, says: 'For Freud, desire for one sex is always secured through identification with the other sex; to desire and to identify with the same person is, in this model, a theoretical impossibility.'[3] As we will see most clearly in *The Good Soldier*, where Dowell explicitly links love to a self-extinguishing identification, Freud's separation of identification from desire is untenable.

The forsaking of the ego which makes these encounters possible is, in fact, a re-enactment of the inaugural loss of every identification.[4] Whether the loss takes the form of failure for Holmes, the death of Florence and Edward for Dowell, or the loss of a love object in general, this protocol of absence distinguishes the truth of identification from that of observation. The riddle of the novel – the human heart, literally and figuratively – seemingly produced by the pitfalls of perspectivism, is finally 'solved' by the post-mortem insights that identification makes possible. Paradoxically, in *The Good Soldier* death enables the novel's only successful strategies for knowing another's heart: identification and autopsy.

Before looking at *The Good Soldier* I want briefly to trace the movement in Doyle's stories from Holmes's triumphalist rhetoric of scientific attention to his own dependence on the protocols of identification. In 'A Scandal in Bohemia' the detective offers his authoritative outlook upon the relation of perceptual difference. To Watson's exasperation at his own failings as a detective, Holmes asserts: 'You see, but you do not observe. The distinction is quite clear' (p. 8). This is the first credo of Holmes's up-by-your-bootstraps theory of knowing. According to Holmes's mechanistic account of the difference between himself and the doctor, both have an object in view, while only he brings his reasoning and concentration to bear upon the object. To extend the earlier metaphor of the 'observing machine', Watson is like a camera without a battery: his optical machinery is present but effectively useless.

However, while Holmes insists upon the undifferentiated visibility of the physical world, he is constantly proven wrong by discrepancies in perspective and access. The relational difference between Holmes and Watson, Watson and the reader, the reader and Holmes intrudes upon Holmes's smug insistence that all we need to do is observe. The concept of identification is already visible here as a producer of structural alliances. First, the reader identifies with Watson on the basis of their shared role as Holmes's sycophantic admirer. Like Watson, the reader hopes to catch the appropriate leads and make the right connections, but is constantly one-upped by the prodigious observational powers of Holmes. Yet this strong textual push for the reader's affective identification with Watson actually masks a subtle and involuntary structural alliance: the reader can only see what Watson, the narrator, reports.

Identification pervades these stories not only as a device which constitutes and constrains the reader but as one of Sherlock Holmes's most basic tools of detection. 'A Scandal in Bohemia' tells the story of Holmes's attempt to recover an incriminating photograph for the King of Bohemia from his former lover, Miss Irene Adler. This story hinges upon the productive power of identification. First, Holmes is able to discover the location of the photograph by identifying with, and then second guessing, Miss Adler. Later, Holmes goes into character, masquerading first as a cabman and then as a clergyman. These transformations, however superficial, are the physical corollary to the psychological identification that Holmes undergoes in order to satisfy his client. But the problem-solving power of identification isn't always in Holmes's favor; 'A Scandal in Bohemia' turns out to be a story of his failure. Miss Adler subsequently masquerades as a young man in order to confirm her suspicion that the clergyman in the house has been the famous detective. Holmes returns to find the woman and the evidence gone; a substitute photograph and an explanatory letter remain. Miss Adler shows that she too knows the problem-solving power of identification. Access to information is augmented by relinquishing the self, by taking on the role and point of view of another.

This story suggests that identification is an ambiguous epistemological tool: it produces truth, but of an unpredictable kind. It is the closeness of love to identification, their ultimate inseparability, that makes identification such a risky epistemological strategy. Watson concludes the story saying: '[Holmes] used to make merry over the cleverness of women, but I have not heard him do it of late. And when he speaks of Irene Adler, or when he refers to her photograph, it is always under the honourable title of '*the* woman' (p. 29). If Freud's 'family romance' has taught us to think of identification and desire as mutually exclusive – identification with one parent positions us to desire the other – this story offers a different picture. Holmes's fascination with Adler is one of erotic respect: she has outwitted him and for that she becomes an icon of desire. In her absence the photograph he retains becomes a medium of identificatory love. The story closes with a reinstatement of the visual, but now as an identificatory rather than scientific conduit of knowledge.

As in the Sherlock Holmes stories, in *The Good Soldier* the strategies of identification enter surreptitiously into an epistemological framework that is explicitly, if unconventionally, scientific. Ford's essay 'On Impressionism' sets up that framework.[5] While strategies of identification present in the novel have not yet emerged here, Ford outlines his theory of human perception – Impressionism – which informs his literary practice. His beginning is deceptively subjectivist: 'all art' he declares 'must be the expression of an ego'. The Impressionist 'will give you nothing but the pleasure of coming into contact with his temperament'. Yet for all the modesty of scope implied by this apparent focus on the individual ego, Ford is far too hot and bothered by questions of epistemology so to limit himself. So, while he speaks throughout the essay of the Impressionist and the Impressionist artist, his insights retain a more general descriptive force. Impressionism is not simply a school of aesthetic production but a theory of human perception, cognition, and response. His account of the nature of human visual perception and its subjection to convention is predicated upon a scientific outlook, insisting upon the production of a local, even technical, verisimilitude: '*Impressionism exists to render those queer effects of real life* that are like so many views seen through bright glass' ('On Impressionism' 41; italics mine). His aesthetic manifesto outlines what Paul B. Armstrong has rightly called an 'epistemological realism.'[6]

This realism is first and foremost visual. In his discussion of Impressionism and audience, Ford asserts that peasants are preferable to English gentlemen. He suggests that while the former's lifestyle affords opportunity for leisurely and unfettered reflection, the latter is overrun by preconceived ideas and class-bound conventionalities. Ford conjures a scene in which the 'peasant intelligence' serves the Impressionist project perfectly: 'Such a man . . . will say: 'Well, I have never myself observed a haycock to be purple, but I can understand that if the sky is very blue and the sun is setting very red, the shady side of the haycock might well appear to be purple' ('On Impressionism' 53). It is the very ability of the peasant to allow the interaction of light and matter to override expectation that Ford values. The purpleness of the haycock is not the solipsistic vision of the alienated modern artist but the product of a shared perceptual machinery. While convention may dissimulate, optics is a universal human truth. Ford distances himself from an aesthetic of the individualized ego in favor of a scientifically predictable epistemological realism based not on opinion, but on near-clinical observation.

The epistemological crisis in *The Good Soldier* consists in the ultimate inadequacy of that empiricism to account for either the epistemological limits its characters face or the solutions they develop. In one early scene from the novel, Dowell offers this anguished summary:

> I know nothing – nothing in the world – of the hearts of men. I only know that I am alone – horribly alone [. . . .] No smoking-room will ever be other than peopled with incalculable simulacra amidst smoke wreaths. Yet in the name of God, what should I know if I don't know the life of the hearth and of the smoking-room, since my whole life has been passed in those places? I don't believe that for one minute [Florence] was out of my sight, except when she was safely tucked up in bed and I should be downstairs [. . .] (*GS* 12)

The structure of emphatic repetition in the first sentence enables a crucial double-meaning. Dowell knows nothing *and* he knows nothing of 'the hearts of men.' In the end of course they are one and the same. In Dowell's schema other people are the epistemological object *par excellence*. Dowell's singularity, what he calls his loneliness, is not simply an existential trial but an epistemological problem. Faced with a loss of faith in what he has seen, Dowell suffers a full scale epistemological crisis, no longer knowing how knowledge is attained or verified. The epistemological crisis of the novel – and the source of

Dowell's mantra, 'I don't know' – is a crisis of vision: the external world has lost all solidity as he finds himself unable to distinguish between real people and their simulacra. The inadequacy of visual empiricism as a total epistemological strategy allows us to assign to his assertion that he 'believes' Florence was never 'out his sight' the same status accorded to religious belief in a secular age: it is not so much a lie as it is a leap of faith of dubious psychological motivation.

The apogee of Dowell's empiricist misdiagnosis of his chronic epistemological problem is his formulation of 'the seeing eye'. Dowell offers an explanation of his epistemological disadvantage, saying of Florence and himself:

> No, we never did go back anywhere [. . . .] We talked of it, of course, but I guess Florence got all she wanted out of one look at a place. She had the seeing eye.
> I haven't, unfortunately, so that the world is full of places to which I want to return [. . . .] (*GS* 16-17)

The rhetoric of 'the seeing eye' concentrates all empirical power onto sight. This eye is like a camera, recording all it sees for posterity and for the satisfaction of the viewer. His lack of the seeing eye makes of him an eternal Watson, following his Holmes in search of the right lead. And, like Watson's, Dowell's observations retard insight, but far more radically. But, in *The Good Soldier,* the reader identifies with Dowell's confusion and epistemological anxiety, only to slowly recognize that Dowell himself is the object of the novel's riddle.

So at the center of this dust storm of contradiction is the narrator Dowell, kicking up dirt and crying that he can't see. The irony of the passage is that Dowell's announcement of his own incapacity is immediately followed by an evocative and minutely detailed account of his travels: '– towns with the blinding white sun upon them, stone pines against the blue of the sky, all carved and painted with stags and scarlet flowers and crowstepped gables with the little saint at the top; and the grey and pink palazzi and walled towns a mile or so back from the sea, on the Mediterranean, between Leghorn and Naples' (*GS* 17). He closes saying 'Not one of them did we see more than once so that the whole world is for me like spots of colour in an immense canvas'. Yet the picture just drawn has none of the evanescent blurriness of an Impressionist painting – if it did, how could we have made out the 'little saints at the top' and other finely drawn details?

For Dowell, the ability to see seems to stand in for another register of epistemological success altogether. Despite his apparent possession of 'the seeing eye' he feels bereft and unsatisfied. The concept of 'the seeing eye' is a red herring, one in a series of unconvincing explanations of his supposed epistemological disadvantage. For even if we were to accept Dowell's shortcomings as illustrating an Impressionist theory of human perception, how would we make sense of those who within the novel appear to have 'the seeing eye' – that is, Florence, Leonora and Edward? Is their relative epistemological success a figment of Dowell's imaginative universe – that is, a displaced fantasy – or does it point to a place where the fragmentary nature of perception is, if only provisionally, reintegrated?

That reintegration can only take place through identification. The epistemological disparity between Dowell and the other characters is the result of his inability, until the second half of the novel, to name any real object of desire. In this light, his obsessive focus on empiricism is understandable; unable to identify with anyone, isolated from any alliance of desire, he has distinctly limited epistemological possibilities. But eventually Dowell's libidinal rectitude gives way, offering in the process a hint about his particular and acute myopia. Speaking of identification directly, Dowell suggests that sexual passion and identification are two ways of describing a unitary desire. He says:

> As I see it, at least, with regard to man, a love for any definite woman – is something in the nature of the widening of the experience. With each new

111

woman that a man is attracted to there appears to come a broadening of the outlook, or, if you like, an acquiring of new territory. A turn of the eyebrow, a tone of the voice, a queer characteristic gesture – all these things, and it is these things that cause to arise the passion of love – all these things are like so many objects on the horizon of the landscape that tempt a man to walk beyond the horizon, to explore. He wants to get, as it were, behind those eyebrows with the peculiar turn, as if he desired to see the world with the eyes that they overshadow [. . . .] But the real fierceness of desire, the real heat of a passion long continued and withering up the soul of a man is the craving for identity with the woman he loves. He desires to see with the same eyes, to touch with the same sense of touch, to lose his identity [. . . .] (*GS* 79)

If we juxtapose this passage to the one in which Dowell expounds upon his lack of 'the seeing eye' we can see two contrasted, but linked, forms of seeing. In both, traveling is a metaphor for a visually-based epistemology; the touristed landscape of Europe becomes a trope for the erotic explorations the novel narrates. Yet, whereas in the former Dowell describes an emotionally neutral mechanistic eye function, in which the registering of both the detail and the vista are the explicit terms of success, this latter framework implies both desire and the specificity of individual personality. The tourism metaphor invoked here employs the language of exploration, of the intrepid individual quester. Paradoxically, the power of the individual ego is invoked at the moment of radical compromise to its integrity: the moment of identification. For as Dowell sees it, the process of loving entails the relinquishing of one's own perspective for identity with that of the love object.

In searching out the traces of the romantic procedures that Dowell outlines, it would be hard to miss his explicit identification with Edward Ashburnham. In keeping with the rampant visuality of knowledge in *The Good Soldier*, Dowell's central trope of identification – the love object's eyes – is foregrounded. Dowell describes Edward's: 'I had forgotten about his eyes [. . . .] When you looked at them carefully you saw that they were perfectly honest, perfectly straightforward, perfectly, perfectly stupid [. . . .] And that chap, coming into a room, snapped up the gaze of every woman in it, as dexterously as a conjurer pockets billiard balls. It was most amazing' (*GS* 26). Edward Ashburnham, stony-faced as a catwalk model, is not only the object of Dowell's gaze but of all the women in the dining room. Dowell imagines Edward's vacuity as somehow active and possessive, but in truth he is an empty container, made up of other's expectations and idealizations of him. As Dowell puts it, 'he remained dumb' (*GS* 154). Edward's silence is part of what makes him so attractive; Dowell needs others' silence to justify his own ignorance. Like a good soldier or a gun for hire, Edward becomes what others need him to be.

Dowell's identification with Edward is quite explicit. In the passage quoted earlier in which he imagines love as a desire to identify with the loved one, Dowell accurately describes his own love relationship to Edward. At the end of the book Dowell muses:

> But I guess that I myself, in my fainter way, come into the category of the passionate, of the head-strong, of the too-truthful. For I can't conceal from myself that the fact that I loved Edward Ashburnham – and that I love him because he was just myself. If I had the courage and the virility and possibly also the physique of Edward Ashburnham I should, I fancy, have done much what he did. (*GS* 161)

Dowell's insistence that he belongs in the same category as Edward is based not on his actions, not in the empirically known world, but because he identifies himself, through love, with him. For Dowell is not, in his actual practical life, any of the things he describes, although 'too-truthful' may be defended on narrow Impressionist grounds. In Dowell's visions of Edward's suffering, this identification is increasingly apparent. He says 'Those two women pursued that poor devil and flayed the skin off him as if they had done it with whips. I tell you his mind bled almost visibly. I seem to see him stand, naked to the waist, his forearms shielding his eyes, and flesh hanging

113

from him in rags. *I tell you that is no exaggeration of what I feel'* (*GS* 152; emphasis added). Dowell has lost a sense of the boundaries between himself and the man that he loved, and thus substitutes his own feelings for Edward's: what Dowell feels in the last sentence is ambiguously both the 'feeling' that Edward was treated sadistically, and his sensory 'feeling' of the whip against his own unblemished skin.

Dowell's identification with Edward ultimately enables the resolution of the novel because the conflict of different points of view, of values and of interests was the basis of contradiction. It is only when Dowell chooses sides, when he abandons the singularity of his own visual, perspectival 'point of view' that judgment is possible. His famous underestimation of the 'sex instinct' is finally belied by what, for lack of a more subtle term, can best be termed desire – specifically, desire for Edward Ashburnham. The sadness of the story, at least in part, is that such productive identifications can only occur in the face of an insuperable loss, which, in *The Good Soldier,* is almost always death. In this the novel follows Freud closely, who said: 'If one has lost a love object, the most obvious reaction is to identify oneself with it, to replace it from within, as it were, by identification.'

The novel's seemingly arbitrary pattern of revelation can be reconstructed, incident by incident, as effects of the epistemological opportunities that death and its identificatory response bring. The death of Maisie Maidan at the close of Book I is the first such incident, providing Dowell with the opportunity to narrate the sordid tale of Edward's philandering. From the point of Florence's suicide onward, we learn that Dowell wants to marry Nancy, that Edward attempted to seduce Nancy, and that his death was a suicide. Indeed, the power of identification to produce a form of truth that is discursive, evaluative and memorializing is testified to in nothing less than the novel as a whole. Begun at the empty Ashburnham place where Dowell tends, like Edward's ghost, over the perpetually child-like Nancy, Dowell's novel-long monologue is the product of his identification with the late Edward Ashburnham.

The nature of identification's post-mortem insights are not objective, scientific or even optical. Rather, identification is a way of choosing among a multiplicity of evaluative positions. The result is an acknowledgment of the importance of point of view, but a rejection of the isolated solipsism with which modernism is frequently defined. While visual epistemology is inadequate to penetrate interiority, identification can overcome such boundaries, even in the face of the death or indifference of the other. *The Good Soldier* paints in miniature, in Dowell's identificatory love, an epistemology of autopsy. Just as the demise of Grandfather Hurlbird reveals a deformity of the lung rather than of the heart, the death of Edward enables a whole series of post-mortem, post-identification insights. Each instantiation of an enigmatic human interiority is subject to dissection. *The Good Soldier* enacts the possibility of a coherent version of truth, *and* an increased dependence on knowledge of the human heart. That knowledge is accomplished through both the autopsy-like possibilities for verification that death brings and the incorporative intimacies of identification.

NOTES

1. Arthur Conan Doyle, *The Adventures of Sherlock Holmes* (New York: Oxford University Press, 1998), p. 5.

2. Ford, *The Good Soldier*, ed. Martin Stannard (New York and London: W. W. Norton & Company, 1995), pp. 9-10. Subsequent references to this edition appear parenthetically in the text using the abbreviation *GS*.

3. Diana Fuss, *Identification Papers* (New York: Routledge, 1995), p. 11.

SALLY BACHNER

SALLY BACHNER

4. Sigmund Freud, 'Mourning and Melancholia', *General Psychological Theory: Papers on Metapsychology* (New York: Collier Books, 1963), pp. 164-79.

5. Ford, 'On Impressionism,' *Critical Writings of Ford Madox Ford*, ed. Frank MacShane (Lincoln: University of Nebraska Press, 1964), pp. 41-55.

6. Paul Armstrong, 'The Epistemology of Ford's Impressionism' *Critical Essays on Ford Madox Ford*, ed. Richard A. Cassell (Boston: G. K. Hall and Co., 1987), pp. 135-42.

THE UNKNOWN FORD MADOX FORD

Roger Poole

The great Modernist novelists are James Joyce, Marcel Proust, Virginia Woolf and Ford Madox Ford – to stop for the moment at that comparatively safe point in history.

In re-formulating thus the canonical judgement of F. R. Leavis at the beginning of *The Great Tradition*, I intend to state a major value judgement of my own, about the Modernist tradition, and that is: that Ford Madox Ford, in spite of the fact that he has had almost no acknowledgement at the technical level, is as great a novelist, technically, as his three peers. He died in 1939. The very first conference ever held on his work was organised in Bologna, in 1989. Even now, he remains a figure in the shadows, off-stage, waiting.

Why is it that critical technical and formal analysis of the work of Joyce, Proust and Woolf, those masters of the stream-of-consciousness, should have been so prolific that it is customary to trace various 'traditions' in the scholarship about them, while Ford cannot claim even a single 'tradition' of scholarship? Those who have written about him seem to do so half-heartedly, with reserves, almost with embarrassment.

For there may not be a tradition of scholarship about Ford's writing, but there is certainly a continuity of attitude in the evaluation. It is always implied that, although Ford was a writer who on occasions shows brilliance, even genius, he was also a muddler, a careless or even slapdash littérateur, who wrote too much and too fast, and whose indifference to 'facts' was such that he was quite incapable of constructing a coherent plot-line or time-scheme. With friends and supporters like these, who needs enemies?

Nowhere is this continuity of attitude, this critical condescension to Ford, more evident than in the accounts given of the best-known of his novels, *The Good Soldier*. Even the most respectful of critics writing about this novel, Thomas Moser for instance, or Frank Kermode, or Martin Stannard, or John Sutherland, seem to agree about one thing: that the famous and repeated use of the date '4 August 1904' amounts, in the end, to nothing more or less than a muddle, that Ford had lost grip on his time-scheme as he revised his manuscript, and that he was too careless or too indifferent to bother to co-ordinate his various uses of this date before he sent the novel to his publisher.

My contention in what follows (and in a previous, much longer, analysis dating from 1990, upon which this new account has to rely for much of its supporting documentation)[1] is that the time-schemes in *The Good Soldier* (for there are *two*, both centering on 4 August 1904) fit together perfectly, once we get the modality and intentionality of the narrator's consciousness right.

For the reason why the critics, even the well-disposed ones, have never yet seen the coherence in the use of the date '4 August 1904' is that they have never properly 'fixed' the game that the narrator, Dowell, is playing with this date. By making the initial and unexamined assumption that Dowell, as narrator, is a narrator on the model of Henry James's narrators (partly understanding, struggling to piece together motive and action from a limited 'point of view' and with inadequate or partial information), these critics have not realised that Ford has carried out, in the figure of Dowell, a major transformation of intentionality.

Dowell is not just misled, struggling to understand, partly informed and possessed of inadequate information (though of course, he is *also* all of these!) but his recital of the events covers over (but only just) a recreation of a criminal intention. This intention started out from the typical Jamesian motif of a young man marrying a sick heiress for her money so that he could later marry his long-time lover, but it builds over this, modifies and adapts the Jamesian device, and

118

tells the story of how the narrator (and his accomplice) actually achieved this aim. It should be remembered that Ford Madox Ford himself was the 'model' for Merton Densher in *The Wings of the Dove*, and it is a novel, therefore, that Ford will have studied particularly carefully. What more likely than Ford should have picked the plot-line of this very novel to show that he could go one better than the Master? In Harold Bloom's terminology, the 'ephebe' places his poem where the precursor's poem was, and insists that it is the better work.

In few words, if we do Ford the elementary courtesy of assuming that he knew what he was doing, instead of assuming that *The Good Soldier* was thrown together in a high wind, we will descry that the two time-schemes which centre on '4 August 1904' fit together perfectly and represent the perfect alibi for the narrator's crime. We have all come to accept Frank Kermode's decision that 'the illusion of the single right reading is no longer possible' and I am not arguing, in what follows, that I have a reading which is 'right'. But I do argue that we gain a great deal if we add in the possibility that Dowell is not the weak-wristed, effete, sexless, motiveless, passive spectator which most commentators have assumed, but that on the contrary Dowell's intentions are reprehensible and criminal. If we make the new decision to distrust Dowell, we shall see, at last, how the two parallel time-schemes which centre on '4 August 1904' actually *work*.

A second value judgement, then, which I want to add to my first, is that Ford carried out, in 1915, a shift in fictional praxis which puts him actually in advance of the Modernist achievements of the other three. We should remember that 'The Saddest Story' appeared first in *Blast* in 1914, and, as it stands there, it represents a complete mystery. In what ways is this apparently maudlin, sentimental piece fit to be included next to Pound and Gaudier-Brzeska and Wyndham Lewis? The puzzle is resolved if we suppose for a moment that Ford is introducing a completely novel departure in the technique of the 'narrator': the criminal narrator. Ford offers a meretricious piece, which involves a transumption of genre in what concerns the intentionality of the 'narrator', a departure from the praxis of James and Conrad which would be apparent only to the discriminating eye. Why is Ford Madox Hueffer's fiction 'The Saddest Story' wedged in between 'Enemy of the Stars' by Wyndham Lewis and 'Indissoluble Matrimony' by Rebecca West? And why do we pay no attention to the subtitle which is so prominently featured in the *Blast* lay-out: *Beati Immaculati*? The reference is to Psalm 119:

> Thou has charged: that we shall diligently keep thy commandments.
> O that my ways were made so direct : that I might keep thy statutes!

Why are we always so *unsuspicious* of Ford and his 'narrator' Dowell? What would happen to our reading of the '4 August 1904' if we once assumed that the misprision has been ours, and not Ford's?

'They don't get the irony!' groaned a frustrated Ezra Pound. It is at least arguable that the great reading public has never, even yet, got the irony of *The Good Soldier*. Consider the plot-line of that novel as it is commonly received in the literary world:

> A lonely and embittered man in his late forties sits and tells what he calls 'the saddest story I have ever heard'. He is speaking to an imaginary guest as they sit by the fire. 'The saddest story' turns out to be the story of how he, the narrator, Dowell, married a woman called Florence, and how she then betrayed him over a period of years with a man called Ashburnham.
>
> He met Florence by chance in her home town of New York. She, bored by a provincial American life, was anxious for 'a European establishment', and therefore agrees to marry the narrator, Dowell, provided that he take account of the fact that she has a 'heart' and, in view of the strain that sexual activity might put on her heart, that he agree to what amounts to a 'marriage blanc'. This is odd, because only a few years before, and in the company of a benign old Uncle called Hurlbird, she had gone on a world tour accompanied by a lover of repulsive aspect called Jimmy (described

by Dowell as 'lugubrious, silent, morose, with a stomach like a man of forty and six golden front teeth)'. Nevertheless, Florence had developed with Jimmy what Dowell assumes to be a fairly advanced standard of sexual expertise.

On 4 August 1901, Florence descends from her room by a rope-ladder in the middle of the night, and she and Dowell are married at 4 in the morning. They have just time for breakfast with Florence's 'dazed' Aunts, before they take the 'Pocahontas' at 1.30 p. m. They arrive in Europe and here they fall in, at a fashionable spa in Germany, with another couple, English this time, the Ashburnhams of Branshaw Teleragh. On one and the same day, 4 August 1904, they meet these two people at dinner in the evening, and also take a trip together to the neighbouring town of Marburg. Considering that this is the first day they met, the degree of intimacy implied in a conversation between Dowell and Mrs Ashburnham, Leonora, is puzzling. On a little terrace overlooking the Lahn outside the Castle of Marburg, Leonora and Dowell seem to be deep in some kind of plot. 'Do accept the situation' says Dowell, and Leonora answers 'Oh, I accept the situation if you can'. The 'situation' seems to involve someone called 'poor Maisie' who has been brought over from India by Leonora as a companion for her husband Edward. Even though Leonora knows that her husband is infatuated with Maisie, it never occurs to Leonora that any sexual activity might take place.

Oddly enough, on the same day that the couples meet for the first time in the evening, which happens to be the very day that they have already spent the afternoon in Marburg, Maisie Maidan is found dead on their return to the hotel. She had fallen head-first into her own travelling-trunk. She had died 'grotesquely', but 'she had not committed suicide. Her heart had just stopped.'

For year after year, then, this unhappy foursome inhabit the same spa, morning, noon and night. They eat together, walk together, take the waters together, dance together, all in each other's sight. Yet (Dowell tells his silent listener) dreadful things had been going on all this while. Dowell had no suspicion that his wife Florence was having a passionate affair with the elegant and distinguished Ashburnham, and this right under his very nose! Heavens! (Dowell reflects again and again) how could he not have noticed? How could he have been so imperceptive? When on earth could Florence have managed these passionate encounters? When was there even time for it? Maybe when he was doing his 'Swedish exercises', might it have been then? Or perhaps in her bedroom, whose door was always locked? (She had given Dowell an axe to hack down the door 'in case she ever failed to answer my knock').

It is odd that Dowell had never suspected that Ashburnham might have had designs upon his wife, considering that Dowell has spent much of the novel chronicling the string of liaisons and affairs which this officer and gentleman had notched up over an active sexual career. He had kissed a servant girl in a railway carriage; tried to arrange (between the episodes of total inebriation) financial terms with the mistress of a Grand Duke; and relied upon the wife of a fellow-officer in India for a great deal of sympathy and understanding.

Meanwhile, there is another series of events which Dowell finds it impossible to understand. There is a girl called Nancy Rufford. Dowell refers to her often as 'the girl', and it would seem that both Ashburnham and Dowell himself are very fond of her, but in ways which it is difficult to determine. Nancy Rufford, whose birth is obscure, is brought up by a 'violent madman' called Major Rufford and his slatternly drunken wife Mrs Rufford, who is nevertheless mysteriously called 'Leonora's dearest friend'. When Nancy is thirteen, Leonora suddenly withdraws Nancy from their care, and takes her to live with Ashburnham and herself. No explanation for this action is given. Nancy thus comes to occupy the place of an honorary daughter to both of them.

For some reason which Dowell cannot understand, Leonora tries to force Nancy to become the mistress of her husband. Nancy joins in this plot. Firstly they abuse and terrify Ashburnham. Then they begin to torture him 'like a couple of Sioux who had got hold of an Apache and had him well tied to a stake.' Then Nancy goes one night to Ashburnham's room and says 'I am ready to belong to you – to save your life'. Shocked and horrified, Ashburnham refuses. Edward decides that Nancy should go to her father in India. On her way out there, in Aden, she reads in a newspaper of the suicide of Edward Ashburnham. As a result, she goes mad. Dowell goes out to Ceylon to bring her back and installs her in his house at Branshaw Teleragh, of which he has become the new owner. Nancy sits there gibbering madly about 'shuttlecocks' while Dowell reminisces and attempts to understand. Why Ashburnham had committed suicide it is hard to guess. The immediate cause seems to have been a telegram sent by Nancy from Brindisi saying that she was having a 'rattling good time'. Such cheerful news is obviously enough to send Edward's mind definitively off the rails, and he commits suicide, not (as one might imagine a military man might do) with a revolver, but with 'quite a small penknife'.

Meanwhile, 'the saddest story' continues, the amorous license of the 'heart' victim, Florence, has brought her to her own death by suicide. When she married Dowell she made it clear that she had a 'heart', and she also makes it clear that excitement might kill her. The ship's doctor on the 'Pocahontas' 'discreetly suggested to me that I had better refrain from manifestations of affection'. To which Dowell adds 'I was ready enough'. She was very rich, so doubtless Dowell had settled from the beginning to the sexual privation. Florence had an uncle, who was also very rich, and who was thought to suffer from a 'heart'. After twelve years, uncle Hurlbird suddenly dies, leaving 1.5 million dollars to Florence. Post-mortem examination shows that he did not in fact have a 'heart'.

By an amazing co-incidence, it is only five days after the discovery that Uncle Hurlbird did not have a 'heart' that Florence dies. Dowell asserts that it was suicide. The reason for her committing suicide is this: she overhears Edward Ashburnham, sitting out in the gloaming after dinner with Nancy, whom he regards as a 'daughter', just as she regards him as a 'father', declaring that she is 'the person he cared for most in the world'. This sends Florence into a rage of jealousy. She rushes back to the hotel. As she goes past the window, she sees her husband, the narrator Dowell, sitting in conversation with a man called Bagshawe. As she runs past, all distressed, her mind goes back accurately to the 4th August 1900, and she realises that Bagshawe, who saw her emerging from Jimmy's room at 5 am on that day, would spill the beans about her affair with Jimmy, and thus expose to her husband her real lascivious nature. She rushes upstairs, writes a long letter to her two aunts in America, admitting to all her affairs and liaisons, seals it up, lies on her bed, swallows a bottle of prussic acid, composes her limbs neatly, and passes into another and a better world. (Dowell had believed that her little bottle contained nitrate of amyl for her angina pectoris).

Dowell goes upstairs to find his wife dead. From this moment on, Dowell's thought-process seems to become more and more markedly economic. Florence's death is an inconvenience, for Uncle Hurlbird's 1.5

million dollars and Florence's 800,000 dollars now come to him, and he has the tedious task of having to go to America to accept this sudden windfall of 2.3 million dollars. The two old aunts, who have received the last self-accusing letter from Florence written just before she took the prussic acid, seem to have only one desire, which is to ensure that Dowell should at least get *something* out of his relationship to their erring and licentious niece. So, in order to please them, Dowell has to accept the fortune of 2.3 million dollars.

Leonora marries someone called Rodney Bayham, who looks like a rabbit. Dowell buys Branshaw Teleragh. He sits there in his country house, with his new fortune and a mad Nancy, and tells 'the saddest story he has ever heard'. It is also one he insists he cannot understand. Given the plot-line as he tells it, that is perhaps not surprising.

No, this cannot possibly be the plot-line. The sheer incongruity of everything should give us reason to pause. What is going on here? What kind of literary game is being played? What are the rules? No plot-line which plays so fast and loose with all verisimilitude can be treated without suspicion.

I would suggest that Ford is experimenting with the limits of a certain genre or convention of which the contours were known and agreed. This genre or convention would be the type of novel written by Joseph Conrad and Henry James, in which the narrator is confused, or only partly-informed, in which too he has to make an effort to understand the significance of what he has to relate. But I suspect that Ford was not developing this convention, so much as submitting it to a radical formal extension. For there is something uncapturable about this novel – all readers feel that. It escapes on every side, it is limitless, it has no known outer contours. This might be because a radical extension of a literary genre is being undertaken, while the reader is still working in terms of the expectations of an older and known literary genre? In Jauss's terms, it is operating a transcendence of 'the horizon of expectation'.

In a recent and incisive account of the problems of reading *The Good Soldier*, John Sutherland has reminded us of the fundamental scepticism of Frank Kermode. He quotes Kermode as saying: 'We are in a world of which it needs to be said *not* that plural readings are possible (for this is true of all narrative) but that the *illusion of the single right reading is possible no longer.*'[2] That is doubtless to be accepted. But, by that very token, it follows that we are not obliged to believe the 'single right reading' that Dowell offers. For it is the case that the tradition of blunt reading, which is the main tradition in Ford criticism, takes Dowell's story at what amounts to face value. The preceding account of the story line as told by Dowell is, in fact, embarrassingly enough, what most scholars and exegetes agree to accept as their raw material.

But how can we make literal sense of what Dowell tells us? No cow could ever hitch its horns under the stomach of another one and throw it into the middle of a narrow stream (*GS* 35); no two members of the social élite in New York would escape down a rope-ladder in the middle of the night, get married at 4 in the morning, and yet turn up for breakfast with two 'dazed' aunts before taking a ship to Europe (*GS* 61-2); no character who was 'lugubrious, silent, morose', who never shaved sufficiently, who was too fat, who had 'a stomach like a man of forty' and who had 'six golden front teeth' is conceivable as the young beau that would introduce a New York socialite into the erotic life; nor is it conceivable that any Uncle, however dotty, would have considered taking an unattached man on the trip round the world with his niece and protégée (*GS* 82); nor is it conceivable that an unattached man should join Dowell and his new bride on their honeymoon ('He met us at Havre': *GS* 63) and tell the bridegroom that he must not enter his wife's bedroom at night (*GS* 64); nor is it conceivable that, at a spa like Bad Nauheim, and in conditions of almost obsessive correctness, a bride should provide her husband with an axe 'in case she ever failed to answer his knock' (*GS* 64); nor is it credible that an officer and a gentleman like Ashburnham should use his sword to hack down flowers in a Burmese garden (*GS* 112); nor that he should offer to provide for la Dolciquita for life if she would come and live with him (*GS* 107); even less probable that a man truly in the grip of desire should 'drink like a fish and spread himself all over the tables' (*GS* 107); nor is it credible that a military man, standing only feet from his own gun-room, should commit suicide with 'quite a small pen-knife' (*GS* 162).

There are in fact, on every page, examples of what we can only call 'put-ons'. Ford is testing our gullibility, making us read the text in the participative manner that Roland Barthes would have called 'scriptible' as opposed to merely 'lisible'. We are constantly being challenged as to *limits*: no, surely he couldn't mean that?; no, surely, that's impossible?; no, surely, that wouldn't have been possible under the etiquette of the time?; no, surely, that is not characteristic of that particular 'type' of person?

The Impressionism which Ford carries out in *The Good Soldier* is a constant and subtle departure from what is expected. This relation of a description to the world described was characterised by the early Structuralists as *vraisemblance*. Julia Kristeva, for example, writing in 1969, sees *vraisemblance* as the artistic play between resemblance and difference: 'Any discourse which is in a relation of similarity, identification or reflection upon another, is vraisemblable. The vraisemblable is a combination of two different discourses of which the one is projected upon the other and serves as a mirror to it'.[3] Roland Barthes, writing a year later, puts the theory of *vraisemblance* to work by examining in detail a short story of Balzac, *Sarrasine*.[4] In *S/Z* Barthes reads *Sarrasine* as a collocation and variation of five 'codes' which allow the reader to judge, to differentiate and to infer what is at stake in any particular reference. The reader has to 'fill in' what is not stated, to connect the cultural signifiers to their signifieds, and to make value judgements in terms of the generally agreed ('natural') background to the story. In particular, the codes which Barthes called 'hermeneutic' and 'cultural' give considerable purchase on the values inherent in the story. The 'hermeneutic' hints allow the reader to build up a series of hypotheses about the mystery which lies at the heart of the tale; while the 'cultural' hints insist that the reader pass judgement on what is or is not 'permissible' or 'natural' in that particular society. Roland Barthes' five 'codes' allows us to make discriminations within a known social context. They allow us, to use now the terminology of Jacques Derrida, to note the effects of 'difference'. In effect, the technique that Ford is deploying in *The Good Soldier* is a deliberate and controlled series of mishandlings of *vraisemblance*. The world described by a novelist sets up certain norms and expectations. The reader does not expect to see these violated. When and if they are violated, the reader notices them. There is a departure from the expected, the 'natural' text, from the *vraisemblable*. These mishandlings of *vraisemblance* in *The Good Soldier* are echoed at a higher level by the liberties that Ford takes with the relation of the novelist to the novel itself. In a comprehensive review of the Structuralist theory of *vraisemblance*, Jonathan Culler lists five main ways in which the literary practice can be observed.[5]

The most obvious kind of *vraisemblance* is that in which a novelist conforms to, and departs from, the convention of a 'real world' What goes on in the 'real world' appears 'natural', but Ford, constantly, constantly, in every line, stretches our sense of what we would expect to happen in Bad Nauheim in 1904, while at the same time mocking the idea that *anything* might be called 'natural' in a world inhabited by sexual savages, so that even the 'natural' world of Bad Nauheim is progressively deprived of 'reality'. Dowell's oft-repeated phrase 'I don't know' is a constant subversion of the first kind of *vraisemblance*, as indeed are some of the events which he recounts – events that would not be 'natural' in *any* world that we know. With regards to the *vraisemblance* of what Culler calls 'the cultural text', Ford plays havoc with this, at once including his reader as a social equal who would naturally recognise the types of 'good people' who enjoy the life-style of the idle rich at an expensive spa in Germany, and yet at the same time constantly disappointing the expectations which he builds up in such a reader. Culler refers thirdly to the 'specifically literary intelligibility' which one might call style, the sense of being at home in 'an author's imaginative world'. Here I believe Ford is at his most radical, here his Modernism is the most uncompromising. He presents a world which looks and feels like the world of Henry James, and then describes a series of actions which would be unintelligible within it. 'The conventionally natural', Culler's fourth type, allows an author to declare overtly his independence of the conventions and rules of his genre, but here there is a further duplicity in Ford. Ford does not overtly claim that he is going to break with the conventions of the novel of 'good people', but, by emphasising how closely he is following the rules of 'natural' description, he distracts the reader's attention from the fact that he is in fact violating every one of them: he describes a world so fantastic, so unbelievable, so Expressionistically crazy, that the reader is bedazzled and confused, and accepts the puzzled helplessness of the narrator at face value. This leads naturally to the fifth of Culler's categories, that of 'parody and irony'. Ford is ironising over Jamesian practice until he reaches the point of parody, but since he has never explicitly announced that he was breaking with 'the conventionally natural', the new genre he is using or inventing has no name. So successful is the device, however, that the learned world has been taken in ever since 1915. Whether or not *The Good Soldier* is ironic transumption, or actual parody, is a theme we are now, at last, in a position to evaluate.

In deliberately creating his text in terms of an unannounced send-up of Henry James's precursor novels, however, Ford can be seen to be ironising the 'honest Joe' quality of the Jamesian narrator, absolutely in the manner of the fifth kind of *vraisemblance*, parody. For Dowell, in all his bumbling incomprehension, is a parody, surely, of the 'honest Bob' figure in *The Golden Bowl*, Colonel Assingham, who for page after page trails helplessly in the wake of the subtleties adumbrated by his wife, always two or three steps behind, always missing the point. In *The Golden Bowl* there are, again, two marriages, but forming a chiasmus of betrayal, as Charlotte Stant marries Mr Verver purely in order to be near her lover the Prince. It is at least arguable that, both in *The Wings of the Dove* and in *The Golden Bowl*, marrying someone in order to achieve adulterous unity with an old lover is a criminal act. When Maggie finally faces the Prince with her new knowledge of his affair with Charlotte, just after Mrs Assingham has smashed the meretricious 'gilt cup', the word 'know' is repeated again and again, until 'the effect of the word itself, her repeated distinct "know, know"' begins to grate on the Prince's nerves (end of Chapter 34).

It seems to me that the plot-line of *The Good Soldier* makes no sense at all. This is partly because great pains are taken by the author and narrator to muddy and confuse all forms of ordinary narrative comprehensibility. But, if I may offer a brief résumé of my published case, then I would suggest that the real lines of force are not between Florence and Ashburnham (as Dowell constantly asserts) but between Dowell himself and Leonora. For a moment, grant me the benefit of the doubt! Suppose that this is the case, and that there is a secret affair, going back perhaps years, and having, as its intended outcome, the possible marriage of Dowell and Leonora after the death of Florence. Then an enormous amount of things begin to 'fit' in the plot-line as told. For example, the fact that no time and place for the passion of Ashburnham and Florence is ever established, or even possible. For example, the fact that we have no evidence whatsoever that Dowell was a rich man, or had means of his own. But if we accept my alternative hypothesis, then at least a comprehensible *motive* is introduced: for the death of Maisie Maidan (who presumably found out what was really going on between Dowell and Leonora); for the death of Florence (if she had indeed taken prussic acid, she would have died in convulsions of agony, not been found laid neatly out on her bed); and for the death of Edward Ashburnham himself, whose life alone now stands between Dowell and Leonora and the satisfactory conclusion of their plan, part of which is to possess Branshaw Teleragh. Further, it would explain the invention of 'Jimmy'. I do not believe that 'Jimmy' ever existed – his physical description would be enough, but the idea that he 'accompanies' an unmarried girl on a trip round the world with Uncle Hurlbird and then 'accompanies' Dowell and Florence on their honeymoon surely flags up two sheer impossibilities in the cultural codes of the time? My alternative hypothesis would also make intelligible (in terms of motive) the endlessly repeated assurances on the part of Dowell that he does not understand the sex instinct, is virtually without desire, and cannot make head nor tail of the sexual drives in others. This, which is repeated to the point where we have to take Dowell almost for a freak or an imbecile, would now appear as what it clearly is: a smoke screen to cover his very real desire for Leonora – *not* for Nancy, for whom he has quite different emotions, concerned and protective. (Why do we never read the *tone*, the tonality, of Dowell's meditations carefully? His reflections on Nancy are deprived of all erotic content. They are, however, remarkably paternal). The ambiguous and menacingly real dialogue which Dowell reports as having taken place outside the Castle at Marburg now fits: it has (I believe) an acoustic reality which is never there when Dowell is lying, as he most often is.

I advance all of this case in the full awareness that Frank Kermode is surely right when he writes: *'the illusion of the single right reading is possible no longer'*. That has to be the fact. But, that said, the plot line as recounted *by Dowell* makes no sense: the plot line as reconstructed (from this new point of vantage) at least makes narrative sense. What has to be emphasised is that Ford, careless though he may have been, and given to inconsistencies of all kinds, was indeed capable of *having in mind* a perfect plot line, one which corresponds to a coherent mental entity. I believe that, after all the editorial difficulties have been acknowledged, and the difficulties due to editing, copying, transmission, proof-correcting and publishing taken account of,[6] there remains, in *The Good Soldier*, a brilliantly coherent plot-line – *once we have got the point*. My contention is, that up to now, we have not got the point, we have 'not got the irony'.

It was in an attempt to establish and analyse that irony that I undertook that first analysis of *The Good Soldier* in 1990. In order to focus on the point at issue (*vraisemblance,* genre) I attempted to isolate four kinds of 'refusals of coherence': refusals of coherence in the description of character; refusals of coherence in the organisation of the plot, including the 'double' time-scheme for 4 August 1904; refusals of coherence to do with the career of Florence herself, in what pertains to her 'heart', her sexual career, and her alleged 'suicide'; and refusals of coherence in organising time-schemes generally, in particular the events on the evening of Florence's 'suicide'. To these I add a section on the concept of 'the repressed', in which I deal with Dowell's infatuation with Leonora and his ambiguous relations to Nancy. Dowell's obsession with the body of Leonora (her shoulders, her arms, her wrist, the little ornament at her wrist) begin to operate as a Derridean 'supplement'. The textual conundrum is whether Dowell allows this obsession to be noticed, in an attempt to lead the reader away from the question of his relation to Leonora and to Nancy; or whether Ford allows him to be simply unaware of his own repressed emotions, and hence to 'give himself away'.

The Good Soldier: A Tale of Passion – by tradition we ignore the subtitle. True, it was the publisher Lane who decided to use a joke for a title and who invented the subtitle. Yet his is an early 'reader response' to the text. So: whose passion then? Max Saunders has suggested, in his recent biography that, 'the girl with whom Ashburnham has become infatuated might be his own illegitimate daughter'.[7] The implications of this have been taken up by John Sutherland in his recent essay 'Whose daughter is Nancy?' which I have already cited. I have myself suggested that Nancy might very well be Dowell's own daughter, a daughter with Leonora (the time-scheme allows for this), which would explain why Leonora reclaims her at the age of thirteen from the Ruffords. ('Nancy Rufford was her name: she was Leonora's only friend's only child, and Leonora was her guardian, if that is the correct term' – one could hardly suppose that Mrs Rufford was 'Leonora's only friend'; if Dowell himself was 'Leonora's only friend' then Nancy would be the daughter of them both; and 'guardian, if that is the correct term' has its usual duality of implication).

Be that as it may: Nancy might be the daughter of Ashburnham, or she might be the daughter of Dowell – the only certainty is that we are never going to be certain. But it doesn't matter which she is. It is obvious that Nancy is not the daughter of Major Rufford and almost equally obvious that Nancy is not the daughter of Mrs Rufford. But the duality of Nancy's status raises yet again the doubtful status of Dowell as narrator. Once again the question has to be asked: is he a continuation of the 'confused' narrator of James and Conrad; or is he a new kind of narrator, one who actually represses most of what we need to know in order to make sense of his story?

If Nancy is indeed Ashburnham's daughter, then we have the almost intolerable problem of why Leonora pushes her so vehemently to 'belong' to Ashburnham in order to 'save his life'. Again, Max Saunders has emphasised that the word 'incest' is never mentioned in the novel but that its possibility is everywhere.[8] If however Nancy is Dowell's daughter, then many of the delphic utterances and anacoluthons of Dowell at the end of the novel, as he sits and watches the crazy Nancy, 'enigmatic, silent, utterly well-behaved as far as her knife and fork go', take on a kind of tragic overtone.

But deft Ford has given the reader a clue even in the most apparently disconnected comments of Nancy.

> And as for Nancy. . . . Well, yesterday at lunch she said suddenly: "Shuttlecocks!" (*GS* 160)

The reference is to the first page of the Preface to the 1909 New York edition of Henry James's *What Maisie Knew:* 'The wretched infant was thus to find itself practically disowned, rebounding from racquet to racquet like a tennis ball or a shuttlecock.'[9] So Nancy's experience of her life is that of being a mere shuttlecock hit to and fro between opposing players, herself largely ignorant of what is going on. But who were the racquet-players?

Again Dowell, the duplicitous:

> And she repeated the word "shuttlecocks" three times. I know what was passing in her mind, if she can be said to have a mind, for Leonora has told me that, once, the poor girl said she felt like a shuttlecock being tossed backwards and forwards between the violent personalities of Edward and his wife. (*GS* 160)

But were those the names that Nancy in fact mentioned? Once admit that Nancy is not the daughter of Major and Mrs Rufford, and the play of forces around her becomes undecidable. Part of the literary breakthrough which Ford is carrying out is the sudden widening of possibility. The whole theme of dual personality and indeed schizophrenia (which the manuscript suggests was originally central to Ford's intention) can occupy any one of the characters at a time, while continuing to set up a general field of terror and indecision which is common to them all. In this general field of terror and self-division, Nancy is ignorant of certain facts about herself until very late on, and the erratic nature of her emotional commitments reflects this. Some of her acts make no sense without this assumption. If she *knew* herself to be the daughter of Ashburnham, for instance, her infatuation with him, and her offer of herself to him, would be incestuous, and we know enough about Nancy's radical innocence to know that she would have refused to offer herself. So we can deduce that she did *not* regard Ashburnham as her father in anything but a formal or an 'adoptive sense'. But to whom else in the field of force might she have felt filial relations? Is not Dowell himself at least possibly one of them?

This, like everything else to do with *The Good Soldier*, can only be a hypothesis. Yet, the final evidence would be acoustic. In *The Wings of the Dove,* which I believe to be the direct model for *The Good Soldier*, Kate Croy is trying to convince Merton Densher that he must court, and if possible marry, Milly Theale:

> 'Since she's to die I'm to marry her?'
> [. . . .] But her lips bravely moved. 'To marry her'.
> 'So that when death has taken place I shall in the natural course have money?'
> [. . . .] 'You'll in the natural course have money. We shall in the natural course be free.'
> 'Oh, oh, oh!' Densher softly murmured.
> 'Yes, yes, yes,' But she broke off. 'Come to Lady Wells.'
> He never budged – there was too much else. 'I'm to propose it then – marriage – on the spot?'
> [. . . .] 'You'll have a free hand, a clear field, a chance – well, quite ideal.'
> 'Your descriptions' – her 'ideal' was such a touch! – 'are prodigious. And what I don't make out of it is how, caring for me, you can like it.'
> 'I don't like it, but I'm a person, thank goodness, who can do what I don't like.'[10]

Compare:

And at last I worked myself up to saying:

'Do accept the situation. I confess that I do not like your religion. But I like you intensely. I don't mind saying that I have never had anyone to be really fond of and I do not believe that anyone has ever been as fond of me, as I believe you really to be.'

'Oh, I'm fond enough of you,' she said. 'Fond enough to say that I wish every man was like you. But there are others to be considered.' She was thinking as a matter of fact of poor Maisie. She picked a little piece of pellitory out of the breast-high wall in front of us. She chafed it for a long minute between her finger and thumb, then she threw it over the coping.

'Oh, I accept the situation,' she said at last, 'if you can.' (*GS* 51-2)

Dowell and Leonora standing on the little terrace overlooking the Lahn outside the Castle of Marburg. The Brahmsian theme of Kate Croy and Merton Densher has been given a new and subtle harmonisation. There is no innocent work, and Dowell is no innocent narrator.

NOTES

1. Roger Poole, 'The real plot-line of Ford Madox Ford's *The Good Soldier*: an essay in applied deconstruction,' in T*extual Practice,* 4:3 (Winter 1990), 391-427. The detailed reasons why I think that there are *two* time schemes based on '4 August 1904', and why I think one is an alibi for the other, are spelt out there, and I have no space to repeat the analysis here, but I rely upon my reader to consult it. It represents one 'half' of my total case.

2. John Sutherland, 'Whose Daughter is Nancy?', in *Can Jane Eyre be Happy?* (Oxford: Oxford University Press, World's Classics, 1997), p. 210. Frank Kermode's essay, which dates from 1974, is reprinted in Martin Stannard's Norton Critical Edition of *The Good Soldier* (1995), pp. 330-7. John Sutherland's quotation comes from p.

336. All references in this essay to *The Good Soldier* (*GS*) are to the Norton Critical Edition.

3. Julia Kristeva, *Semiotiké* (Paris: Editions du Seuil, 1969), p. 212.

4. Roland Barthes, *S/Z* (Paris: Editions du Seuil, 1970).

5. Jonathan Culler, *Structuralist Poetics* (London: Routledge and Kegan Paul, 1975), Chapter 7.

6. See Martin Stannard, 'A Note on the Text', in the Norton Critical Edition of *The Good Soldier,* pp. 179-193.

7. Max Saunders, *Ford Madox Ford: A Dual Life* (Oxford: Oxford University Press, 1996), vol. 1, pp. 421-2.

8. Saunders, *op. cit.*, pp. 423-4.

9. Henry James, *What Maisie Knew* (Harmondsworth: Penguin Books, 1971), p. 5; the text taken from the New York edition (1909).

10. Henry James, *The Wings of the* Dove (Oxford: Oxford University Press, World's Classics, 1984), pp. 378-9; and Part III of Book Eighth, *passim.*

THE GOOD SOLDIER: EDITORIAL PROBLEMS

Martin Stannard

In my Norton Critical Edition of *The Good Soldier* (1995) I tried to explain the general difficulties facing an editor of this text. They fall into several categories: (a) the provenance of the text through its various states; (b) footnoting; (c) the history of the text as an aspect of Ford's life and opinions; (e) the correction of factual inaccuracy; and (f) the choice of copy-text. At the root of all the problems lay the choice of copy-text, and the challenge to conventional theories of copy-text by literary theory.

Conventional theories (Greg, McKerrow, Bowers) assume that an editor, through a 'scientific' analysis, can restore a text of ideal intention. Structuralist and poststructuralist thinking, however, has undermined the notion of traceable authorial intention and constructs the text as an immaterial weave of signifiers. In response to this, a new breed of theoretically informed textual critics has emerged (McGann, Greenblatt) who talk rather of the sociology of the text and of the poetics of culture. Where Greg and his fellows were formalists, in some ways similar to the Practical Critics,[1] seeking to treat the text as an extra-historical phenomenon with its own internal logic, McGann *et al.* try to replace the historical context as integral to a text's meaning in its various forms while at the same time retaining the multiplicity of those forms' 'meanings'. Two major responses to this new way of thinking about textual criticism have been hypertext (producing all states and all contextualising material, e.g. McGann's Rossetti project at Virginia), and the *Cornell Wordsworth* (printing the earliest complete versions of the poems with massive textual apparatus to explain subsequent emendations). Both hope to avoid the problem of a text which melds various states. The current wisdom appears to be that to do so merely produces something the editor has invented. And it is true that when one examines applications of the conventional theory of copy-text, something odd emerges: that 'copy-text' as such is never printed. It is 'virtual', a choice of template which, as soon as the editor gets to work on it, changes into something else.

Conventional editors attempt to purify a text of its corruption by third parties. Modern practice stresses that the author may be one of these 'corrupters', either through simple mistakes, misplaced faith in later revisions, or self-censorship. The only answers appear to be parallel texts or the earliest complete version. My edition attempted to find a happy, or at least not neurotic, medium between these two positions. It is a single text. It does meld various states. But I hope to have removed most of the arbitrary aesthetic decisions of conventional editing by inventing a methodology for the sifting of pre-publication variants, and by creating a section at the back of the book called 'Manuscript Development and Textual Variants'. The latter lists all substantive variants and offers the reader open access to the editorial procedure, explaining what decisions were made and, in difficult cases, why. In some ways it presents a printed version of hypertext which the reader could use to reconstruct the text as s/he wishes should there be disagreement with my decisions. The basic principle was complete frankness about the editorial process.

Let me first deal with intention. *The Good Soldier* was never given this title by Ford. It was intended to be, and is in all pre-publication states, *The Saddest Story*. And the sub-title, 'A Tale of Passion', is also the publisher's invention. Ford tells an amusing story (as usual plagued with inaccurate historical detail) of how John Lane bullied him into changing the title for fear that a book called 'The Saddest Story' would never sell in wartime. Having achieved fame as *The Good Soldier*, the novel went on being produced thus – in the belief that no-one would recognise it otherwise. My first difficulty, then, was what to call the book – and its author. For Ford first published it under his earlier name Ford Madox Hueffer. But I was no more exempt from the financial considerations of producing an expensive text under an ambiguous title or with a obscure author. Although I put the idea to Norton that to do this would restore Ford's original conception, they sensibly discouraged this as purist fantasy.

Other interesting issues arose from what I take to be Ford's mistakes. If he misspells the name of a painter, for example, should the editor correct it? Or should this simply be left as an example of Dowell's inaccuracy? Ford's 'Dedicatory Letter' to Stella Bowen is quietly proud of his management of the book's complex interweaving of cross-references. He does not explicitly mention the chronology but the implication is that it all hangs together in the deepest sense. As we now know, it does not add up at all,[2] and trying to untangle the chronology has become a favourite party game for Ford scholars. An editor could probably make the chronology coherent by altering one or two of the dates but were s/he to do that, the book would lose its power of self-deconstruction. In short, the editor of a text with an unreliable narrator is caught, impossibly trying to distinguish between those 'errors' the author 'intended' to mark off this figure as unreliable, and those which are the result of the author's inaccuracy. I made a distinction between matters of fact (e.g. the 'correct' spelling of proper nouns) and impressions (e.g. the dating of events in a fiction). The former were standardised to clarify meaning; the latter were left unmolested.

A particular difficulty arose with punctuation. Ford corrected the extant typescript which, it is usually assumed, was the text from which proofs were set up. One would expect the punctuation of the first edition largely to correspond with this typescript, particularly where Ford has made punctuation corrections. It doesn't. The whole thing has been standardised in a quite different fashion. Short, 'ungrammatical', sentences have been tacked onto the beginning or end of longer ones. The general conversational tone has been straightjacketed by conventional usage. Unfortunately, we have no corrected proofs and so cannot be certain that these alterations were not Ford's. Even so, it seemed to me to be unlikely that he was responsible for them. It was much more probable that a house style had been imposed. I had settled on taking the first British edition (which is identical, apart from the title page, to the first American edition) as copy-text on the grounds that this was the last edition certainly overseen by Ford. The problem with the punctuation, however, obliged me to make an awkward decision: to modify the original printed text wherever possible, replacing its punctuation with that of the typescript. Only later – and with great relief – did I discover that Robert Kimborough had done a similar thing with his Norton Critical Edition of *Heart of Darkness*.

Footnoting a text like this also makes an editor hesitate. To footnote it at all is in many ways to prostitute its spirit. Dowell is, as Ford often was, deliberately careless about detail: '(I am not really interested in these facts but they have a bearing on my story.)' Florence is condemned for pretension in trying to impress others with information and, as I say in the 'Preface', 'The "bearing" that the facts have on Dowell's story can be construed as the impression of Florence's trying to use them as a weapon of sexual warfare.' There is, it seems, a distinction in Ford's mind between truth (data) and reality (the tumult of impressions, infinitely plastic, created by the conscious and unconscious mind's engagement with data). Ultimately, and particularly in the theory of literary Impressionism, these data have the status of truth only in so far as they log certain 'events': the deaths, for example, of Maisie, Florence, and Ashburnham. But these events only have 'reality' (perhaps it would be more accurate to say 'are only *given* reality') first by the perceiving consciousness, and second by the desire to 'render', or to communicate, that perception. The 'facts' of Dowell's narrative are, of course, notoriously obscure and still lead critics (see Roger Poole's essay here) to unearth motivations disguised by the narrator. Indeed, the withholding of information persistently creates a vacuum which the craving for meaning must occupy.

Nevertheless, there is a quite specific historical backdrop to the novel: the site of the Marburg Colloquy in the Schloss, and we know from Violet Hunt's account of her visit to Marburg with Ford that he uttered words very similar to Florence's about the devastating effects of the Protestant split from the Catholic Church. In Marburg the Colloquy was thrashing out the doctrine relating to communion and transubstantiation. As Carol Jacobs points out, this turns on the interpretation of the words 'This is my body', and is raised in the novel during a scene which Dowell only understands in retrospect, when Florence is effectively offering her body to Ashburnham.[3] Ford's eccentric Catholicism was constantly confronted by his desire, like that of Philip the Magnanimous, to sleep with more than one woman. Ford described the novel once as a discussion of the 'polygamous desires that underlie all men'.[4] Luther offered this freedom to Philip by granting him a special dispensation bigamously to marry a second wife. Protestantism for the first time countenanced divorce. Ford, it could be argued, was thus a Catholic by religious temperament who craved Protestant liberality to resolve the otherwise unbearable strains of his sexual psychology. The details of the Lutheran debate, therefore, need to be clear, even if Dowell and Ford were muddled about them. One of the local myths I discovered about Philip the Magnanimous was that he was a pious man who reputedly had three testicles and an insatiable sexual appetite. His study in the Schloss was said to have had two doors: one leading to the chapel and the other to his bedroom. It is possible that Ford would have heard this story, as I did, in Marburg, and would have expected the subtle reader to detect the analogy with the rest of his tale.

I decided, then, to footnote thoroughly rather than half-heartedly or not at all, even though Ford would probably have hooted with laughter at the idea. The sociology of the text is important, not only in this case to reclaim historical context which would be unknown to most readers, but also to reconstruct the history of the production of the text. Close examination of the manuscript reveals that Ford put a great deal more work into it than his airy assertion in the Dedicatory letter would suggest. There he talks about holding the whole novel in his head and dictating it quickly. He also speaks of finishing the book before the outbreak of war, thus presenting his choice of the date 4 August 1914 as uncannily perspicacious. I have given my reasoning for suspecting his statement about the date of completion in my edition, and shall not repeat it in detail. But I can now take the argument a stage further, and raise another difficulty about how the text was physically produced. Both ideas revise some of my statements in the edition.

Ford used three amanuenses: Brigit Patmore, H. D., and Richard Aldington. But one notices immediately that the 'manuscript' is not all holograph. Rather, it is a complex patchwork of holograph in the three hands of the amanuenses, ribbon-copy typescript, and carbon-copy typescript, the whole corrected, at least twice, by Ford, once in pencil and once in ink. Examining the typescript sections, one finds that they are spliced into the flow of holograph, yet what I term the 'internal pagination' (i.e. the contemporary pagination of the various sections of composition which recommences at '1' when a new section begins) remains continuous. There are no deletions of page numbers and insertions of revised ones when the holograph by an amanuensis begins again. This suggested to me that Ford often stopped dictating and re-wrote or scrapped large sections as he progressed, only starting the dictation again when he had adjusted the preceding matter. I felt that one could distinguish between that text typed by Ford and that by a third party if the text included what most textual critics would take to be strong signs of spontaneous composition. And these typed pages do display these signs: deletions with a series of 'x's, additional remarks crammed between lines etc.

To double-check, I contacted Caroline Zilboorg, editor of H. D.'s and Aldington's correspondence. She kindly offered to examine a copy of the manuscript to see whether she could confirm that the section Ford scholars have always assumed to be in H. D.'s handwriting was in fact her work, despite the fact that her performing this task is not mentioned in Barbara Guest's biography of H. D.. Zilboorg agreed that it was certainly H. D.'s hand and, as an expert on the woman's life and work, was intrigued by the fact that H. D. scholars apparently knew nothing of her acting as Ford's secretary. We then went on to discuss the typed sections interleaved with H. D.'s holograph. I explained my theory about how one might distinguish typing by Ford, and that the only alternative explanation I could think of for those signs of spontaneous composition would be that Ford was dictating to a typist. This seemed unlikely to me given that there was obviously more of the holograph, now lacking and replaced by typescript (holograph sections not infrequently conclude in mid-sentence). Zilboorg, however, was less certain. Characteristic eccentricities in the layout of the typing suggested to her that it might be H. D.'s work, although there was not world enough and time for Zilboorg to perform the detailed analysis necessary to prove this. If, however, anyone ever *does* do this analysis and Zilboorg's instincts are substantiated, this might raise editorial problems. Was H. D. merely taking dictation, squeezing in those extra phrases, deleting others, under Ford's supervision? Or was she typing up sections of her own holograph, perhaps sections which would otherwise have been largely illegible? If the latter, there is just a chance that, given what we know of her practice elsewhere, she might have had a stab at improving the text herself. This was not an editorial problem for me because, in the system for sifting variants I have employed, any such alterations would have been implicitly validated by Ford's correction of the manuscript, and by his later correction of the typescript and, presumably, proofs. Another editor using another system, however, might want to take these putative H. D. interventions into account.

The second problem – the date 4 August, 1914 – also remains unresolved, but has taken on an interesting twist. In my edition I presented all the biographical evidence and concluded, with Moser,[5] that the section for which Aldington acted as amanuensis, the last two chapters, was probably written after the declaration of war. I didn't, however, accept Moser's idea that, because the crucial date first appears in a section in H. D.'s hand, a section almost certainly written before the war, this is evidence for the 'amazing coincidence' theory. While it is possible that Ford coincidentally picked on the date once, it seems, to say the least, improbable that he could have elaborated on this choice as he did, to make it the lynch-pin of the novel's chronology, before 4 August, 1914. Its resonance as an historical moment was certainly not lost on him, and another theory suggested itself: that although there might have been one example of coincidental dating, he corrected the text's dating *as a whole* after war had broken out. The crucial page here is manuscript page 180 where it is clear that although the date appears once in H. D.'s hand, the extension of this date as a structural motif is Ford's correction, squeezed into the left-hand margin. The question is: 'When was this correction made?' If it was contemporaneous with dictation then the 'amazing coincidence' theory holds up. If, however, it was made after 4 August, 1914, we have a logical explanation of how Ford was able to develop this dating in the light of recent events. If the latter is true, then engaging critical possibilities open up in the opportunity legitimately to review the novel not merely as a commentary on the epistemological collapse of Edwardian society, but also as a war book – indeed, that these two issues might be seen to be intimately connected.

Examining the insertion itself, I fear, will not resolve this difficulty, until someone invents something like a carbon-dating method for the precise chronological location of a piece of handwriting. We might be talking here about a matter of days. Ford wrote to Lane requesting 'the fifty pounds that became due to me on the delivery of the ms. of the "Saddest Story"', dating his letter 12 (or 10?) August, 1915. There is a dispute surrounding this date, too, centring on whether it should have read '1914'.[6] But debating this will not help us to establish the point of completion. Ford was a fast worker. There is no reason why he could not have dictated those two last, brief, chapters in the week before sending this letter and after the outbreak of war. On the other hand, there is strong evidence to suggest that Ford's '1915' is accurate. Lane's account book, for instance, suggests that he wasn't paid anything until 16 February, 1915. Why? It is all, as Dowell might have said, a muddle.

One crucial piece of evidence concerning the book's completion date remains obscure. On the last page of Ford's corrected typescript there is a date stamp. It is very faint but reads:

RECEIVED
J. LITTLE & IVES CO.
OCT 3 1[?]1[?]19 AM 19 1[?]4[?]

The final date is indecipherable, even with ultra-violet light, but 'Oct 3' is clear enough, the third digit of the year must be a '1' and the fourth a '4'. It can't possibly have read '1915' since the book was published on March 17, 1915. Mizener assumes 'J. Little & Ives' to be the book's British printer. On this he bases his argument about the book's completion before the war: 'Oct. 3, 1914, would be just about the time the printer would be likely to receive the ms. if the novel had been completed when Ford said it was' (565). But there is no mention of J. Little & Ives in Lane's London account book. There is mention of carriers and cases and binders for the book but none of the date-stamp firm or of any printer for it. Neither the British nor the American first edition cites a printer. To my amazement, I discovered that there is no comprehensive guide to twentieth-century British printers. I did check *Kelly's Handbook*, however, for all the major British cities. No trace. In my edition I therefore speculated that J. Little & Ives might be a typewriting agency rather than a printer, which, if true, would push the date of completion clearly beyond the war.

It now seems that I was misguided in this speculation. On a trip to the Humanities Research Center (University of Texas at Austin) I examined some of their books on printing history and discovered J. Little & Ives. They were printers – American printers and publishers. The entry was infuriatingly vague. It suggested merely that they had been a famous firm of nineteenth-century New York printers. It implied that they had also been bookbinders. But there was no reason for Ford to send a typescript to a binder (especially not one in New York) and it was certainly not his practice to preserve pre-publication matter in this way. The manuscript is not bound but in loose sheets. No, Mizener's guess was half-right: J. Little & Ives were almost certainly the printers of *The Good Soldier*.[7]

In itself this may seem a discovery of startling dullness. It signals, though, something interesting about the book's publishing history. Mizener assumes, as everyone has assumed until now, that the 1915 first edition was printed in Britain and sheets sent to the USA. In fact, the reverse seems to have been the case: the book was printed in the USA and sheets sent to Britain, possibly because of wartime paper quotas. This does not necessarily damage the case for Ford's completing the manuscript after the outbreak of war. He could easily have sent it to Lane during the week after 4 August, and Lane could have had it typed and dispatched it to New York by 3 October, even allowing five weeks for the sea crossing. It does, however, add something to the sociology of this text. One of the puzzles surrounding it is the length of time it took to appear in print. This mystery might to some extent be resolved by an American printing and the need to get sheets back across the Atlantic during wartime.

Trying to reconstruct the textual history of a Ford novel is like trying to establish the details of a dream. He was so chaotic in his business affairs, so charmingly inaccurate in his public statements, so careless of his papers that one can only smile at the way his ghost frustrates the seeker after facts. Frank Kermode once told me a Ford anecdote which seems now like a metaphor. The major archive of Ford's papers is at Cornell. When the university had settled terms with the estate, Allen Tate and Janice Biala packed a truck with Ford's literary remains and set off for the north. Driving along a freeway, they noticed something like confetti floating about in the rear-view mirror, then realised that the back doors had sprung open. You can't stop on a freeway. By the time they eventually managed to pull up, a quantity of their precious cargo had been distributed across the countryside. Perhaps all the crucial links in the puzzles surrounding *The Good Soldier* went with them. How Ford would have laughed. If *The Good Soldier* is about anything, it is about how we think we come to know things. It would surely have delighted him that we shall probably never come to think that we know the history of his text.

NOTES

1. A point made by D. F. McKenzie in *The Panizzi Lectures 1985. Bibliography and the Sociology of Texts* (London: The British Library, 1986).

2. See Vincent J. Cheng, 'A Chronology of *The Good Soldier*', *English Language Notes* 24 (September 1986), 91-7; reprinted in the Norton Critical Edition of *The Good Soldier* (1995), pp. 384-8.

3. Carol Jacobs, 'The (Too) Good Soldier, "A Real Story"', *Glyph*, 3 (1978), 39-45; reprinted (revised) in Carol Jacobs's *Telling Time: Levi-Strauss, Ford, Lessing, Benjamin, de Man, Wordsworth, Rilke* (Baltimore: John Hopkins University Press, 1992), pp. 75-94.

4. See Sondra J. Stang, (ed.), *The Ford Madox Ford Reader* (Manchester: Carcanet, 1986), p. 477.

5. *The Good Soldier*, ed. Thomas C. Moser (Oxford: Oxford University Press, World's Classics, 1990).

6. See Arthur Mizener, *The Saddest Story. A Biography of Ford Madox Ford* (London: The Bodley Head, 1971). Mizener (p. 565) cites this letter as belonging to the Naumberg collection and adds: 'the exact day appears to be the 10th, but the second digit is not unquestionably clear.' He then goes on to date it as 1914 and to provide a rather far-fetched scenario to explain away the other material in the letter which would seem to date it clearly in 1915. See Richard M. Ludwig, ed., *Letters of Ford Madox Ford* (Princeton: Princeton University Press, 1965), p. 61. Ludwig dates it, surely more reliably, as 12 August, 1915.

7. See, for instance, *War Nurse: The True Story of a Woman who Lived, Loved and Suffered on the Western Front* (New York: Cosmopolitan Book Corporation, 1930). This, a story from Corinne Andrews's diaries, ghosted by Rebecca West to be serialised in *Cosmopolitan* (NY), later appeared in the book form cited 'Printed in New York by J. J. Little & Ives'.

FICTION AND HISTORY:
REREADING *THE GOOD SOLDIER*[1]

Bernard Bergonzi

Ford Madox Ford's novel, *The Good Soldier*, first published in 1915, is highly regarded by critics and practising writers – Graham Greene was a devoted admirer who constantly returned to it – but has never become a popular favourite. John Bayley has called it the most over-rated novel of modern times, while Ruth Rendell has described it as one of the great novels of the century. That kind of disagreement about a book is a sign of life, more so than unbroken acclaim and a safe classic status. Having recently reread *The Good Soldier*, for, I suppose, the third or fourth time in my life, I unhesitatingly go along with Ruth Rendell's opinion. It is a great novel, if on a small scale, almost unbearingly moving in places, where the intricacies of form are at one with the subtleties of feeling. Martin Stannard's critical edition in the Norton series (1995) does the book ample justice. It admirably shows the process of composition of *The Good Soldier* and the problems involved in its publication. It is immensely interesting to learn, for instance, from Ford's revisions that he altered the character of the 'good soldier' and Edwardian gentleman, Edward Ashburnham, to make him more of a sentimentalist and less of a libertine. The last part of this edition contains a representative selection of critical opinions. They include such influential readings of the novel as Mark Schorer's study of it as a great work of comic irony, told by the ludicrously inadequate narrator, John Dowell, and Samuel Hynes's exploration of its epistemological uncertainties, which have set the tone for much later discussion.

I have long been interested in how *The Good Soldier* relates to history. We know that Ford began writing it on his 40th birthday in December 1913 and finished it some time during the latter half of

1914; Stannard's edition shows that we cannot be sure when, though there is circumstantial evidence suggesting October as a terminal date. At all events, it is very probable that Ford was still working on the book when Britain declared war on Germany on 4th of August. *The Good Soldier* is not a war novel, though the title might have misled some readers when it was published, after unusually long delays for that period, in March 1915. Nevertheless, the war left its mark on it; the publisher, John Lane, thought that Ford's orginal title, *The Saddest Story*, under which the opening section had appeared in *Blast* in the summer of 1914, was too gloomy for wartime and asked Ford to think of a better one. According to Ford's account he sent a telegram to Lane, which said, in 'hasty irony' as he put it, 'Why not *The Good Soldier*?';[2] he was horrified to find, months later, that Lane had taken him at his word and published the novel under that name. In fact it seems to me a good title, better perhaps than *The Saddest Story*, and it has served the novel well.

Stannard's edition reveals another curious way in which the war affected the text of *The Good Soldier*. The manuscript shows that Dowell cannot stand Belgians, and makes several disparaging remarks about them, referring to the way they let the French trains miss their connections at Brussels as 'a mean dirty trick, typical of the Belgians'. Stannard plausibly suggests that Ford disliked the Belgians because of their oppressive imperialism in the Congo, as exposed by Conrad in *Heart of Darkness*; he actually quotes a phrase from that novella, 'the dark places of the earth', in *The Good Soldier*. But the offensively anti-Belgian phrases do not appear in the published text, having been deleted in proof; after Germany had invaded and brutally occupied Belgium in August such sentiments were inappropriate, and public opinion became strongly pro-Belgian. As, indeed, did Ford himself, as shown by his poem, 'Antwerp', commemorating the sufferings of the Belgian people.

Most of *The Good Soldier* was written in peacetime, but its composition was affected by the outbreak of war, which had been going on for months when it was finally published. The way of life it describes, of rich, rootless cosmopolitans like the Dowells and the Ashburnhams – that phrase presents itself so effortlessly that it has become a cliché – travelling round Europe from one resort to another, was to be destroyed by the Great War. In the light of history, we know that only too well, but Ford did not know it when he was writing the novel, though he may well have had his suspicions of what was to come, like many far-sighted people at the time. It is, I think, illuminating to compare *The Good Soldier* with two major novels from the Germanic world with which Ford, who was born Hueffer, had connexions, and where most of his novel is set. They look back to that vanished era and way of life, but were written after the war in the full knowledge of later events. Thomas Mann's *The Magic Mountain* isolates his consumptive cosmopolitans over several years in a Swiss sanatorium; in a different context, and with different health problems, the Ashburnhams and Dowells might have encountered them at Bad Nauheim. History is excluded from most of *The Magic Mountain*, but in the end war breaks out and breaks in, and our last sight of the central character Hans Castorp is on the battlefield.

Robert Musil's immensely long but still unfinished novel *The Man Without Qualities* is set in imperial Vienna over a few months in 1914, precisely the period during which Ford was writing *The Good Soldier*. Musil's characters – bureaucrats, politicians, businessmen, soldiers, intellectuals, artists – are involved in planning a great commemoration of the Emperor's seventy years on the throne, which will take place in 1918. They do not know, as we do and Musil does, that none of this will happen, that the Austrian empire is going to be swept away by war, though Musil stops short his narrative before the actual outbreak of war. We use the word 'irony' far too loosely these days, but *The Man Without Qualities* really is a work of sustained massive irony. In addition to these major novels, I shall mention a more recent English work, much slighter but still excellent, Isabel

Colegate's *The Shooting Party*, published in 1980. This describes an aristocratic shooting party at an English country house in the autumn of 1913, and concludes with the greater shooting party which breaks out a year later.

Returning to *The Good Soldier*, as the novel opens we find Dowell talking of the 'saddest story' of adultery, betrayal and suicide that he is about to tell us, in terms appropriate to national disaster:

> You may well ask why I write. And yet my reasons are quite many. For it is not unusual in human beings who have witnessed the sack of a city or the falling to pieces of a people, to desire to set down what they have witnessed for the benefit of unknown heirs or of generations infinitely remote; or, if you please, just to get the sight out of their heads. Someone has said that the death of a mouse from cancer is the whole sack of Rome by the Goths, and I swear to you that the breaking-up of our little four-square coterie was such another unthinkable event. (*GS* 11)

Dowell goes on this hyperbolic fashion, deploying images of the dissolution of harmony, of order, of civilization itself. He emphasises that he had suspected nothing, had been totally deceived in his conviction that all was well, that life could continue that way indefinitely: 'And, if you come to think of it, isn't it a little odd that the physical rottenness of at least two pillars of our four-square house never presented itself to my mind as a menace to its security?' (*GS* 12). Ford, writing several months before the outbreak of war, gives to Dowell's account of the sad fate of two wealthy couples the metaphors that were to be freely used about the collapse of European order once the war had started. As, for instance, in a well-known passage from an agonized letter that Henry James wrote on 5th August:

> The plunge of civilization into this abyss of blood and darkness by the wanton feat of those two infamous autocrats is a thing that so gives away the whole long age during which we have supposed the world to be, with

whatever abatement, gradually bettering, that to have to take it all now for what the treacherous years were all the while really making for and *meaning* is too tragic for any words.[3]

James, in his seventies, had a deeper sense of what the war meant, and would mean, than did the cheering patriotic crowds all over Europe who welcomed the war and were eager to see some action before it ended in a few months, as was the general expectation. James's tone and imagery have a noticeable continuity with those of the fictional Dowell. It is understandable that many readers have come to think of *The Good Soldier* as a war novel *avant la lettre*.

Let us go back one day, to 4th August, when war was declared. Here we come to an element in Ford's novel which has long puzzled me and many other readers, for 4th August is what Stannard calls the 'spine date' of the narrative. It is Florence's birthday; on that date in 1899 she begins a trip round the world with her uncle; on 4 August 1900 she embarks on an affair with the young man called Jimmy, and on that date two years later she marries Dowell and sets out for Europe with him. 4 August 1904 is the date of one of the great dramatic set-pieces of the novel; the Dowells and the Ashburnhams, having met up at Bad Nauheim, take a trip to the castle of Marburg, which contains a founding document of the Reformation. There Leonora Ashburnham has a hysterical outburst; she tells Dowell, and he believes her, that it is because she is a Catholic, conscious of all the evils that Protestantism has brought to the world. In reality it is because she has suddenly become aware of her husband Edward's sexual interest in Florence. That same evening, back in their hotel, his erstwhile mistress, little Maisie Maidan, dies of a heart attack, falling grotesquely head first into a trunk. Then, nine years later, on 4 August 1913, the novel moves to its frightful climax. Florence, long Edward's lover, sees him in the park at Bad Nauheim with his young ward Nancy and believes he is transferring his affections to the girl. She runs into the hotel and is spotted by an obnoxious guest who had known about her affair with Jimmy years before. She rushes upstairs and poisons herself, though the poor deluded Dowell at first believes she has succumbed to her non-existent heart condition. It is the end of the world for him; as he later writes, 'Permanence? Stability! I can't believe it's gone. I can't believe that long tranquil life, which was just stepping a minuet, vanished in four crashing days at the end of nine years and six weeks' (*GS* 11). Precisely one year later, on 4 August 1914, the European world really did come to an end.

What was Ford doing? How did he come to make this historically crucial date so central to his novel? In the past I assumed that it must have been done deliberately, and that even if the bulk of the novel was written before 4 August 1914, Ford went back over it and inserted the date, so as to make the collapse of his little world a proleptic metaphor for the great collapse that was to come, rather in the way that Isabel Colegate deliberately used the shooting party in her novel. In the absence of definitive evidence to the contrary one could go on believing that. But now Martin Stannard's edition, with its impressive textual appendices, moves the question towards resolution. As he describes, the original manuscript of *The Good Soldier* at Cornell contains material taken down from Ford's dictation by three amenuenses, Brigit Patmore, Hilda Doolittle, otherwise 'H. D.', and Richard Aldington, together with material typed by Ford and others. The 'spine date' first appears in Chapter One of Part II, which opens, 'The death of Mrs Maidan occurred on the 4th of August 1904. And then nothing happened until the 4th of August 1913'. This identifies the date clearly enough and the rest of the paragraph refers to the earlier occurrences of the date in Florence's life. From the textual commentary on this page, we see that Ford had second thoughts about the year – 1903 is changed to 1904 – but not about the date: 4th August stands without any alteration. Dowell, or Ford, repeats this information in Chapter One of Part III. The editor's textual commentary shows that Ford inserted several lines into the manuscript dictated to H. D., the appropriate page of which is reproduced in the edition. This holograph addition, though, does not add anything to what has already been established in Part II. Stannard remarks that Ford may have been wanting to emphasise the significance of this date once the war had started, but he admits that the reference to 4th August was already there on the page in H. D.'s writing. Personally I think it more likely that Ford was wanting to remind the reader of the multiple associations of this date, first stated in Part II, rather than to allude to a very recent historical event. In the early weeks of the war, which was widely expected to be over by Christmas 1914, 4th August may not yet have acquired its later resonance. And on the European scale the war had started several days earlier, when Austria declared war on Serbia on 28th July, followed by Germany on Russia on 1st August and on France on the 3rd.

Disconcerting though it may be, I think we have to conclude from the textual evidence Stannard supplies that Ford selected that date well before the outbreak of war. This is what commentators on Ford such as Arthur Mizener and Thomas Moser have called the 'amazing coincidence' theory. Stannard seems to accept that that is the way the evidence points, but still resists it, referring to 'the unlikelihood of the "amazing coincidence" theory being true'. I can't see why it should be unlikely; in fact what we are faced with seems to me not an amazing conicidence but a very ordinary one. In the real world we frequently encounter concidences of dates. If I might refer to my own experience for a moment: my wife has the same birthday as my late father; my son shares a birthday with my step-grandson, and one of my daughters with her cousin's wife. When I was a small boy back in 1937 I had to have an operation on my ear, which took place on St Patrick's Day, 17th March; in adult life I came to need another operation on that ear, which as it happened was done on 17th March 1971, precisely 34 years later. Reading a fictional text, one would be prompted to speculate about the 'significance' of such a correspondence, but in life it just happened.

In fact, the odds against Ford settling on 4th August by chance were not all that great. It is one of the *donnés* of the story that the Dowells and the Ashburnhams spend every August together at Bad Nauheim, so it has to be a date in that month when the major scenes take place, which gives a one in 31 chance; once Ford had fixed on 4th August when planning the novel it was easy enough to bring the earlier references to the date in line. What one might call the 'internal' coincidences of the spine date – which Dowell refers to as 'half-jocular and altogether merciless proceedings on the part of a cruel Providence' – may be more taxing than the 'external' one with 4th August 1914 – but there is nothing impossible about them. My only difficulty is on the level of plot; the events of 1904 and 1913 take place on Florence's birthday, which does not seem to be marked or celebrated in any way.

The drama of 4 August 1913 is in one sense the climax of the novel, but Ford avoids clear resolutions and there is a lot more story to come, with Florence's suicide being followed by Edward's later in the year. Stannard's edition includes a very useful essay on the chronology of *The Good Soldier* by Vincent J. Cheng, which traces Dowell's movements after 1913. He goes to Ceylon, brings back the deranged Nancy, and settles with her in Branshaw Teleragh which he has bought from the widowed Leonora; she, meanwhile, has married her old admirer Rodney Bayham and is expecting a child. Dowell begins writing down the 'saddest story'. By this time it is late 1915 or early 1916 in the scheme of the novel, and it is still a world at peace. Fiction and history seemed momentarily to coincide but thereafter they went in different directions.

There are other ways of looking at *The Good Soldier* and of relating it to history. One of them is suggested by a very acute essay, 'What Dowell Knew' by Eugene Goodheart, included in the Norton Edition. Goodheart picks up the theme of epistemological uncertainty which has directed earlier discussions of the novel, and directs it to the subtitle, 'A Tale of Passion'. He relates Dowell's images of collapse and dissolution to the confusions that have beset sexual life in the twentieth century, which were recorded by Lawrence and Freud and Musil and many other prophets. Dowell, the passionless man surrounded by the passionate and doomed, is very conscious of these confusions as he writes his narrative, however deluded he had once been. Goodheart sees Ford's novel as having something in common with Freud's *Civilization and Its Discontents*, but looks further back: 'It is not the repression of passion that makes for unhappiness, but the expression of passion that makes for the most intense happiness for the moment and for the deepest sadness, for it too must pass. Dowell here sounds the note not of Freud but of Ecclesiastes'. Goodheart goes on to say that:

> *The Good Soldier* is a story whose vividness and intensity are in excess of its meaning - or lack of meaning. Ford's famous commitment to impressionism is a statement that we have nothing but impressions. Yet the impressions bespeak not an emptiness but a felt absence [. . . .] All permanent, meaningful structures (God, character, the virtues) have disappeared, but not the desire for them. (*GS* 382-3)

He discusses *The Good Soldier* with the seriousness it deserves, and a kind of wisdom that is not common in academic criticism. His account is one of the best things in this valuable edition.

NOTES

1. Earlier versions of this essay appeared in the *London Magazine*, new series, 39:3-4 (June-July 1999), 46-53; and in Bernard Bergonzi, *War Poets and Other Subjects* (Aldershot: Ashgate, 2000).

2. *The Good Soldier*, ed. Martin Stannard, Norton Critical Edition (New York and London: W. W. Norton & Company, 1995), p. 5. Subsequent references to this edition (abbreviated to *GS)* appear parenthetically in the text.

3. Henry James to Howard Sturgis, continuing a letter of 4 August 1914: *Letters of Henry James*, ed. Percy Lubbock, 2 vols (London: Macmillan, 1920), vol. 2, p. 398.

III

FORD, THE WAR AND THE POST-WAR:
ENGLISHNESS, SOCIETY, HISTORY

REMAINS OF THE DAY:
TIETJENS THE ENGLISHMAN

Dennis Brown

Englishness is not what it was. In 1972 Philip Larkin wrote in 'Going, Going':

> And that will be England gone,
> The shadows, the meadows, the lanes,
> The guildhalls, the carved choirs.
> There'll be books; it will linger on
> In galleries; but all that remains
> For us will be concrete and tyres.
>
> Most things are never meant.
> This won't be, most likely: but greeds
> And garbage are too thick-strewn
> To be swept up now, or invent
> Excuses that make them all needs.
> I just think it will happen, soon.[1]

Since then, many poets have made the break-up or decay of Englishness a major theme. Tony Harrison has given us an England of them and '[uz]', further frayed into multi-ethnic complexities.[2] More recently the 'Bloodaxe poets',[3] hailed as a triumph of margins over the centre, have almost revelled in metropolitan and suburban decay. Peter Reading, connoisseur of neo-Thatcherite grot, the second volume of whose *Collected Poems* was published in 1996,[4] has yoked horrendous tabloid news items and cardboard box-land by violence together to conclude in quasi-Anglo-Saxon apocalypse:

> ...horror unbearable
> universal insanity   senility wrath
> weariness indolence   insomnia earth shall

('Untitled')[5]

Even the urbanely New Formalist Glyn Maxwell has looked beyond the zany hyperreality of a teenager's Welwyn Garden City to notice: 'The Burnt-out, the Despite,/The muffled in their homes and heaps'.[6] While Linton Kwesi Johnson has given us all a right dubbing throughout his protest-poem – 'Inglan's a Bitch'.[7] So on the poetry front, at least, Englishness is not what it used to be. But then it never has been.

In *Englishness: Politics and Culture 1880-1920*, edited by Robert Colls and Philip Dodd, Robert Colls notes:

> Englishness has had to be constantly reproduced, and the phases of its most intense reproduction – borne as its finest moments – have simultaneously been phases of threat to its existence from within and without.[8]

In his contentious book *England and Englishness*,[9] John Lucas has succeeded in indicating that a poetic battle of Britain has been waged since at least the Glorious Revolution of 1689, so the 'Moment of Bloodaxe', as some might call it, is not so exceptional. What Colls and Dodd's book calls particular attention to is the way the Great War, especially, caused a 'threat' to Englishness – that war, of course, which Ford Madox Ford fought in, and which is represented at the heart of his *Parade's End*.[10] In a chapter from *Englishness*, Alun Howkins quotes an anecdote from Clive Aslet's *The Last Country Houses* where an officer at the front had the magazine *Country Life* 'sent out to the trenches as a symbol of what he was fighting for'.[11]

Whatever quite Ford was fighting for, it probably included 'two gross of broken statues/…a few thousand battered books' (as Ezra Pound put it in 'Hugh Selwyn Mauberley'), and I think the tetralogy's commitment to cultural continuity makes it reasonable to consider it in terms of contemporary discussions about both Englishness and masculinities. Certainly, Ford's earlier work indicates his 'fascination with Englishness'[12] – especially in the trilogy *England and the English*.[13] The key figure in *Parade's End* is Christopher Tietjens, an Englishman, whose distance from, say, Edward Ashburnam has much to do with the Great War and Ford's modern memory. So my primary instance from the book will not be the often-noticed opening in the railway compartment, but one where Tietjens is at the front – mediating in idealised fashion among such highly-strung 'Britishers' as Cockneys, Canadians, Welshmen, ex-miners or millenarians. The passage is from the second volume, *No More Parades*:

> The other captain rambled on in front of him. Tietjens did not like his talk of the circle and the millennium. You get alarmed, if you have any sense, when you hear that. It may prove the beginnings of definite, dangerous lunacy. . . . But he knew nothing about the fellow. He was too dark and good-looking, too passionate, probably, to be a good regular officer on the face of him. But he *must* be a good officer: he had the D.S.O. with a clasp, the M.C., and some foreign ribbon up. And the general said he was [. . . .] He wondered if General Campion knew what a Vice-Chancellor's Latin Prize man was. Probably he did not, but had just stuck the piece of information into his note as a barbaric ornament is used by a savage chief [. . . .]

The repressions of the passionate drive them mad [. . . .] He seemed to see his draft: two thousand nine hundred and ninety-four men he had had command of for over a couple of months – a long space of time as that life went – men he and Sergeant-Major Cowley had looked after with a great deal of tenderness, superintending their morale, their morals, their feet, their digestions, their impatiences, their desires for women. . . . He seemed to see them winding away over a great stretch of country, the head slowly settling down, as in the Zoo you will see an enormous serpent slowly sliding down into its water-tank [. . . .]

Intense dejection, endless muddles, endless follies, endless villainies. All these men given into the hands of the most cynically care-free intriguers in long corridors who made plots that harrowed the hearts of the world. All these men toys, all these agonies mere occasions for picturesque phrases to be put into politicians' speeches without heart or even intelligence. (*PE* 295-6)

The enemy of Englishness here is not 'Fritz' nor the German High Command, but individual 'lunacy' or corporate anarchy.

So Ford, brought up among arty Pre-Raphaelites, Ford the collaborator with Conrad (inventor of Kurtz), Ford editor of the radical *English Review*, Ford who rolled on the carpet at Ezra Pound's poetic archaisms, Ford contributor to *BLAST* – whose wildness led to the editor, Wyndham Lewis, being summoned to 10 Downing Street for an explanation – Ford the passionately adulterous creator of the 'Good Soldier', constructs an even better soldier – one whose fundamental Englishness will survive whatever intrigue or High Explosive may throw at him: 'I am the master of my fate:/I am the captain of my soul'.[14] A key proto-Modernist is here playing a conventional late-Victorian card to shore up the ruins of English manhood. For English manhood is synonymous with sanity. Everything that threatens this becomes foreign. Talk of the millennium suggests 'dangerous lunacy' and its utterer 'too dark and good-looking, too passionate', whatever his officer-credentials. General Campion, Tietjens' preposterous god-father, who will later both demote and appear to cuckold him, evidently sponsors this 'foreigner' so his remark about Latin Prize men is rendered 'a barbaric ornament [. . .] used by some savage chief'. The men under his command – potentially anarchic Cockneys, Canadians, Welshmen etc – with their 'morale, their morals, their feet, their digestions, their impatiences, their desires for women' become animalised as 'an enormous serpent sliding down its water tank'. And the politicians playing with all these lives are wholly reified – 'without heart or even intelligence'. Anything which threatens our Englishman's sanity is alien. In this the 'other captain' has a point in objecting to noise. 'By God, he was perfectly right'. The heart of darkness must be kept at bay at all cost.

Faintly ridiculous as some of the idiom may now appear, Tietjens stands for a psychic reality beyond either nationality or gender – the fragility and necessity of what Freud tended to call Ego or even Superego but has more recently been reworked by British psychoanalysis in terms of a model of containment. The model has particularly been developed by another Great War veteran, who also produced a fine book about the war (*The Long Week-End*),[15] Wilfred Bion, one-time President of the British Psycho-Analytical Society. In *Attention and Interpretation,* Bion wrote:

> According to his background a patient will describe various objects as containers, such as his mind, the unconsciousness, the nation; others as contained, such as his money, his ideas.[16]

Donald Meltzer has described the container more lyrically:

> At the nucleus of this private core is the mysterious, sacred nuptial chamber of the internal objects, to which they must be allowed periodically to withdraw to repair and restore one another...these internal gods [. . .] are the superior, most evolved segment of the human mind [. . . .][17]

The 'container' needs to be able to withstand or incorporate all possible forms of 'lunacy'. At the beginning of the Second World War, Wilfred Bion was set by the War Office to study forms of officer leadership, and began developing group psychoanalysis.[18] The group leader, to be successful, must act as a form of 'container' for the anxieties of the group as a whole, to preserve it from anarchy. A loss of containing ability either on the personal or group plane might lead to Craiglockhart War Hospital, as it were – a historical shattering of English manhood recently examined in Pat Barker's trilogy.[19] Even when a shell-burst erases three weeks of his life and his memory-stock, Tietjens merely returns home to restock his mind from the *Encyclopaedia Britannica*. I am simplifying the issues, but arguably Ford does too. He knew enough about the psychic realities at stake (as well as the psychoanalytic jargon of the twenties) to wish to preserve his hero's sanity and leadership role, and hence his status as Englishman, against all the odds.

This determination gives rise to one of the most extraordinarily weird and wonderful discussions of Englishness in twentieth century literature. It is in *Some Do Not . . .*:

> It has been remarked that the peculiarly English habit of self-suppression in matters of the emotions puts the Englishman at a great disadvantage in moments of unusual stresses. In the smaller matters of the general run of life he will be impeccable and not to be moved; but in sudden confrontations of anything but physical dangers he is apt – he is, indeed, almost certain – to go to pieces very badly [. . . .]

> Tietjens had quite advisedly and of set purpose adopted a habit of behaviour that he considered to be the best in the world for the normal life. If every day and all day long you chatter at high pitch and with the logic and lucidity of the Frenchman; if you shout in self-assertion, with your hat on your stomach, bowing from a stiff spine and by implication threaten all day long to shoot your interlocutor, like the Prussian; if you are as lachrymally emotional as the Italian, or as dryly and epigrammaticaly [*sic*] imbecile over unessentials as the American, you will have a noisy, troublesome, and thoughtless society without any of the surface calm that should distinguish the atmosphere of men when they are together. You will never have deep arm-chairs in which to sit for hours in clubs thinking of nothing at all – or of the off-theory of bowling. On the other hand, in the face of death – except at sea, by fire, railway accident or accidental drowning in rivers; in the face of madness, passion, dishonour or – and particularly – prolonged mental strain, you will have all the disadvantage of the beginner at any game and may come off very badly indeed. Fortunately death, love, public dishonour and the like are rare occurrences in the life of the average man, so that the great advantage would seem to have lain with English society; at any rate before the later months of the year 1914. (*PE* 178-9)

Englishness betokens normality, as opposed to the 'later months of the year 1914' – abnormality, 'lunacy', foreignness: the Other. And such Englishness is specifically linked with an ideal of masculinity.

The context of Tietjens' somewhat batty meditation is an interview with Lord Port Scatho resulting from the sinister machinations of his fiendish wife Sylvia, who represents a restless, inchoate, destructive 'feminine' Otherness to our hero's sane English normality. It does not seem to occur to Tietjens (or perhaps Ford?) to question Sylvia's behaviour as abnormal, un-English or even 'lunatic'; she is, after all, a woman. The binary opposition involved is as compulsive as Toril Moi in *Sexual/Textual Politics*[20] might wish it to be. And, of course, such a masculinist construction survived the Great War and way past the second one. Both Antony Easthope in *What a Man's Gotta Do*[21] and Lynne Segal in *Slow Motion: Changing Masculinities Changing Men*[22] have interesting things to say about typical 1950s men. Segal, with Lacan's writing in mind, sums it up like this:

> the promise of phallic power is precisely this guarantee of total inner coherence, of an unbroken and unbreakable, an unquestioned and unquestionable masculinity.[23]

Tietjens' masculinity, however, is represented as neither 'unbreakable' nor 'unquestioned'. Ford teases the reader at various points not only with the possibility that his hero might break down – 'he was mad and seeing himself go mad' (*PE* 564) – but also that he has broken down – as his girl Valentine believes: '"He appears to be mad"' (*PE* 653). Valentine does not see 'lunacy' as a loss of either Englishness or manhood. Indeed, it is precisely at this point in the story that she is willing to become Tietjens' physical lover. But Ford does seem to see it in those terms – some, after all, do not; and a man can only stand up if he can keep his head when all around are losing theirs. And even Mark, Christopher's brother and rival, does not break down when he succumbs to paralysis in *Last Post*: in fact, he self-consciously makes an Iago-like decision: '*From henceforth he never would speak word*' (*PE* 679), similarly pluming up his will.

In the major decade of literary modernism, when selfhood was typically represented as dynamically fragmentary, *Parade's End* is remarkable for bringing a highly modernist stylisation to bear on shoring up traditional English manhood, even in the post-Great War era when Groby House will pass to an American woman and the title to a French woman. There'll always be an Englishman, even if he is marginalised away from the national centre of a low dishonest decade. The Groby Great Tree – proto-Lacanian phallic signifier – may be cut down, and Tietjens' legitimate heir alienated from him by Sylvia, but he has Valentine and the coming child to sustain him. As Mark reflects: 'Christopher no doubt was wise in his choice. He had achieved a position in which he might – with just a little more to it – anticipate jogging away to the end of time, leaving descendants to carry on the country without swank' (*PE* 831). What more could a true Englishman desire? The drift is similar to that in D. H. Lawrence's near-contemporaneous *Lady Chatterley's Lover* – the authentic Englishman is no longer to be found in the Country House or in charge of the nation's affairs. Yet he remains, unbowed if somewhat bloodied: 'A good man', as the dying Mark says to Valentine.

However, *Parade's End* renders the 'Condition of England' as one of decline if not fall – of 'remains'. And it does so partly by using a shortened genealogy. As Alun Howkins shows in *Englishness*, a dominant myth of the time was of an Elizabethan 'Merrie England', lasting until the 1680s. That is where the Tietjens' line is about to begin. As Valentine ruminates toward the end: 'Christopher was eleventh Tietjens of Groby [. . . .] Number one came over with Dutch William, the Protestant hero!' (*PE* 811). This is an almost Irish Unionist mythology of Britishness holographed over a simulacrum of Yorkshire grit. Guilt towards a usurped catholic family is linked to a fanciful genealogical curse in Ford's post-war mythologisation. Perhaps the shorter time-span is deployed to salvage the overall historical destiny of Englishness. George Herbert of Bemerton, after all, lived well before the Glorious Revolution – an inheritance which the Tietjens put roots *into*, as it were. And while the wooden butler-narrator of Kazuo Ishiguro's Booker Prize book *The Remains of the Day*[24] has served the appeasing, if not fascist, Lord Darlington – whose weekend parties seem traceable back to Ford's 'endless muddles, endless follies, endless villainies' (*PE* 296) – it is arguable how representative of their land most Englishmen would find this 1930s' butler's almost unbelievable up-tightness. England is the land he sees – and the other characters he meets who are more inclined to 'bantering'.

'Get you to bed. . . . I will come and examine you' (*PE* 836), says the 'much-liked' doctor to pregnant Valentine at the end of the tetralogy – Englishness will continue. From the standpoint of the double millennium, *Parade's End* stands out as perhaps the most comprehensive fictive exploration of Englishness which the twentieth century produced, and one highly relevant to current multi-ethnic and post-devolution Britain. For, to repeat Colls's point: 'Englishness has had to be constantly reproduced'. 'History is now and England'[25] remains a priority for cultural thinking in terms of national identity. Derek Walcott, a St Lucian who has, nevertheless, recently been championed (unsuccessfully) for the Laureateship, has hymned, as it were, a transplanted England:

> A green lawn, broken by low walls of stone,
> Dipped to the rivulet, and pacing, I thought next
> Of men like Hawkins, Walter Raleigh, Drake,
> Ancestral murderers and poets.../
> My eyes burned from the ashen prose of Donne.[26]

There is a similar ambivalence about the English legacy in Derek Jarman's *The Last of England* (1987) – a title pointing directly back through allusions in *Parade's End* to the famous painting by Ford's grandfather, Ford Madox Brown. However, Jarman has also published more positive-sounding titles – *Little England/A Time of Hope* and *Today and Tomorrow.*[27]

In addition, the inter-nation complexities of *The Last Post* (final book of *Parade's End*) – Mark Tietjens' belief in a 'single command' (French) to bring European peace, Christopher's implication in selling the country's antique heritage to Americans, Marie-Léonie Riotor's transformation into Lady Tietjens – not only speak to current political squabbles between Europhiles and Little Englanders but also foreshadow the wry, trans-national and multi-ethnic pyrotechnics of Salman Rushdie's *The Ground Beneath Her Feet* (1999) – 'Lord Methwold is recently dead [. . .] his wife is the sole – and uncontested – beneficiary [. . . .] This country mansion is now hers; also the town house at Campden Hill Square [. . . .] Spenta Carma has received the news of her good fortune [. . .]'.[28] However, recent poems also continue Ford's gentler English infatuation:

> Leave it now, leave it; give it over
> to that all-gathering general English light,
> in which each separate bead
> of drizzle at its own thorn-tip stands
> as revelation.
> (Geoffrey Hill, 1998)[29]

> A dream of English watercolourists
> all spread out on the hills: the sky is blue..../
> Hills on the horizon
> breed and open till the light has all....
> (Glyn Maxwell, 1998)[30]

Something lovely of Englishness endures 'without swank', and akin to those lines of Herbert which help Tietjens preserve his sanity against all that the Great War can throw at him:

> Sweet day, so cool, so calm, so bright,
> The bridal of the earth and sky....

NOTES

1. Philip Larkin, *Collected Poems*, ed. Anthony Thwaite (London: The Marvell Press and Faber and Faber, 1988), p. 190.

2. For 'them & [uz]' I and II, see Tony Harrison, *Selected Poems*, second edition (London: Penguin Books, 1987), pp. 122 and 123. For 'multi-ethnic complexities' see, e.g., 'v', *Ibid*, pp. 235-49.

3. See, especially, *The New Poetry*, ed. Michael Hulse *et al.* (Newcastle upon Tyne: Bloodaxe Books, 1993), including the Introduction.

4. Peter Reading, *Collected Poems 2: Poems 1985-1996* (Newcastle upon Tyne: Bloodaxe Books, 1996).

5. *Ibid*, p. 295. See also further 'Untitled' poems in Peter Reading, *Work in Regress* (Newcastle upon Tyne: Bloodaxe Books, 1997), pp. 43, 50, 54, 57.

6. From 'In Herrick Shape for Her', Glyn Maxwell, *Out of the Rain* (Newcastle upon Tyne: Bloodaxe Books, 1992), p. 78. For 'a teenager's Welwyn Garden City' see 'Tale of the Mayor's Son', Glyn Maxwell, *Tale of the Mayor's Son* (Newcastle upon Tyne: Bloodaxe Books, 1990), pp. 10-14, and for 'Garden City Quatrains', Glyn Maxwell, *Rest for the Wicked* (Newcastle upon Tyne: Bloodaxe Books, 1995), pp. 51-3.

7. Linton Kwesi Johnson, 'Inglan's a Bitch', *The New Poetry*, pp. 187-8.

DENNIS BROWN

8. See *Englishness: Politics and Culture 1880-1920.*, ed Robert Colls and Philip Dodd (Beckenham: Croom Helm, 1986), p. 299. Since writing this essay, I have become aware of the flood of commentary on Englishness and the British which has attended the issue of constitutional devolution. See, for instance, the republication of Linda Colley, *Britons: Forging the Nation 1707-1837* (London: Vintage, 1996) and Bill Bryson, *Notes from a Small Island* (London: Doubleday, 1995), Jeremy Paxman, *The English: A Portrait of a People* (London: Michael Joseph, 1998), Norman Davies, *The Isles: A History* (London: Macmillan, 1999), Simon Heffer, *Nor Shall My Sword: the Reinvention of England* (London: Phoenix/Orion, 2000), Andrew Marr, *The Day Britain Died* (London: Profile, 2000). There have also been many recent books on nationalism and 'place myth'. My own more recent thoughts on Englishness have been somewhat prompted by some essays in *Contemporary Writing and National Identity*, ed Tracey Hill and William Hughes (Chippenham: Sulis Press, 1995) and are reflected in my chapter 'The Last of England', Dennis Brown, *John Betjeman* (Plymouth: Northcote House, 1999), pp. 36-50.

9. John Lucas, *England and Englishness: Ideas of Nationhood in English Poetry 1688-1900* (London: The Hogarth Press, 1990). Some of the issues have been updated in John Lucas, *The Radical Twenties: Aspects of Writing, Politics and Culture* (Five Leaves Publications, 1997).

10. All references to Ford Madox Ford, *Parade's End* (London: Penguin, 1988): henceforth *PE*.

11. *Englishness: Politics and Culture*, p. 78.

12. The phrase is from Colin Edwards' essay 'Dates and Infidelities: Ford Madox Ford and national history', in *Contemporary Writing and National Identity*, pp. 93-101. Edwards effectively quotes Ford's 'conviction' that: 'I was not English'; however, I do not think it 'rash to presume' that Tietjens represents 'some kind of ideal form of "Englishness"' (p 99). My earlier view about this is indicated in 'No Brain Could Stand More', Dennis Brown, *The Modernist Self in Twentieth-Century English Literature: A Study in Self-Fragmentation* (London: Macmillan; New York: St Martin's Press, 1989), pp. 58-66.

13. Ford Madox Hueffer, *England and the English*, comprising *The Soul of London*, *The Heart of the Country* and *The Spirit of the People* (New York: McClure, Phillips, 1907). See also *An English Girl* (London: Methuen, 1907). For details of Ford's (Hueffer's) earlier career see Max Saunders, *Ford Madox Ford: A Dual Life*, Vol. 1:

The World Before the War (Oxford: Oxford University Press, 1996). I am grateful for discussions about Ford's early work with my Ph.D. student Jenny Plastow.

14. W. E. Henley, *Echoes*, IV, 'Invictus. In Mem. R. T. H. B.' (*Bloomsbury Dictionary of Quotations*, 1994, p. 178).

15. Wilfred R. Bion, *The Long Week-End 1897-1919: Part of a Life,* ed. Francesca Bion (London: Free Association Books, 1986). Bion was in the early Tank Corps and would probably have been awarded a Victoria Cross had he not spoken his mind, after a disastrous attack, to a Campion-like superior.

16. Wilfred Bion, *Attention and Interpretation* (New York: Jason Aranson, 1923), p. 122.

17. Donald Meltzer, 'Foreword', Meg Harris Williams and Margot Waddell, *The Chamber of Maiden Thought: Literary Origins of the Psychoanalytic Model of the Mind* (London: Tavistock/Routledge, 1991), p. xvi.

18. See, for instance, W. R. Bion, *Experiences in Groups and Other Papers* (London: Tavistock, 1972).

19. See Pat Barker, *Regeneration* (London: Viking, 1991), *The Eye in the Door* (Viking, 1993) and *The Ghost Road* (Viking, 1995). For a discussion of the psychological issues involved and their relation to notions of English manhood, see Dennis Brown, 'Pat Barker's Trilogy: Total War, Masculinities, Anthropology and the Talking Cure' in *Pat Barker*, ed Sharon Monteith (forthcoming).

20. Toril Moi, *Sexual/Textual Politics: Feminist Literary Theory* (London: Methuen, 1985).

21. Antony Easthope, *What a Man's Gotta Do: the Masculine Myth in Popular Culture* (London: Paladin, 1986).

22. Lynne Segal, *Slow Motion: Changing Masculinities Changing Men* (London: Virago Press, 1994).

23. *Ibid,* p. 102.

24. Kazuo Ishiguro, *The Remains of the Day* (London: Faber and Faber, 1989).

25. T. S. Eliot, from 'Little Gidding', *The Complete Poems and Plays of T S Eliot* (London: Faber and Faber, 1969), p. 197.

26. From 'Ruins of a Great House', Derek Walcott, *Collected Poems 1948-1984* (London: Faber and Faber, 1992), p. 20. There is also a magically diffused 'Englishness' within his *Omeros* (London: Faber and Faber, 1990).

27. See Derek Jarman, *The Last of England* (London: Constable, 1987); *Today and Tomorrow* (London: Richard Salmon, 1991); *B Movie: Little England/A Time of Hope, 1981* in *Up in the Air: Derek Jarman's Collected Film Scripts* (London: Vintage, 1996). Jarman's films *Jubilee* (1978) and *The Tempest* (1979) are also highly relevant. Elsewhere, I have suggested connections between Jarman's and Sir John Betjeman's rendering of England. See *John Betjeman*, pp. 42 and 68, n. 11.

28. Salman Rushdie, *The Ground Beneath Her Feet* (London: Jonathan Cape, 1999), p. 310.

29. Geoffrey Hill, *The Triumph of Love* (London: Penguin, 1999), pp. 26-7.

30. From 'Edward Wilson', Glyn Maxwell, *The Breakage* (London: Faber and Faber, 1998), p. 33.

FORD'S AND KIPLING'S MODERNIST IMAGINATION OF PUBLIC VIRTUE[1]

Robert L. Caserio

In a formulation that remains cogent, Lionel Trilling writes of 'the bitter line of hostility to civilization'[2] which is characteristic of modern literature and especially characteristic of modernist fiction. One motive for the hostility is literary modernism's sympathy with Freud's claim that civilization and the State together repress creative Eros and transform a State-upheld civilized super-ego into a death-driven id. But, in the light of this bitter line, Ford's *Parade's End* shows up queerly. For *Parade's End*, instead of objecting to the repression of Eros, objects to the repression of sexual abstention and of chastity; above all, *Parade's End*, instead of opposing the State and civilization, objects to the repression of *them*: of what they are and stand for, or ought to stand for. These objections are summed up in Valentine Wannop's loving appreciation of Christopher Tietjens' surmounting of Eros: 'His abstention not only strengthened her in her predilection for chastity; it restored to her her image of the world as a place of virtues and endeavors'.[3] The public world, *the* place of virtues and endeavors, can only be made possible by civilization and the State. What are the latter but that place itself? Public virtues and endeavors are the repressed whose return *Parade's End* seeks to bring about – in loving alliance with 'abstention' and without bitter hostility to civilization. Is Ford's novel at all modernist, then; or shall we have to endorse Trilling's formulation yet supplement it, in order to re-envision a modernism various enough to include Ford's oddness?

In asking this question, I propose that we be of two minds about modernism. Being of two minds, however, is part of a modernist problem that *Parade's End* seeks to get us beyond. Modernist rebellion against civilization partly results from the belief that 'civilized' culture wrongly represses the duplicities, ambiguities and indeterminacies that inhabit history and Eros. No less than the bitter hostility to civilization, ambiguity and double-minded indeterminacy have seemed to us to be characteristic of modernism. Yet these duplicities and ambiguities are the trouble in *Parade's End*. They are identified as the trouble, even though Ford is a master of the representation of the self-contradictious duality, or multiplicity, of life. Max Saunders's critical biography shows Ford's creative saturation in the modernist medium of double-mindedness. Nevertheless, we must continue to meditate on Ford's attitudes towards this medium. Was double-mindedness for him a constant and normative condition of art and experience; or does he identify it with a specific historical condition, which must be opposed? In Ford's transit from *The Good Soldier* to *Parade's End*, his attention turns from doubleness and duplicity in Eros and language, to doubleness and duplicity in the public realm. The State order that produces the Great War deliberately fissions its actions and meanings so that its right hand does not know, can not and will not know, what its left hand is doing. This is the dualism that hides the virtues and endeavors which Valentine wants returned to her world. 'In every man,' Christopher thinks, 'there are two minds side by side, the one checking the other' (*PE* 87). Ford's fiction forms itself on the model of self-divided mind; but there is a new motive outside fiction, in history, which inspires the innovation.

The unprecedented global crisis produces an unprecedented historical construction of self-contradictory psychology. Christopher wants to go to the front for a second time, and he insists on going, when faced with a War Office official who offers to keep him at home. "'Some do [go]. Some do not'", the officer intones (*PE* 225). Why is Christopher, instead of flouting the title of Ford's book, not on the side of the some who do not go? He rushes back to the front not because he has made a choice, but to express his warring desires and to put an end to them by getting killed. The warring desires are not just personal. Tietjens typifies the suicidal way out for a self-contradictory double-minded era of public life.

The British state shares the psychic self-contradictions of individual figures in *Some Do Not . . ..* The State invests in the self-alienating contradictions, as do the characters. Christopher's suicidal purpose derives from the contamination of the brilliant work he does as a statistician for the Civil Service, whose Department of Statistics has been asked to rig some of its figures so that the British can manipulate, and even betray, their French allies. Going against the grain of his own convictions and showing off ("'in the lightness of my heart!'" [*PE* 253]) to a colleague how to accomplish the statistical fakery, Tietjens sets into motion a state-required betrayal of administrative principle and public accountability. But perhaps it is not betrayal? The facts speak not only one way; how they speak is indeterminate, since they can be made to speak at least two ways at once. Christopher can instance this unsettled duplicity even with figures. Christopher's colleague passes on to those who want them the faked figures, which translate fact into fiction. In adopting the fiction as fact, the State shows how easily it can adopt self-contradiction, the unclear line between truth and lie, the ambiguity and indeterminacy of the Freudian psyche's dual life, as a public mode of conduct. But perhaps the early-twentieth-century State, mired in imperialism's self-contradictions, *originates* the psychic division and self-contradiction of its citizens – which Freud then portrays as an ahistorical public norm! The State can shrug off inconsistency and manipulation as an inevitable strategy of political life, if it appears to be an inevitable psychological formation. This appearance I think Ford's emphasis on the *historical* determinants of ambiguity intends to correct. Fordian-Freudian self-division is symptomatic not of any universal psychic state, but of a specific European history. To punish himself for his part in indeterminacy and duplicity, to escape his wife's sudden conversion to a monogamy he is not single-minded about, Tietjens sends himself to the trenches. He defers his pursuit of Eros and Valentine by departing from those who do not go into battle. He thereby defers, or represses, two things: honest administration of public order, and conscientious objection to the War. He represses the former because, having stood up against his Department, he has been unable to withstand its manipulations of fact. He has also stood up against the War Office on the subjects of mismanaged economies and the maltreatment of soldiers at Command Depots. But having lost the battle in both stands, Christopher capitulates. Like Ford in real life, he does not choose to be a 'C. O.' – or 'conchie' (*PE* 270). Valentine's brother is a conchie, and it is in fact his drunken presence which prevents the lovers from making love on the night before Christopher 'goes out'. The brother falls asleep on the couch on which Valentine had hoped to lose her virginity. Curiously, the brother's snores sound to Christopher like 'the laughter of unknown races from darkness' (*PE* 252) – like, one might say, the voices of peoples oppressed by the State's double-minded and double-dealing empire. This narrative event – whereby, in effect, conscientious objection intervenes against the lovers' adultery – means that, albeit secretly, conchie-ism does go to the front with Christopher. It is there as the deferment of Eros; it is there when he longs for something in Valentine that is not 'couched' in Eros, but is chaste and is detached from the adulterated morality of Tietjens' class; and conchie-ism is there as his desire not to follow through on his suicide, but to get out of the war instead – to be among those who do not fight, after all. In this example, the secret spreading of conchie-ism into the hero's life is for good. It consolidates the virtues and endeavors which Valentine loves. Unfortunately, Tietjens' conscientious objection at first is not grasped by him *consciously*.

How is a world of virtues and endeavors to emerge out of these ambiguous psychic cross-currents so that Christopher's great administrative competence can become practicable? At the end of the episode in which the famous collision of vehicles in the mist takes place, Christopher damns all principles, but then exclaims: "'But one has to keep on going . . . Principles are like a skeleton map of a country – you know whether you're going east or north'" (*PE* 144). Chastity and conscientious objection – not just to war but to the State's dishonesty and to the common duplicity of psychic life – are among the principles, or the principle-like concerns, which will liberate the lovers from the

War and the State. They are the principles that also might master and redeem the public administration of the State. Included among the liberating agents are what Tietjens calls 'exact and constructive intellects' (*PE* 231), which the lovers want to use to master indeterminacies and divisions of all kinds, and to achieve definitive union. To be sure, it does not seem a sign of their search for unity when Ford has the hero say to Valentine, who objects to his support for the war: "'I support it because I have to. Just as you decry it because you have to. They're two different patterns that we see'" (*PE* 221). Apparently *not* trying to unify a double vision by resolving it into single focus, Christopher's statement is varied later, when he asks:

> 'Do you know these soap advertisement signs that read differently from several angles? . . . You and I are standing at different angles and though we both look at the same thing we read different messages. Perhaps if we stood side by side we should see yet a third' (*PE* 234).

The hero strains, and the author too perhaps, to express the wish for a 'third' message, a coalescence – into a single determinate unity – of the indeterminacies and conflicting double perspectives, which are produced by, and include, modern political history (another kind of soap advertising). 'Principle' might be a name for the true, unified message. As the tetralogy unfolds, Tietjens replaces the double messages, in which his psyche and his culture are caught, with a single-minded integrity. Valentine mostly commands this integrity all along. When both lovers are united in determination, their capacity decently to administer life grows.

To see Ford trace the lovers' turn away from ambiguity and indeterminacy, and towards principle and truth, is to see modernism on the move against itself – if we believe that bitter opposition to civilization and heightened ambiguity and indeterminacy exclusively characterize modernism. But a counter-movement like Ford's also characterizes it – or should be recognized as characterizing it. Certainly, after *Parade's End*, in the work which has no canonical status, Ford cultivates the surmounting of the duplicity-minded ambiguity that wrecks the characters in *The Good Soldier* and that, at first, drives Tietjens towards suicide. As if in protest against the suicidal tendencies of modernist life, Ford makes himself into an anti-modernist modernist. Better principle and ideals, he seems to say, and distance from reality, than the misty particulars and double visions of impressionistic truth. Ford's later novels declare that, if the mist of modern impressions permits the conflation of fact and desire which is instanced in the State's and the ruling class's manipulation of truth, then fiction will have to cleanse itself of realistic mists, including those created by self-contradictory dualisms and indeterminacies.

Having attained a renewed single-mindedness in *A Man Could Stand Up –*, Christopher becomes a 'conchie' in the peace. The peace-time conchie objects to the imperialist political order as itself an undeclared self-divided and continuing war; and he does whatever possible to withdraw himself from the conflict. While the withdrawal looks like an instance of modernism's 'bitter line', the withdrawal is not an escape into a pure or mere privacy, opposed to civilization and the State's public virtue. The withdrawal is an enactment of public norms which must be kept alive in acts of secret resistance at very local sites by civic principles that might yet come back into common use. The very resistance of these norms to party affiliations or to collective-sounding names or slogans marks their political virtue. Public values are hidden away, or abducted, in the conchie's withdrawal from the State's decline into a life which makes peace the double of war. One of Ford's terms for this hiding is 'small producer'. *No Enemy* (1929) is a small producer's bible. But small production, in Ford's sense, does not only mean growing one's vegetables. Ford's garden plots function more comprehensively. The small producer is minor, is of minor importance, has a minority status; and just this is what makes the small producer's sheltering of public virtue both possible and significant. Minority protects the world of conscientious virtues and endeavors by preserving that world in deliberate single-minded obscurity.

What critics dislike about *Last Post* is its single-minded resolution of history's cross-currents and psychic and erotic self-contradictions. No wonder that Graham Greene, whose fiction depends on modernist ambiguity of thought and feeling, objects to *Last Post's* crystallization of *Parade's End* into decided commitments and definite peace. What is crystallized, of course, in *Last Post's* pastoral world are the values that most can serve the public sphere. But the evocation of these values in *Last Post* is criticized, for example by the intelligent commentator Robert Green, on the grounds of single-mindedness: the novel 'is too nakedly preceptive'.[4] Robert Green's is a kind of literary criticism which considers itself too tough to countenance the idea that public virtues can be kept alive in spheres of narrowed and hidden endeavor. The idea is evaluated by such criticism as mere utopianism, too feeble for an effect on reality, or even any intersection with reality. Green's *Ford Madox Ford: Prose and Politics* goes back to 1981, but its politically-based evaluation of Ford remains current. Green assumes that *Parade's End* signals the collapse as well as the high-point of Ford's desire to enlist fiction in the service of public values. The critic's assumption depends, significantly, upon the belief that both modernist subjectivity and modernist aesthetics are hostile to collective political responsibilities and public virtues. The assumption is another version of Trilling's formulation, although it is attached to a different value-judgment. Trilling respects modernism's attack on all aspects of culture, including politics; latter-day critics attack the attack. In doing so, however, they maintain the idea of modernism's unqualified and invariant lack of interest in the public endeavors to which the hero and heroine of *Parade's End* are devoted. Green's story about Ford is that Ford emerges from *Parade's End* in the grip of politically-nefarious modernism: in the late 1920s he wants art to aspire to the condition of music; to be without content, ahistorical and apolitical: 'Ford's philosophy in these [latter] years' – especially after *The English Novel*, a small production from 1929 – 'was founded on "the gourmandisation" of politics', on a 'willed isolation' rather than on community. Ford makes a choice, Green claims, for which 'a [high political] price must be paid' (Green 176, 167).

For Green the price is a hermetic sealing off of Ford from 'contact with a living reality of exertion and disappointment' (Green 177). Green's diction here echoes Ford's phrase about virtues and endeavors, even as the critic is faulting Ford. He faults Ford for not pursuing, beyond the first three volumes of *Parade's End*, an art of fiction that 'is fashioned by imperatives that lie outside the boundaries of the text, by the author's desire to construct a work of fiction that will modify human behavior' (Green 130). But Ford did continue to pursue this artistic goal, and was able to. Green will not recognize the continuity and the ability, because he confines himself to narrow assumptions about 'reality' and modernism. Green assumes that reality is solely historical, that history is the only identifiable common agent of art and political responsibility. On this assumption, if novelistic invention flees to some corner of the world in order to escape the available spectrum of politicians and political ideologies, it can not encapsulate public virtues. For Green, Ford-Tietjens' ultimate conchie-ism merely offers us 'magic' as a way to 'cure that social malaise so well-analyzed' (Green 165) earlier by Ford when his head temporarily was clear and 'in contact' before *Last Post*. Yet Green shows that his own assumptions are not as secure as his condemnations. He admires Ford's treatment of Tietjens for making the character not 'true to life,' not 'strictly realistic,' but, in spite of this failure of truth, '"living"' (Green 142). Apparently, then, untruth to life in Ford *is* compatible with political impact, since three-quarters of *Parade's End* use a myth-like hero to engage real history. Clearly the nature of artistic 'contact' with history is not simple. An artistic 'magic', an aesthetic conscientious objection to mere reality, can secure art's grappling with historical concerns; a small production, a retirement from the world, can be vitally worldly, public in effect. Having allowed himself his honest admission in praise of Ford's not-so-life-like but 'living' characterization, Green is left with only critical prejudice on which to base his picture of late Ford as too 'relaxed or enervated'

(Green 181) for political relevance.

It is not my intention to be wantonly aggressive towards Green's excellent book, however. Green and I both are interested in finding public and political importance in Ford, and in modernism too. Such importance can't be recovered or realized, however, if we assume that political virtues and public-minded endeavors must be tied to a politics or an aesthetics that depends on history-centered realism; or, according with that assumption, if we also assume modernist politics has to be identified with political models already established and at work in real history. Indeed, the modernist exceptions to Trilling's bitter line are tragic imaginations of public virtue precisely because of their attachment to actual historical politics: Pound's, for example.

But between attachment to the State and civilization at their imperialist or fascist worst, which forecloses the authentic world of virtues and endeavors, and bitter adversarial detachment from State and civilization altogether, there is a middle way. It is a middle way as modernist, arguably, as are the extremes; and Ford belongs to it. Another novelist in Ford's world also belongs to it: Kipling. I invoke him side by side with Ford for several reasons. Kipling and Ford, the two great modern English writers produced by the ancient lights of pre-Raphaelitism, continually slip away from our narrow assumptions about what is modernist. In Kipling's case, this in part is because the aesthetic experimentation that characterizes modernism seems to be missing from his work. But this is seeming merely. Kipling's condensation and compression of novelistic elements into short forms (another kind of small producing) constitutes one of the great modernist experiments in fictional narrative. More importantly, of course, Kipling slips out of the modernist category for us because, in imaging figures of public virtue – and restoration of the public world of virtues and endeavors is indeed an essential aim of his writing – he seems to attach his imagination to the State at its worst. But this attachment is not what we always have made of it. It characterizes what Kipling says outside of his fiction rather than in it. Kipling commits art to history, but Kipling also (prefiguring Ford) strongly suggests that a world of virtues and endeavors has no continuity with the historical imperialist State as it exists. In fact, Kipling's fiction repeatedly demonstrates the continuity with public virtues of a withdrawal, just like Christopher's and Valentine's, from the historical world to a last post beyond worldliness and beyond historical realism. In terms of his art, Kipling seems to have set up an internal conscientious objection to the values which, at the conscious level, made him side with the State and 'civilization' against independence for Ireland and India. It is Kipling's conchie-ism that is being noted when Angus Wilson remarks that Kipling's 'artistic heart' is not in his collectivist-imperialist dreams but is in the 'proper realisation of the meaning of individual suffering'.[5] One of the fountain-heads of suffering is the State's manipulative practice of self-division: even among the often politically distasteful Stalky stories, one finds 'The Flag of Their Country' (1899), which portrays the obnoxious effects of the contradictious character of imperial civilization's 'public' life. In this story Stalky and his friends learn that their public virtues and endeavors will belong to a world they will have to make separately and apart in an unacknowledged integrity. Ford's vision of the nefarious duplicitous State and of virtue's response to it is continuous with Kipling's.

If, like Ford, Kipling finds fault with even the dishonestly dual state, if Kipling does so in terms of a single-minded resolution that compels even *him* to represent public virtues and endeavors in terms that are unworldly, or magical, and sympathetic to a minoritarian and small-producer's model (for example, in *Puck of Pook's Hill*), then we have reason to claim that modernism is more varied than what is comprehended by the bitter line. Modernism includes, in writers as various as Ford and Kipling, a common drive to restore, for the sake of renewed public norms, the values that Valentine sees Christopher restore to the world. A like sense of values shared by Ford and Kipling partly might explain the tendency of literary critics to give Ford only an uncertain place in the modernist canon. That canon, as Martin Green has argued, was constructed in hostile reaction to Kipling and his politics.[6]

Critics who follow Robert Green's evaluations might be intuiting suspiciously the affinity between Ford's sense of political heroism and Kipling's. Thus because of the political cloud we keep Kipling under, we have not noted Ford's affinity with him; we are likely to pair Ford more with Pound, and yet to feel jittery about the reaction implied by *that* constellation. Of course, our discomfort attests to the conflicting imaginations and models of public virtue that roil the consistency of modern literature's hostility to all of civilization. But at least, by pairing Ford with Kipling, we might begin to see that *Parade's End* is, in its time, not an isolated imagination of political virtue; and to see also that the form Ford's imagination takes, and the form Kipling's takes, is not inevitably tied to reaction. Here is the alternative to both the bitter line and the modernist attraction to *fascist* 'civilization'.

I think it would be hard to call this alternative, and its single-minded aim to preserve an ideal of public endeavors, reactionary in either Ford or Kipling. Written after *Parade's End* and curiously resonant with it, a Kipling story like 'The Church That Was At Antioch' (1929), about a good soldier named Valens, who is a Roman Tietjens, surely is neither a reactionary nor even a conservative tale. It pictures a single-minded personal model of public virtues, an exemplary agent in the cause of resolving the imperialist world-state's double-minded injurious ambiguities and duplicities. It accepts and makes use of the latter, to be sure; but it treats them as both ancient and modern problems, which must be surmounted and in response to which some resolved and unified stance or principle must be reached. A single-minded principle of public conduct, albeit familiar with ambiguities, will map the return of hope for the public world.

Working for the police force in first-century Antioch, Valens has to keep a peace that respects a multicultural environment and that sets up a democratic norm whereby to regulate one or another bid for domination by one or another culture within the imperium. Unfortunately, the Christian sect at Antioch, which Valens protects but which he also dislikes for bastardizing his own Mithraic cult, turns up the Apostle

Paulus, a ravening imperialist who hopes for Christian empire and who resembles the hostile literary-critical version of the ravening imperialist Kipling. Now the actual artist Kipling deliberately produces in 'The Church That Was at Antioch' contrasting dual ways of seeing his story's elements. On the one hand, Valens, his uncle the prefect of police, and Paul the Christian, are all the same imperialist under the skin. There is no choosing among them, apparently, if one looks for alternatives to Empire. On the other hand, Valens' democratic impulses discipline his imperialism and make him more egalitarian in impulse and action than either the higher ranking Roman rulers or their Judeo-Christian subjects. The timid, time-serving Christian Petrus, under the thumb of empire-hungry Paul, tacitly acknowledges that Valens nurtures an egalitarian balance between rulers and ruled and among competing cultural identities and allegiances. And, indeed, when Valens is fatally stabbed by the vengeful brother of a criminal whom Valens has prosecuted, Valens' dying words – inspired by his Mithraism – are not imperialist but antinomian: he asks his policeman uncle not to prosecute his assassin, because law is fallible and his murderer 'doesn't know what he is doing'.[7] The scene of Valens' death, in which the Roman is surrounded by Peter and Paul and by a former prostitute whom Valens has made his concubine (and who thinks of Valens as 'her God'), exhibits Kipling's aesthetics and their ideological complement: antinomianism hostile to the world, especially to the world of political dominations. We have seen two Valenses, the imperialist and the antinomian; but in the finale we see only one:

> Petrus stood like one in a trance. The tremor left his face as he repeated [Valens' words]:
> '"Forgive them, for they know not what they do." Heard you *that*, Paulus? He, a heathen and an idolator, said it!'
> 'I heard. What hinders now that we should baptize him?' Paulus answered promptly.
> Petrus stared at him as though he had come up out of the sea.
> 'Yes,' he said at last. 'It is the little maker of tents. . . . And what does he

now – command?'

Paulus repeated the suggestion.

Painfully, that other raised the palsied hand that he had once held up in a hall to deny a charge.

'Quiet!' said he. 'Think you that one who has spoken Those Words needs such as *we* are to certify him to any God?'

Paulus cowered before the unknown colleague, vast and commanding, revealed after all these years.

'As you please – as you please,' he stammered, overlooking the blasphemy. 'Moreover there is the concubine.'

The girl did not heed, for the brow beneath her lips was chilling, even as she called on her God who had bought her at a price that he should not die but live.[8]

The struggle for public command and public virtue here is crucial, and Peter's momentary accession of unworldly command goes hand in hand with what Paul the imperialist takes to be Peter's blasphemy against Christ's empire. Betraying the Christ of this world, so to speak, Peter protects the anti-imperialist side of Valens' character against the worldly ambitions of Christianity. Although the crucified one is the Roman soldier, it is hard to see this as an imperialist tableau, especially in light of Kipling's treatment of Paul, who clings to the imperializing intention of his worldly legalisms, who cowers in the face of Valens' and Peter's spiritual anarchism, and who uses the concubine, in a sour grapes fashion, to suggest that Valens isn't repentant, and isn't spiritually fine enough, anyway, to be baptized.

What underscores the anti-imperialist moral of this is Kipling's minimalizing, his small producing, of the means of expression for communicating the single-minded antinomian moral. Whereas the imperialist in the scene is heavy-handed, the artist is more like Peter: handicapped by – in the artist's case – a self-imposed commitment to use a restricted means of expression (one-sentence paragraphs; demonstration rather than narration of what is happening) to deliver a large significance. It is as if Kipling, in his self-confinement to modernist experimentation with the short story form, economizes all the narrative elements so as to inhibit his manipulation of language and his own text – as if he wanted to liberate an experience, or a subject, and not dominate it. Even the 'translatese' elements of the story might be read as a gesture towards the autonomy of (as well as towards the self-conscious textual mediation of) Kipling's subject. Kipling's art, whatever its relation to imperialism, seems to favor aesthetic means that belie command. And where and when command is in evidence, or clearly must be practiced, the artist identifies with Valens so that command is re-defined by him not as Pauline mastery and meanness, but as a tolerance for keeping differing cultural intentions and traditions in equitable play.

Part of the equitable play is the art's ambiguous, because simultaneously multiple, representation of things: in the last sentence of the passage above, the external narrator shares the woman's view of her god Valens, but the external narrator also mingles the indirect conveyance of the woman's words with a bitter protest against any god (even the antinomian one) who wastes the value of his creatures and who has no power over death. The celebration of Valens thus is, simultaneously, a protest against him and his values; the condemnation of Paul thus also comprehends Paul's desire to master the mortal vulnerability conceded by the dying man, to not waste life and value. In spite of this honest engagement with contradictions and ambiguities, however, what matters more is the emerging image of a conduct that moves from indeterminacy and self-contradiction towards integrity and resolve. To be resolutely and scrupulously true to conflicting commands upon one's attention, no matter their self-contradictory complexity, appears to be both the imperialist artist's and the imperialist public figure's vocation. It appears even more to be a programme for an *anti-imperialist* artist's and public figure's vocation.

Valens turns out to be the better man in 'The Church That Was at Antioch'. The conflict between Valens and Paul, which is about finding the best personal and public strategy for making order and sense out of a war among competitors for worldly dominance, and which suggests that the better strategist – the one whose virtues and endeavors are the very sort needed by the public world – is the one bound to fail in worldliness under the burden of scrupulous attention to competing interests, is central to Kipling's work. Unworldly, even mystic, worldliness is the paradox that inspires Kipling's aesthetics and his politics; and a like mystic worldliness inspires Ford's art and politics. Valens, Christopher and Valentine are curiously imbricated vehicles of a like political value. But to speak of 'politics' here is to speak coarsely. The unworldly worldliness, which is articulated by Kipling and Ford alongside a rejection of Christian transcendence, is a public virtue shadowing itself forth, a public standard or norm which needs first to be in play in order for politics, or history, or reality, to make the sense one needs them to make.

The shadowing forth of a place of virtues and endeavors in *Parade's End*, and in Kipling as well, expresses a convinced single sense of what is currently dislocated in their world, and of what needs, paradoxically, to be maintained in its dislocation, at its obscure last post. Public virtue, in its modernist literary version, must be hidden to preserve its single-minded integrity against the State-generated double-mindedness and duplicities that produce the dislocation. Of course, there are many occasions when that single-minded virtue, which in its exile appears to be merely fantastic, must be re-located, brought out of obscurity into public action, and translated into 'reality'. One possible occasion is the moment of conscientious artistic production, whereby dualisms and ambiguities are brought into play and, under the pressure of imaginative impulse, newly unified. Ford's modernism instances such an occasion. Another like occasion, for both Ford and Kipling, is the moment of history. History starts up in their fiction as the moment when, magically no less than really, the imagination of hidden past or present virtues and endeavors suddenly breaks through into current life. This happens thanks to the conchie-ism of art: its conscientious objection, in the service of an alternative virtue, to the current public character of civilization and the State.

NOTES

1. An earlier version of this essay appeared in Caserio, *The English Novel 1900-1950: Theory and History* (New York: Twayne–Simon & Schuster Macmillan, 1999), pp. 90-108.

2. Trilling, *Beyond Culture: Essays on Literature and Learning* (New York: The Viking Press, 1965), p. 3.

3. Ford, *Some Do Not . . .: Parade's End* (New York: Knopf, 1961), p. 267. Subsequent page references to this edition will be given in parentheses in the text using the abbreviation *PE*.

4. Robert Green, *Ford Madox Ford: Prose and Politics* (Cambridge: Cambridge University Press, 1981) – henceforth 'Green'; p. 167. Subsequent references to this book appear in the text.

5. Angus Wilson, *The Strange Ride of Rudyard Kipling: His Life and Work* (New York: The Viking Press, 1977), p. 242.

6. Martin Green, *The English Novel in the Twentieth Century: The Doom of Empire* (London: Routledge & Kegan Paul, 1984).

7. Rudyard Kipling, *Short Stories: Volume 2*, ed. Andrew Rutherford (New York: Penguin Books, 1971), p. 253.

8. *Ibid.*, p. 254.

CONSTRUCTIONS AND RECONSTRUCTIONS:
NO ENEMY

Cornelia Cook

No Enemy, Ford Madox Ford's memoir of the Great War calls itself 'a Reconstructionary Tale'. Not quite a novel, but not, either, the essays ('English Country', *New Statesman*, 1919) on which it is largely based, it resists becoming autobiography and affronts the apparent responsibilities of historiography.[1] Through its dual narrative, combining the reminiscences of Gringoire the poet and the commentary of his 'friend' the Compiler, this generic oddity engages the mechanics and the mechanical necessity of remembering and reconstructing. Gringoire's memory is an essential tool in war and peace and the agency of surprising visions and re-visions. The Compiler sifts and arranges written records and memories – his own and Gringoire's – to memorialise the soldier-poet and the war experience itself. *No Enemy* calls attention to its own textuality at every opportunity and also alludes widely to other constructions: not only those of memory, but also of 'history', myth, propaganda, architecture, cartography, poetry, fiction, political rhetoric and trench engineering. The 'Reconstructionary Tale' describes a world of reconstructions. In doing so it submits the notion of Reconstruction to probing critical scrutiny.

No Enemy opens with the observation that:

> . . . you hear of the men that went, and you hear of what they did when they were There. But you never hear how It left them. You hear how things were destroyed but seldom of the painful process of Reconstruction.[2]

'Reconstruction' was a wartime political buzzword which became a post-war political agenda. Ford and his critics have associated the word with a number of his post-war writings. It is relevant in various ways to them all and in the kaleidoscopic *No Enemy* the word has more than one aspect. Superficially this is obvious: 'Reconstruction' alludes to a nation and individuals in it rebuilding their society and lives in the aftermath of war *and* to the processes of recovery of the fragile bodies and psyches disabled or disassembled by injury in war. Locally it describes the 'whitewashing, papering, glazing . . . digging out of foundations, and fertilising an abandoned and ill-treated garden' (*NE* 149) which transforms Gringoire's Gingerbread Cottage from a ruin to a home. Both war and narrative are signalled as reconstructive agencies in the statement: 'How the war changed [Gringoire's] heart is here recorded' (*NE* 18). And we discover that, with the aid of 'pencils, tablets and erasers', the Compiler will reconstruct for us Gringoire himself: 'Gringoire, Gallophile, Veteran, Gardener, and above all, Economist, if not above all Poet' (*NE* 10).

The agenda of historical record in '. . . you hear of the men that went, and you hear of what they did when they were There . . . but seldom of the painful process of Reconstruction' might be set alongside the report of the Ministry of Reconstruction's Committee on Adult Education (1917) that 'in . . . lectures, study circles, and classes . . . activity has been directed towards the study of the historical background and causes of the war, but attention is now being turned to the problems of Reconstruction.'[3] Both the Compiler and Gringoire spend their days engaged in what may be seen as versions of the War Cabinet's project of Reconstruction: 'not so much a question of rebuilding society as it was before the war, but moulding a better world out of the social and economic conditions which have come into being during the war'.[4] The Compiler 'instructs classes in English Literature and Physical Development' – typical elements of the enlarged national education programme.[5] The poet Gringoire aims 'to teach persons forced to live on minute incomes how to lead graceful, poetic and pleasant lives and so to save the world' (*NE* 11). The narrator's proposal to tell the story of Gringoire the poet 'just after . . . Armageddon' (*NE* 9) pits an impressionist reconstruction of personal experience, the 'war-reminiscences of a contemplative and sensitive soul' (*NE* 11-12), against a postwar 'Reconstruction' rhetoric of science, centralisation, efficiency and State collectivism.[6] This may alert us to potential subversiveness in the statement 'This is therefore a Reconstructionary Tale' (*NE* 18).

The way the text of *No Enemy* is constructed participates in the significance of the 'Reconstructionary Tale'. Three of Ford's war poems frame the text's divisions. The patterns of these poems shape time and space into ways of seeing. The passage from 'Footsloggers' which is the epigraph to *No Enemy* presents a moment which brings a hidden knowledge to consciousness. It describes an epiphany which exposes an internal relationship to the external ('one's land'), and it registers two different kinds of experience in time:

> What is love of one's land? . . . .
> I don't know very well.
> It is something that sleeps
> For a year, for a day,
> For a month – something that keeps
> Very hidden and quiet and still
> And then takes
> The quiet heart like a wave.
> The quiet brain like a spell,
> The quiet will
> Like a tornado – and that shakes
> The whole of the soul.

The poem which prefaces Part Two, figures the destruction of the old houses of Flanders as an extinction, in a naturalised moment, of their own capacity to see: 'old eyes that have watched the ways of men for generations/Close for ever.' The poem 'Clair de Lune', which concludes the body of the book, juxtaposes two versions of a nocturnal landscape. A vision of ruined churches, a battlefield, star-shells and verey lights is, in a noiseless pause, 'For a minute . . ./ For ten . . .', returned to a vision of long avenues, trees, untroubled stars, the clear of the moon. Time and space are reconfigured and reinterpreted in these poems; like their conceptual and representational derivatives history and landscape, they take shape from the constructions in which they occur. Vagaries of vision, found in these poems, will be characteristic of the text of *No Enemy;* several strategies of narrative construction and representation in the book evoke multiple consciousness and undermine, like the book's title itself, the habitual – and persisting – binaries of wartime rhetoric.[7]

A constructed allegorical suggestiveness marks the painterly images which give titles to Part One, 'Four Landscapes', then Part Two, 'Certain Interiors'. Gringoire's dogged reiterations emphasise 'four' (actually five) structuring 'moments' of vision provoked by landscape and the four individual figures, Private Morgan, the Lincolnshire Private, Henri Gaudier, the Quartermaster of the Wiltshires (five if you add the equally significant and symbolic Rosalie Prudent), that shape and signal his relationship to the war, to his country and to his art.

The double act of Compiler and Gringoire calls attention to the mechanics of narrative construction. 'I have purposely omitted to mention . . .' says the poet, crafting his account. And the Compiler decides, at the opening of Part Two, to 'let Gringoire speak for himself' in a comic act of reader-friendliness and self-defence:

> The paraphernalia of inverted commas interspersed with indirect speech is apt to become wearisome to a reader. It is difficult – nay, it might even prove dangerous – to The Compiler. For who shall say what powerful enemies the present writer might not make by omitting inverted commas and appearing to speak for himself? (*NE* 147)

Free indirect speech, employed by the Compiler, promotes a notable slippage in pronouns: 'he . . . one . . . we . . . one' and sometimes 'you' merge their points of view. Pronominal confusion sometimes makes the joint 'authors' appear like the two ends of a pantomime horse:

> Here then is Gringoire's prose, the original French of which he says was written at Pont de Nieppe during September 1916 after his visit to the French Ministry which he will describe in my next chapter. (*NE* 130)

Beyond the shared discourse by which one writer's experience is constructed as another writer's book is the unconcealed fact that the writings of The Compiler *and* of Gringoire are Ford's.[8]

The poet constructed by the Compiler as 'Gringoire, Gallophile, Veteran, Gardener, and above all Economist, if not above all Poet' has already been subject to reconstruction as a character from a story. Gringoire is not his name but a nickname given the schoolboy poet out of a tale by Daudet about a goat, a wolf, poets and starvation – a story which recurs as a nightmare of creative failure in this text. This figure (who will discover his own experience reconstructing the 'fictitious-real' of another literary construction – Henry James's *What Maisie Knew*) is introduced in his postwar 'rural habitation', a cottage 'so ancient, frail and unreal that it is impossible to think of it otherwise than as the Gingerbread Cottage you may have read of in the tale of "Haensel and Gretel"' (*NE* 9).

The confectionary construction from a fairy tale is the space in which we both inhabit a moment removed from time and are aware of the precariousness of moments in time (which may bring the encroachments of war or poverty just as the fairy tale itself unfolds danger). In a similar fashion *No Enemy* implicitly locates itself in the Forest of Arden (and thus in a literary construction and an English tradition) as the secure point from which to recall the horrors of the Ardennes. The cottage becomes the meeting place of 'before the war', 'what they did when they were There' and 'the painful processes of Reconstruction', just as it is simultaneously the realisation of the elusive and persistent 'idea' of 'sanctuary' and a scene of domestic, agricultural and artistic struggle. In the soldier/narrator's recurrent 'idea' it is

> a little nook, all green, with silver birches, and a trickle of a stream through the meadow, and the chimneys of a gingerbread cottage out of Grimm just peeping over the fruit trees. (*NE* 70)

It is also, observed by the Compiler, 'a very bad cottage, with a roof that leaks, walls that used to drip with damp, cupboards that . . . smelled of mold and bred the very largest spiders that can be imagined' (*NE* 16).

The Gingerbread Cottage is an image which allows the narrative's pursuit of 'sanctuary' to comment on the public and psychic worlds Gringoire inhabits. The soldier's conscious mind entertains the thought of having 'a garden in a southeastern country . . . as who should say, "After the war we will take a cottage in the country" . . .' (*NE* 66). This practical desire merges with the image of the green nook, the 'inviolable corner of the earth', as the 'subconscious mind' searches for 'sanctuary'. Then, on the Somme, the 'little vision of English country' which 'possibly . . . was really a prayer' realises itself in a landscape at the tip of Mont Vedaigne: 'There, in a small enclosed space, shut in by trees . . . was, precisely, a little gingerbread cottage out of Grimm' (*NE* 72).

The passage which describes this idyllic prototype of Gringoire's leaky post-war English cottage explores the layers of mind whose interactions are recorded and scrutinised by Gringoire and his Compiler. The infantryman's observing mind, 'working in the water-tight compartments of his immediate professional job' (*NE* 78), reconstructs a landscape as points of reference for military intelligence. A further, 'secondary' level of the Infantry Officer's mind recalls practical detail ('of dead ground, field of fire . . . sites for trenches . . . timber'; *NE* 80) including the topographically valueless presence of a cottage and garden. It is inevitable that when Gringoire the infantryman later approaches this cottage for coffee he is given gingerbread. (Reconstructing the scene, the Compiler is compelled to a strained narrative prolepsis: 'The significance of this did not occur to our subsequent inhabitant of a gingerbread cottage'; *NE* 81.) Underlying the 'professional mind' is the 'poet's mind' which watches statue shells over Poperinghe become 'two great white swans' and sees the shells assaulting the German trenches on the Wytschaete ridge as a village cobbler's 'line of brass nails on . . . smooth leather'. A relaxation of the 'professional mind' liberates the 'poet's mind' to see landscape as landscape and to associate the 'little white cottage with the green shutters, a little nook that should be inviolable', with 'the Kentish garden' that 'one might plant' sloping to the sea. With the dusk-enabled view of the sea beyond Dunkirk comes 'an intense longing to be beyond that sea . . . just for the green country, the mists, the secure nook at the end of a little valley, the small cottage whose chimneys just showed over the fruit trees – for the feelings and the circumstances of a sanctuary . . .' (*NE* 86).

The idea of 'sanctuary' realised in a cottage links this place with several aspects of war and peacetime experience in the book. Such 'small, verdure-masked homes' are Gringoire's reason for going to war: 'it was mostly for the sake of the little threatened nooks of the earth that Gringoire found himself on that hillside' (*NE* 68). Like the 'affrighted' houses in war or 'little homes' cowering 'among the stubble fields' of France, their owners absent at war, the cottage associates itself with the soldier-poet's determination that there must be a 'world assured of nooks and houses that never cowered or trembled' (*NE* 175). The image of the cottage implicitly reflects, too, on the notion of 'home': a place of desire and of alienation for soldiers in wartime – variously 'English country' or 'a southeastern county' or an 'old building' – which became an issue of 'Homes fit for Heroes' in Reconstruction.[9]

The literary technique for which Ford adopted the term 'Impressionist' itself debates the nature of historical reconstruction. 'Impressionism' emphasised the subjectively determined character of the experienced moment and located 'reality' in the uninterpreted individual observation. The impressionist text exploits a viewpoint necessarily imperfect, partial, personal. A small change in circumstance, in information, in angle of vision can reconstruct the view ('It was as if the focus of the camera had suddenly clicked, readjusting itself . . .'; *NE* 40). This continually reconstructed 'reality' effectively challenges both the 'history' constructed as 'progress' by Victorian liberalism, then constructed as determined advance by modern materialism, and wartime constructions of contemporary events as Apocalyptic. *No Enemy* exposes ways in which public 'history' is constructed by juxtaposing them with the record of personal, experienced history. It replaces chronological narratives of progress with multi-layered descriptions of wartime landscapes, with reflections on events and their representation, and with narrative patterns of repetition and anachrony which display the endless possibilities for reconstruction in our knowledge and expression.

The war which Gringoire's narrative labours to realise through compelling similes, impressions or descriptive detail is summed up in the Compiler's narrative as 'Armageddon' – an analogy popular with politicians, poets and preachers, underpinning an apocalyptic construction of the event itself. 'History' is documented through the Infantry Officer's professionally 'memorized' observations of war and topography, through anecdote and observed detail, and even in landscape: 'If you looked over the hedge you saw Bailleul, Armentières, away to queer, conical, grey mountains that were the slag-heaps near Béthune, and away, farther, toward the Somme itself' (*NE* 72). 'History' is unrecognised: 'the great beautiful machine – which was . . . the first Handley Page to reach France in safety – passed overhead without Gringoire's thinking of more than that it was beautiful' (*NE* 79). 'History' is dates, places, names, objects: 'a place near Gemminich', 'The Agadir incident', 'the queer, stodgy Victorian mind' – these are already in the poet's *conscious* memory, constructions of political rhetoric, public record:

> I began to think . . . about Albert the Good, and the Crystal Palace . . . I remembered John Brown and John Morley and John Bright and John Stuart Mill and Mr. Ruskin and the rest of them, and mahogany chairs with horsehair seats and Argand lamps and the smoke and steam that used to fill the underground at Gower Street station. (*NE* 128)

But 'History' is also an uncertainty of vision, an 'idea' or 'a feeling, not an intellectual idea':

> on the 4/8/'14, when the Huns crossed the Belgian frontier 'near a place called Gemmenich' it was mainly the idea that a field-gray tide of mud was seeking to overwhelm the small, verdure-masked homes, the long, white thatched farms of the world that forced Gringoire into political action. (*NE* 68)

> . . . he had the feeling that . . . they would have seen the Huns, a white, tumultuous line, like advancing surf or like gnashing teeth. That was, of course, a feeling, not an intellectual idea. He knew that the German lines didn't look like that – though indeed at times they did . . . . (*NE* 69)

History as a 'feeling' becomes a Hardyesque vision

> that for thousands of miles, on the green fields and in the woodlands, stretching away under the high skies, in the August sunlight, millions, millions, millions of my fellow men were moving – like tumultuous mites in a cheese, training and training, as we there were training – all across a broad world to where the sun was setting and to where the sun was rising – training to live a little, short space of time in an immense long ribbon of territory where for a mile or so the earth was scarred, macerated, beaten to a pulp, and burnt by the sun till it was all dust . . . The thought grew, became an immense feeling, became an obsession. (*NE* 128)

The vision is self-evidently a literary construction – reminiscent perhaps of the birds-eye panoramas of *The Dynasts,* the questionings of *War and Peace* or the opening of Barbusse's *Le feu,*[10] but certainly made of the rhetoric of remembrance verse, of Empire, of prophecy. History is constructed by poets as much as by historiographers just as individuals are constructed by the world they inhabit, the names they are given, the books they read. History itself embraces the constructions of religion, myth or fantasy, the creations of human desire or fear: Gringoire observes that the desire for sanctuary 'has given to the world in succeeding ages, The Kingdom of God, the Kingdom of Heaven, the Kingdom of Thule, the Cassiterides, the Garden of the Hesperides, the land of Cokaigne . . .' (*NE* 68).

A continual process of constructing history is emphasised in the text's references to the media – newspapers and propaganda, cameras and film crews – to political 'schemes' and intrigues and rumour and in echoes of political speeches and government documents. Art, too – paintings, writings – generate images which 'become' historical record. National identities and regional identities are constructed in the popular imagination, in propaganda. Essex is a strange place, a 'friendless foreign country' to one who recalls 'the southeastern saying . . . ". . . never you trust a man from the Sheeres!" . . . It is Kent and Sussex against the world – just as no doubt it is Essex and Hertford' (*NE* 35). 'Hun' is for Gringoire 'a convenient phrase to use about what was evil in the people we were fighting against' (*NE* 89), but Brahms is a 'German' composer and 'I should not . . . ever think of calling Holbein a Hun painter or the Brothers Grimm of the fairy tales, Boches' (*NE* 89). He rebukes the Compiler's earlier dismay, when they were 'both writing propaganda', that 'instead of atrocity-mongering' the poet constructed the German troops as 'the gallant enemy' (*NE* 91). Juxtaposing an image of 'forlornly ashamed' German prisoners of war he has seen and 'our own people in that condition' which he has not, Gringoire notes 'they are represented to us as remaining erect and keeping most of their *esprit de corps*' (*NE* 27). Such representations powerfully influence thought and action. An 'excited England, covered . . . with patriotic and colorful placards' (*NE* 140) generates a 'fine wave of enthusiasm . . . confident that we had a great singleness of purpose extending across a world' (*NE* 202).

Gringoire's 'A Cricket Match' letter displays and mocks national stereotypes. The garrulous, demonstrative Frenchman, the taciturn monocled Englishman are seen as contemporary equivalents of the Napoleonic wartime 'caricatures' of the 'meagre, famished' frog-eating 'barber' and 'John Bull, as big as an ox, his belly as big as the belly of an ox'. 'They were stupid, those caricatures, but . . .', Gringoire says, 'The English who fought in France in 1815 sought for what they saw – but they found it. And the same with the French' (*NE* 139-40). And the poet admits that he, too, constructed a notion of the French from an impression of a wartime landscape, 'when I . . . found . . . a France . . . gray, silent and preoccupied, it was natural that I should look for grave people and find them' (*NE* 140). Fear, the need to construct recognisable antagonists or assimilable situations, and the inheritance of earlier constructions all generate those fictions which become the arguments of propaganda and of history. *No Enemy* finds its place among such constructions and comments on them.

In *No Enemy* writing looks at itself, at propaganda, at history and at the effort to begin anew with critical suspicion. The single 'atrocity' detailed in the book is an act of reconstruction: the filming of the sinking *Luisitania* 'for the gloating of others' is 'the most horrible of crimes' (*NE* 109). In Gringoire's view, 'falsehoods' written 'for the newspapers' promote the self interests of officialdom in war and peace. The post-war political agenda itself acquires both a cosmetic and a coercive aspect packaged as 'Reconstruction'. But the danger of deconstruction – of history, of identity, of authorship, of 'a great singleness of purpose', too – finds an illustrative counterpart in the text. In 1916 the knowledge of the Somme 'fiasco', 'of the 38th Division murdered in Mametz Wood' destroyed confidence: '. . . doubt had begun to creep in' (*NE* 202). The doubting soldiers, sensing 'a tenuous, misty struggle of schemes' at home, which Gringoire (construing the uncertainty through recent reading of James) calls 'just the atmosphere of "Maisie"' (*NE* 203), inhabit a Conradian loneliness: 'we were, truly, very lonely out there; truly we were some millions of men, suspended on a raft, in limitless space' (*NE* 202). Gringoire's narrative, even as it records the war's bitter turn, counteracts this tendency to solipsism or despair by invoking the comic-heroic figure of Henri Gaudier. The sculptor's life and death are reconstructed not only (with the aid of Pound's memoir) as a brief biography, but as an epiphany in Gringoire's experience – the discovery in the 'low tea-house' of war the miraculous 'Sacred Emperor' of 'Youth, Beauty, Erudition, Fortune, Genius' (*NE* 215) seemingly lost to the book's world of possibility. Other telling human images – the

CORNELIA COOK

personal models, *'homines bonae voluntatis'* – which replace, or complement, the visions of Part One lead the poet back to himself, his 'duty', his art, and out of war.

In Gringoire's own narrative, 'a great singleness of purpose' cannot sustain itself, but a sharp sense of incongruity can produce critical judgment, or poetry. Gaudier is 'like the appearance of Apollo at a creditors' meeting' (*NE* 207); the 'great walls with their human lining' of the Paris theatre are surrounded by 'a vast black map fringed by conflagrations' (*NE* 221). The continuing 'reconstructionary' character of this book lies in the awareness that (to recall Virginia Woolf's phrase) nothing is one thing. Gringoire is an Englishman with a French name so that the reader confusedly feels him to be French knowing him to be English (he is also long, lean, grey: Germanic; and we may recall that Hueffer reconstructed himself as Ford shortly after the events recorded in this memoir) – just as the gingerbread cottage is both a damp cottage in England and a white cottage in Belgium and a visionary cottage belonging to France, Kent, and fairy tales. Soldiers' French *is* English: 'Ker wooley woo – say la gair', 'appry la gair finny'. In 'A Cricket Match', which appears twice – once in French and once in English, the French officer presents an 'English' mode of behaviour while the English soldiers and the poet himself resemble, in their careless play and gesticulations, 'Gallic' demonstrativeness. The Englishman in the anecdote speaks French, and all the French speakers address him in English. These comic transformations are no more wonderful than the recognition that playing cricket on their return from the trenches, 'whilst the shells of the Germans were passing overhead', itself effects a transformation – a reconstruction, if you like: 'all of a sudden that threatening and superhuman landscape became . . . just a cricket field' (*NE* 143). The act of translation which makes a battleground a cricket field, like the revision which sees the baffled life of the Tommy of the Lincolns as 'a stupendous Odyssey' (*NE* 189) or the multiple consciousness which makes the battlefields of Belgium and France hold visions of England and the English countryside yield up images of war,

202

promotes a creative conception of reconstruction that is aesthetic and moral. It is crucial that even the vision which is the book's constant, recurring, still and stable point is clearly recognised as a construction – of the 'mind', of the desiring 'heart': 'And suddenly, at that point it came – the castle in the air; the simulacrum; the vision of the inviolable corner of the earth' (*NE* 65).

No Enemy ultimately *invites* reconstruction as an activity. The narrative honours a continuing process of reconstruction 'in space and time' (*NE* 266). 'Do you remember, Mr. Compiler,' Gringoire asks, 'the redoubt our regiment made once – Montgomery's Folly?' He describes the engineered fortifications, the 'Regimental Gardens', the furnishings, and exclaims

> Lord! the interiors we have constructed out of such materials and the fun we had. And how they vanished like a drift of leaves when we were drafted away. And how solid they seemed and the work we did in them whilst they lasted, those interiors! (*NE* 266)

The constructions of history, propaganda, politics, science, too, seem solid, and they serve the needs of the moment. But, like the gardens and interiors of trench life, they can be reconstructed as necessity or a change of perspective dictate. If seen in this light, they liberate themselves and the perceiving mind for endless reconstruction. Reconstruction, the book seems to warn its readership in the new post-war society, is not an achieved state, not even a comprehensive blueprint, but a process. Such creative process, too, the activity of narrative reconstruction in *No Enemy* reminds us, is the artist's liberating field of action.

As if to underline this awareness, the notion of a finally constructed Gringoire itself ultimately evaporates. The reconstructionary character of the book lies beyond the rehabilitation of Gringoire and his installation in a Gingerbread Cottage where he is at liberty to oppose Reconstruction institutionalism and collectivism with a politically unreconstructed individualism and 'a spirit of hospitality that was large and open rather than either considered or calculating' (*NE* 19). In *No Enemy's* concluding scene, the voice of the poet both yields and sustains itself as his poetry is recited, misrecited, corrected by the women's voices quoted by the Compiler. The narrative becomes constructive process itself. The book's final act is a shared act of reconstruction. Gringoire, happy, at rest, at peace – reconstructs Spenser's lines ('Sleep after toyle, port after stormie seas, / Ease after war, death after life does greatly please'; *Faerie Queene* I. ix. 359-60) blotting out war and death in a hiatus which, of course, effectively invokes these.[11] We reconstruct the lacuna with our memory of Spenser's lines and our 'memory' (provided or amplified by the book, by Gringoire's 'memories') of a war and a pursuit of 'sanctuary', the reconstruction of which as memorial, history, in national consciousness and countless mythologies, revisions and political changes of 'heart' *is* the story of the on-going necessary process of 'Reconstruction'.

NOTES

1. The work also contains material (chapter 11) reconstructed from the ms., 'Epilogue', written (1917) probably for *Women & Men*. See Ford, *War Prose*, ed. Max Saunders (Manchester: Carcanet, 1999), 52-63; James Longenbach, 'Ford Madox Ford: The Novelist as Historian', *Princeton University Library Chronicle*, Winter 1984, 150-66, and Max Saunders, *Ford Madox Ford: A Dual Life*, 2 vols (Oxford: Oxford University Press, 1996), vol.1, p. 572.

2. Ford Madox Ford, *No Enemy* (1929) (New York: Ecco Press, 1984), p. 9. Subsequent page references to this edition are given in the text, using the abbreviation *NE*.

3. Quoted in Arthur Marwick, *The Deluge: British Society and the First World War* (London: Macmillan, 1965), p. 245.

4. *Report of War Cabinet for 1917*, quoted Marwick, pp. 239-40.

5. Specified in the Education Bill of 1918, a product of developments emerging from the Ministry of Reconstruction 1917-18. Marwick, pp. 239-46.

6. Marwick, (p. 239) quotes the *War Cabinet Report for the Year 1917* (1918) on the 'scientific approach' of the new Ministry of Reconstruction: 'The country is for the first time equipped with a Department devoted . . .to research into questions of political science and to the encouragement of action on the lines of the results ascertained'. The report elsewhere notes, '1917 may be described as a year in which State control was extended until it covered . . .every section of industry – production, transport and manufacture' (Marwick, pp. 249-50). Reconstruction centralisation affected health, education, pensions, food production, agriculture and industry. In 1918, Lord Rhondda urged the War Cabinet to 'the immediate establishment of one Central Ministry of Health, in place of the two or three competing Government Departments' (Marwick, p. 241). The Education Act (1918), the Housing Act (1919), the Ministry of Health Act (1919) and a succession of acts affecting agricultural production from 1916 onward are key pieces of Reconstruction legislation germane to the concerns of *No Enemy*.

7. See Paul Fussell, *The Great War and Modern Memory* (New York and London: Oxford University Press, 1975), pp. 105-6, on the 'adversary habit'.

8. Echoes from or references to Ford's essays written for *The Outlook* in 1915 and 1916 and the propaganda pieces *When Blood is Their Argument* and *Between St. Denis and St. George,* his preface to Violet Hunt's novel, *Their Lives* (1916), the essay 'A Day of Battle' (1916) and the war poems are among those found in the book.

9. *NE* 203. See also Fussell, pp. 88-90, 100.

10. Saunders, *Ford Madox Ford: A Dual Life*, vol. 2, p. 199. Versions of the image occur in 'A Day of Battle' and *Parade's End*.

11. Ford's use of the lines from Spenser also reconstructs their use both as epigraph to Conrad's *The Rover*, and as epitaph on Conrad's grave. See Paul Skinner, 'Just Ford', *Agenda,* 27:4/28:1 (Winter 1989-Spring 1990), 105.

IV

FORD AND MODERN WRITING:
BIOGRAPHY, INTERTEXTUALITY,
AND STYLE

FORD MADOX FORD, VIOLET HUNT, AND THE BATTLE OF THE BOOKS: SEXUAL/TEXTUAL HOSTILITIES

Joseph Wiesenfarth

The flurried years that gave Violet Hunt the title of her memoir are those between Ford Madox Ford's founding of *The English Review* in December 1908 and the beginning of the First World War in August 1914.

PART I of *The Flurried Years* encompasses the time from Violet Hunt's rescuing Ford from suicide in early 1909 to her going off to Germany with him to become his wife – a status which, much to her regret, she never achieved. PART II of *The Flurried Years* takes us from the legal action which Ford's wife, Elsie, brought to prevent Violet from even calling herself 'Mrs. Hueffer' (the *Throne* case of February 1913) to the death of W. H. Hudson. These events bring into sharp contrast Ford's refusal to face an ordeal of social ignominy with Violet and her own total commitment to Hudson as he faced the ordeal of his death.

Both parts of *The Flurried Years* are tailored to present Violet as the Victim of Ford. Indeed, one reviewer regretted not seeing 'the heroine under the influence of other things than persecution'.[1] But Hunt shows us, by making constant allusion to *The Argonauts*, that, when Ford made her a victim, he also made her a Medea who determines, remorselessly, to revenge herself on him as a ruthless Jason: *The Flurried Years* is the uncompliant victim's revenge on her faithless lover.

Hunt's sense of herself and of Ford as utterly different leads her to cast her memoir as a conflict between Love and Genius. She is the one, he the other. Their conflict is complicated by Money and the Law. The law doesn't permit Ford to divorce his wife in England, so he tries to do it in Germany. But Violet has to supply the cash because Ford doesn't have nearly enough. The law is also a problem for Hunt whose sisters object to the way that she spends her mother's money; they even object to the way their mother spends her own money. Since Violet calls her sisters Goneril and Regan, the Jason-Medea motif of *The Flurried Years* becomes intertwined with a Lear motif, with Violet playing Cordelia. Thus her status as Victim of Love is further enhanced by this subtext. So too is the status of her memoir as 'a novelist's book' presenting situations 'as they appear imaginatively'[2] further intensified by these allusions. Consequently, Frank Swinnerton concludes, that 'those who will accept the book as a document are few'.[3]

Fidelity in Love is the moral ideal laid out in the memoir early on when Hunt remarks that 'Conrad's deification of the sense of responsibility in emotional affairs is to me the high-water mark of civilisation'.[4] Neither Hunt's lover nor her family is faithful to her. He is constructed as Genius and Beast; she is constructed as Servant and Beauty. Beauty loves the Beast but he's careless of her; she serves him and her family, and they become ever harder task-masters to her. So Violet becomes ever more the Victim in this allegory as her legal and financial problems proceed from the twin scourges of infidelity and ingratitude.

The Flurried Years confronted Ford with a book that appropriated his literary heritage and used it against him. Violet undermines the claims he made in *Thus To Revisit* (1921) of camaraderie with both James and Conrad. They appear there as mentors and collaborators in the great work of achieving the New Form of the Novel. Hunt presents them, along with Hudson, as models of fidelity in their love for her and thereby as Ford's opposites. He had then to reappropriate his masters in *Return to Yesterday* (1931) with detailed accounts of his friendship with James and his collaboration with Conrad in the days before, during, and after his founding the *English Review*. And he presented the three of them together as undivided in mind during the First World War. So whereas Hunt had argued that a man who was a real man was one who was faithful to his woman, Ford shifted the ground of the debate completely. He redefined a man as faithful to his vocation as an artist rather than as faithful to a woman.

In writing his reminiscences of the flurried years of Violet's title in *Thus To Revisit* (1921), Ford never mentions Hunt at all. But he writes, almost anticipating her memoirs, that 'to report details of private history, affections or intimacies is usually infamous'.[5] Consequently, his memoir, like Violet's, includes sections on James, Conrad, and Hudson; but its subject is the evolution of the New Form of the Novel. Just as in all his memoirs, then, Ford positions himself as an Artist. He emphasizes the way that various 'Movements' starting with the Flaubert-Maupassant-Turgenev circle and going on through *The Yellow Book* years and the Henley 'gang' kept the Art of the Novel going, especially in James's and Conrad's fiction, until Ford himself joined with Conrad in a 'collaboration' to modify it yet once more. W. H. Hudson appears as a contemporary version of Turgenev rendering with meticulous simplicity what he has observed with meticulous accuracy. James, Conrad, and Hudson, whom Violet presents as loyal friends, Ford presents as saviors of civilization: 'So there is re-awakened in the Writer the passionate belief that Creative Literature – Poetry – is the sole panacea for the ills of harassed humanity – the sole alleviator, the only healing unguent' (*TR* 19). But Hunt refuses Ford the luxury of being an artist without being a man. She refuses to allow him to make textual the years she experienced with him as sexual. Moreover, dramatizing Ford as her unfaithful lover, Hunt presents his culture heroes as faithful to her – as her faithful friends. Fidelity is her unguent. James, Conrad, and Hudson not only visited her but also remained faithful to her when Ford did not. By contrasting him and them, Hunt forces herself to admit that she and Ford were unsuited to each other, as she clearly states in *The Flurried Years*: 'F. M. H. would have done very well without me; perhaps better, as I have come to see now' (*FY* 25).

> I make ridiculous attempts to placate the powers, 'going round behind' as it is called, but quite boldly and above board, sitting down on the hornet's

nest, stealing into the camp of the enemy, and offering desperate and romantic concessions. It is never any good, but I have done it. (*FY* 123)

This is the way she appears in her novel *The House of Many Mirrors*, which was published in 1915, the same year as Ford's *The Good Soldier*. In this work Hunt tells the story of Alfred Pleydell and his wife Rosamond. Alfy draws on Ford's character and Rosamond on Violet's. He is an architect whose exquisite work has not found a good market; he also collects antique furniture expertly and plays the piano beautifully, just as Ford did. He's a 'cool and languid' person who stands on his honour, and she's a woman determined to get back the inheritance he lost when he married her.

The novel is set forth as a conflict of character in which Alfy won't move a finger to get his inheritance and Rosamond gives her life for it. Their characters are shrewdly delineated as the action is first projected from her point of view and then shifts to his. Rosamond dominates the first half of the novel, Alfy the second. It presents a careful working out of the affair of their marriage with Alfy sliding toward infidelity and Rosamond boldly approaching death faithfully committed to Alfy. Their happy days together are dramatized as an idyll of married life just as their days apart tear apart this picturesque couple. *The House of Many Mirrors* works out this Affair: this 'one embroilment, one set of embarrassments, one human coil, one psychological progression' (TR 44). It shows, at this moment in time, the maximum influence of Ford on Hunt's technique of fiction, while simultaneously showing her minimal influence on Ford's way of living his life. A roman à clef written as a novel of manners, *The House of Many Mirrors* pays tribute to Ford as an artist but indicts him as a man. It also pays tribute to Joseph Conrad, to whom it is dedicated, with an epigraph from a line of Virgil's *Georgics* (II. 490): 'Felix qui potuit [rerum congoscere causas']. That is, 'Happy is he who can know the causes of things'. The novel explicates, in mirror images of Rosamond and Alfred Pleydell, the causes of fidelity and infidelity in a marriage.

Fidelity has an even more prominent place in *I Have This To Say* (1926), Violet's revision of *The Flurried Years* for the American market. Reviewers in England had complained of an allusiveness in the memoir that allowed only those who already knew the details of Hunt's story fully to understand her book. Such comments led her to add an Envoi for her American readers in which she states that Ford now has a new mistress. Violet also added Appendices in which she reprinted news stories about Elsie's legal actions against her calling herself 'Mrs. Hueffer'.[6] Violet's theme of fidelity is thus reinforced by these as well as other revisions.

Hunt also amplifies her case in *I Have This To Say* by using, in her Foreword, a quotation from Ruskin[7] that emphasizes life-long devotion as an ideal: 'Find someone you can love and trust and then count no sacrifice too great to make in that one's service' (p. v). Given Ford's thorough aversion to Ruskin – 'that most preposterous of all portentous humbugs'[8] – and all that Ruskin stood for, Violet's use of this statement adds insult to injury.

Indeed, she anticipated her revenge on Ford one year before her memoir in a story, appropriately entitled 'The Corsican Sisters', in *More Tales of the Uneasy* (1925).[9] It opens with Lelis Cranmer, age nineteen, married to Cecil De La Garde, son of her Uncle Horace, who, once upon a time, brought two sisters, Matalina and Chilina ('Chili') from Corsica to London where they became the rage as Pre-Raphaelite 'stunners' at the same time as they became indifferent governesses to Lelis and her two older sisters. Uncle Horace was expected to marry Chili, but he did not. The young women subsequently returned to Corsica where Chili died of a broken heart and Matalina married a brigand named Andrea, who gained respectability by killing twenty men in vendettas. When Lelis brings Cecil to Vivario on their honeymoon to visit her former governess, Andrea shoots Cecil with De La Garde's own gun to revenge his father's abandoning Chili, the sister whom Andrea had really wanted to marry. Lelis goes mad.

Hunt writes her story in the Fordian manner by working out one Affair, the vendetta, through a series of time-shifts that render different aspects of it. Thus the story begins with Lelis as a mad young woman about the same age as Nancy Rufford, who has herself gone mad through the death of her beloved in *The Good Soldier*. And it works its way back through events to show just how she has been driven mad. At the same time, the story has that Gothic aspect about it that Ford saw as peculiarly characteristic of Violet's fiction: 'Barbarous ideas rough hewn – a mixture of passion and superstition . . . [not] subordinated to purposes of art' (p. 244). Because Lelis cannot, finally, subordinate feeling to art and tell a good lie by following Cecil's promptings, he is shot dead. Lelis, we read, is 'just a modern girl, a unit of no particular value, as Cecil had often told her, who could practice no arts of any sort, do nothing but love!' (p. 240). Violet Hunt's art shows what happens to artless women. They become, in Ford's words, 'the stuff to fill graveyards'.[10]

One year after *More Tales*, Hunt returned to the attack by emphasizing her claim on Ford: in *I Have This To Say* when she revised *The Flurried Years* to demonstrate in greater detail her contributions to the *English Review*, which Ford did not mention in *Thus To Revisit*. But Hunt's most important revisions introduce the fidelity of W. H. and Emily Hudson to each other as man and wife. Emily's proving a difficult wife to the patient and faithful Hudson is emphasized to suggest that Violet's proving a difficult lover should not have induced Ford to leave her. This new vignette carefully prepares us for the long peroration on Hudson which, in *The Flurried Years*, seemed strange and anomalous at best.

Whereas Violet Hunt is staking a claim to call herself 'Mrs. Hueffer' in both versions of her memoir and thereby staking a claim to Ford's fidelity, she is more than fair to him outside his character as her problematic lover. Indeed, she 'has attained, on the whole to charity', a reviewer remarks, 'if a somewhat contemptuous charity',[11] given that the 'precincts of genius . . . are apt to be unsavoury'.[12]

Violet, another reviewer notes, proves unwilling to turn Ford into a villain. Hunt indicates that those who say that Ford did not support his daughters are liars. She denies that he used individuals in his fiction and thereby damaged their reputations. In a remarkably generous gesture, she defends the novelist's art of amalgamation and transformation even as she smarts from seeing traits of her own in Sylvia Tietjens and traits of Stella Bowen in Valentine Wannop in *Some Do Not . . .* (1924) and *No More Parades* (1925):

> If you wanted something killed you'd go to Sylvia Tietjens in the sure faith that she would kill it: emotion, hope, ideal; kill it quick and sure. If you wanted something kept alive you'd go to Valentine: she'd find something to do for it. . . . The two types of mind: remorseless enemy, sure screen, dagger . . . sheath![13]

With passages like this in mind, Hunt still says in *The Flurried Years* that 'when a literature-picture of a total personality is put together it is non-libellous in effect, being a mere blend – an action of A's, a speech of D's, a look of C, the hair and eyes of F. Surely such a preparation or composite of aliens cannot possibly be dubbed a description of Z'.[14] And when she introduces Rebecca West into *I Have This To Say*, Violet presents West's praise of Ford – 'she chose to compare his work to that of Velasquez, who "painted less with the hand than by pure thought"' (p. 208) – and West's praise of *The Good Soldier*: 'Behind it is a force of passion which so sustains the story in its flight that never once does it appear as the work of a man's invention' (p. 209). And Hunt adds to West's praise praise of her own:

> Dowell, the real hero of the story, Dowell, not Edward Ashburnham the rather pathetic, rather ridiculous, sentimental swashbuckler of a lover – of three women on whom Dowell also has a lien. Dowell, the man who does not know but who can write, dropping on one page after another his little mosaics of character, detail and incident so that, in the end, we know all – and more – about these five people and about other men and women who

might conceivably find themselves in this awful fix, or other fixes like it – there are so many permutations of pain! (p. 210)

There is never any question, in either version of Violet Hunt's memoir, of Ford's merit as an artist. It is his fidelity as a lover that is constantly questioned, which may account for her savaging the sexual Edward Ashburnham and her praising the textual John Dowell. *The Flurried Years* and, even more so, *I Have This To Say* show that the genius and the faithful lover are – Alas! for Violet Hunt! – distinct entities. As Ford himself writes of artists, 'We shall commit acts of immorality and end in the Divorce and the Police Courts' (*TR* 6). The painful result of this dichotomy between writer and lover is implied in the line Violet sees Ford leaving out of his love poem, 'On Heaven', and takes upon herself to supply: 'the great word Agony three times, taking up all one line!' (*FY* 219).

But to Ford's taste Hunt delights too much in Strong Situations expressed without subtlety. Even though his affection for her once moved him to commend her reminiscences of Germany, *The Desirable Alien* (1913),[15] Ford's better knowledge of Germany also moved him to correct her book. And when he finally reviewed it, the critical attitude predominated. Positing that selection based on a sense of values is required for good writing, he does not find it in her work. But he himself demonstrated the effect of such selection in *The Good Soldier,* where the significance of Nauheim and Marburg (the subjects of chapters 6 and 11 of *The Desirable Alien*) is elicited. There the meaning of Luther's Protest in Schloss Marburg and of Kurhaus culture in Nauheim is rendered to show an unmistakable cost to the human spirit. And Ford's lesson was not lost on Hunt according to her biographer, Barbara Belford: 'her five novels written during their affair have a clarity only Ford could have helped to craft'.[16] And when Ford saw Hunt's fiction come to maturity in *Their Lives* (1916), he praised that novel unstintingly in his preface to it.

Their Lives is the story of three sisters, Christina, Virgilia, and Orinthia and of their parents, Henry and Victoria Radmall, he a painter with a Pre-Raphaelite turn, she a sharp-tongued woman who rules their household. Her oldest daughter Christina is Victoria's favorite child; her youngest daughter Orinthia she neglects. Virgilia is ruthlessly self-sufficient and sweeps away everyone and everything in her path. The novel centers on the rivalry among the sisters and is largely projected from Christina's point of view. But it ends with her defeat. The last pages of the novel are given over to Virgilia's engagement, courtship, and wedding. Virgilia has won a husband by being a cunningly correct middle-class maiden, while Christina has proven herself a Bohemian – eminently suited for flirtations and preeminently unsuited for marriage.

Ford wrote his preface to the novel under the pseudonym 'Miles Ignotus'; that is, Unknown Soldier. He presents the novel as an 'attempt to apply the method of Jane Austen' to 'the Eighties'.[17] Ford thought of Austen and Christina Rossetti as the most perfect artist-writers of the English nineteenth century.[18] 'Art is clarity; art is economy; art is surprise', said Ford.[19] By attaining these criteria, Austen and Rossetti became supreme artists.

When, therefore, Ford speaks of Violet Hunt as achieving in *Their Lives* what Jane Austen achieves, he is saying that she has given us a clear, economically presented, no-nonsense picture of domestic life in late Victorian and Edwardian England that is completely truthful. *Their Lives* '*is* history – and it makes it plain', Ford insists. And the significance of his remark lies in our realizing that Ford wrote the preface for the novel on 7 September 1916 from 'Somewhere in Belgium'. That is to say, he wrote the preface from the murderous Ypres Salient on the Western Front during the First Battle of the Somme. He dated it, in fact, the very day that he wrote Conrad that 'yesterday . . . we were being shelled to hell and I did not expect to get thro' the night'.[20] Ford begins his preface to Hunt's novel saying, 'I took the proofs of this book up the hill to read. From there I could see the gas shells bursting in Poperinghe. . . '. If Hunt's fiction can stand up to this, it can stand with Conrad's *Typhoon*, James's *What Maisie Knew*, and Crane's *The Red Badge of Courage*, which

Ford also read at the front (*TR* 108). *Their Lives* is that kind of a book: 'a horrible book' that is 'triumphantly true'.[21]

The critical consensus is that *Their Lives* is Violet Hunt's best book.[22] Given that judgment, it is regrettable that Ford did not have an especial word for *Their Lives* in *Thus To Revisit,* where he mentions single novels of extraordinary merit amid his fuller discussions of James, Conrad, Crane, and Hudson. Certainly *Their Lives* deserved mention and deserved Ford's help in securing it a greater readership than it has. Moreover, Ford risked little in recommending his former lover's novel because it has nothing to do with him. But, too flurried by her sexual failure with Ford, Violet had too much to say about him in the original text and revision of her memoirs. His response to *Their Lives* in their battle of the books was, consequently, the same as his response to her attack on him in both versions of her memoirs. He said nothing – and, in each instance, prevailed.

NOTES

1. 'The Flurried Years', *Times Literary Supplement* (18 February 1926), 111.

2. Review in the *Nation and Athenaeum* (20 March 1926), 870.

3. 'Kissing and Telling', *Bookman*, 64 (1927), 739.

4. Violet Hunt, *The Flurried Years* (London: Hurst & Blackett, 1926) – henceforth *FY*; p. 13.

5. Ford Madox Hueffer, *Thus to Revisit: Some Reminiscences* (London: Chapman and Hall, 1921) – henceforth TR in citations; p. 22.

6. Violet continued to call herself 'Mrs. Hueffer' when she could safely do so. Thus, when she presented the British Museum with four watercolors and sketches by her

father Alfred W. Hunt, she presented them as 'Mrs. Hueffer', and the gift remains to this day officially recorded this way.

7. This quotation from Ruskin appears in *FY* 16; *I Have This To Say* (New York: Boni & Liveright, 1926), p. v.

8. Ford Madox Hueffer, 'Literary Portraits – V. Miss Violet Hunt and "The Desirable Alien"', *Outlook*, 32 (11 October 1913), 497.

9. Violet Hunt, 'The Corsican Sisters', *More Tales of the Uneasy* (London: Heinemann, 1925), pp. 165-287.

10. 'Since the great majority of mankind are, on the surface, vulgar and trivial – the stuff to fill graveyards – the great majority of mankind will be easily and quickly affected by art which is vulgar and trivial. But, inasmuch as this world is a very miserable purgatory for most of us sons of men – who remain stuff with which graveyards are filled – inasmuch as horror, despair and incessant strivings are the lot of the most trivial of humanity, who endure them as a rule with commonsense and cheerfulness – so, if a really great master strike the note of horror, of despair, of striving, and so on, he will stir chords in the hearts of a larger number of people than those who are moved by the merely vulgar and the merely trivial.' 'On Impressionism', *Critical Writings of Ford Madox Ford*, ed. Frank MacShane, Bison Books (Lincoln: University of Nebraska Press, 1964), pp. 48-9.

11. 'Here Are Lions', *Saturday Review* (6 March 1926), 306.

12. *Nation & The Athenaeum* (20 March 1926), 872.

13. *Some Do Not . . .* in *Parade's End*, intro. Robie Macauley, Vintage Books (New York: Random House, 1979), p. 128.

14. *FY* 213. Hunt reworked this passage to less effect in *I Have This To Say*: 'For I submit that there is not, nor ever can be, in fiction any such thing as a true description of X. I should say that a pretty fair description of X, or X-ess, might be detailed in a dozen yards or so of film print comprising the slow crescence and decrescence of her smile and his frown' (p. 202).

15. Violet Hunt, *The Desirable Alien at Home in Germany. With Preface and Two Additional Chapters by Ford Madox Hueffer* (London: Chatto and Windus, 1913).

16. Barbara Belford, *Violet* (New York: Simon and Schuster, 1990), p. 177.

JOSEPH WIESENFARTH

17. In *Sooner or Later: The Story of an Ingenuous Ingénue* (London: Chapman and Hall, 1904), Violet Hunt describes her heroine in a variation on the opening of *Emma*. Hunt tells us that Edith Assheton 'was rich, well connected, handsome, and clever, with the one hereditary weakness skillfully kept out of sight' (p. 3). That hereditary weakness is a liability to bouts of madness! Jane Austen begins her novel this way: 'Emma Woodhouse, handsome, clever, and rich, with a comfortable home and happy disposition, seemed to unite some of the best blessings of existence . . . .' But by the fourth paragraph we see that Emma's problems, 'at present so unperceived', are her having 'rather too much her own way' and 'a disposition to think a little to well of herself'.

18. Ford Madox Ford, *The March of Literature from Confucius' Day to Our Own* (New York: Dial, 1938), p. 785. For an extended discussion of Ford on Jane Austen and Christina Rossetti, see Joseph Wiesenfarth, 'Ford Madox Ford and the Pre-Raphaelites or How Dante Gabriel Rossetti Started the First World War', *REAL: Yearbook of Research in English and American Literature*, ed. Herbert Grabes, Winfried Fluck, and Jürgen Schlaeger (Tübingen: Gunter Narr, 1993): 9 (1993), 109-48.

19. Ford Madox Ford, *Portraits from Life* (Boston: Houghton Mifflin, 1936), p. 51.

20. *Letters of Ford Madox Ford*, ed. Richard Ludwig (Princeton: Princeton University Press, 1965), p. 75.

21. This was Ford's description of *What Maisie Knew*; see 'Escapes', Literary Causeries, *Chicago Tribune Sunday Magazine* Paris ed. (9 March 1924), 3, 11.

22. May Sinclair, Hunt's contemporary and friend, wrote that if 'Violet Hunt had written nothing but *White Rose [of Weary Leaf]* and *Their Lives* and *Their Hearts*, these would have been enough to establish a reputation for more than mere cleverness. If only she had written nothing else she would have been recognised as one of the most sincere, uncompromising, and serious of psychological realists' ('The Novels of Violet Hunt', *English Review*, 34 [1922]: 106-7). Barbara Belford asserts that 'except for *Their Lives* and *Their Hearts* and one or two of the romantic novels, Violet's writing has not stood the test of time' (*Violet*, p. 282). And Robert and Marie Secor have written a substantial appreciation of *Their Lives* (1916) and its sequel, *Their Hearts* (1916), in 'Lives and Hearts in Pre-Raphaelite England: The Autobiographical Novels of Violet Hunt', *The Pre-Raphaelite Review*, 2 (1979), 59-70.

'DRAWN FROM LIFE':
STELLA BOWEN AND FORD MADOX FORD

Ros Pesman

Remember, dear, you have not lost the battle because you really have got
Something out of life, and you have created yourself.
Edith Sitwell to Stella Bowen, 1928.[1]

Stella Bowen, the Australian painter and companion of Ford Madox
Ford from 1919 to 1927, created herself most surely and elegantly in
her book, *Drawn From Life*, published two years after Ford died. And
it was above all in her portrait of Ford and in the telling of the story of
her relationship with him that Bowen constructed the image of self
which has come to be so admired.[2] It is this autobiography that is also
a biography that is the subject of this essay.

Ford Madox Ford's personal life and his relationships with
women have always aroused considerable comment but about this
part of his life he himself was very reticent. As he wrote to his mother
in 1919, protesting about remarks that his sister, Juliet Soskice, had
made about his private life, 'I never comment on anybody'.[3] Just as
the name of Violet Hunt, Bowen's predecessor in Ford's affections,
does not occur in his 1921 reminiscences, *Thus to Revisit*, Stella
Bowen is not mentioned in Ford's 1933 autobiography, *It was the
Nightingale*, although over half the subject matter covers the period
when she lived with him, first in Sussex and then in France. Ford's
women were less reticent. In the Preface to his 1948 biography of
Ford, *The Last Pre-Raphaelite*, Douglas Goldring wrote that his was
only the fourth book to deal with the career and personality of Ford.
The preceding three were Goldring's own *South Lodge* and the books
written by women who shared Ford's life – that is Violet Hunt's, *The
Flurried Years* and Stella Bowen's *Drawn From Life*.[4] Goldring went
on to doubt whether any woman:

However loyal and affectionate, however clear sighted and perspicacious, can ever see a man, especially so elusive and complex an individual as Ford, except in the slightly distorting mirror of her own emotions.[5]

In the case of Stella Bowen, later commentators on Ford have not been so uncertain.

In 1966, while Arthur Mizener was in England collecting material for his biography of Ford, Oliver Edwards wrote an article on Ford for *The Times*; he hoped that Mizener, who was approaching his subject 'with American zeal and thoroughness', would spend quite a number of pages 'telling us all he can about Stella Bowen'.[6] Edwards recommended *Drawn From Life* to anyone interested in Ford: 'There is no book in which Ford shows up better'; indeed no man could have asked 'for a better epitaph'. Mizener, unsympathetic to Ford and writing in the days before the feminist challenge to traditional biography and history and before the development of interest in partnership and collaboration in artistic creativity, raided *Drawn From Life* as a source for events but not for Ford as persona. Bowen herself was a peripheral figure, just another of Ford's women.[7] Writing Ford's life twenty years after Mizener, Alan Judd was more inclined to concur in Oliver Edward's opinion: *Drawn From Life* contained 'an unmatched portrait' of Ford.[8] In Max Saunders' biography of Ford, while Bowen is still just another in the long line of Ford's women, those women are now given a far more central role in Ford's living and writing. Saunders observes that in *Drawn From Life*, Bowen makes 'one of the few genuinely understanding comments on Ford's art, the proximity between his impressionism in literature and his impressionism in life'.[9]

It was in 1940, in an England awaiting the expected German invasion, that Stella Bowen completed *Drawn From Life*. She herself gave her desperate need for money as the motive for the book. To Ford and Elsie Martindale's daughter, Katharine Lamb, Bowen wrote in 1947 that she had only told her story because she was absolutely broke and she had been offered an advance of £100.[10] Janice Biala, Ford's last companion and his fiercely devoted champion, accepted this explanation: 'I understand that you wouldn't have done it if you hadn't been desperate for money'.[11]

There is no doubt that Bowen was in dire financial straits, but there may have been other motives. She had appeared in literary texts in far from flattering guises. Mrs Braddocks in *The Sun Also Rises* is an unsophisticated and naïve colonial. Jean Rhys in *Quartet,* the fictionalised account of her own relationship with Ford, portrayed Bowen in the character of the wife, Lois, as someone thrilled to be moving among the talented and famous and as impressed by the supposed daring of her life, which in Rhys's eyes was far from *louche.* Bowen may have wished to give her account of the relationship of Ford and Rhys; the other three participants had published their versions between 1928 and 1932, engaging in what has been termed a kind of fictional 'debate' among witnesses to the same event.[12] She may also have wished to salvage the reputation of Ford, the father of her daughter Julia, after the publication of Violet Hunt's memoirs. And lastly, since Ford had erased her from the public record of his life, Bowen may have been claiming her place.

If Stella Bowen wrote *Drawn From Life* to make money, its selling point was not Bowen herself but her relationship with the recently deceased and reputed womaniser Ford, and the life that this relationship had given her among the modernists in Montparnasse. And much of the book is taken up with Bowen's time with Ford and in Paris; less than 10% is concerned with her life after she left Paris for England. When Bowen was dying of cancer in 1947, two decades after her separation from Ford, she sent for Janice Biala as being the only person with whom she could talk about her 'real life', that is her life with Ford.[13] Without Ford there was not only no audience but also no story to tell. While the autobiography may in large part have taken the form of a biography of Ford, as Janice Biala recognised, *Drawn From Life* was primarily about Bowen not Ford: 'it really is about you'.[14] In the same letter Biala told her predecessor of the 'fear and trembling' with which she had first opened *Drawn From Life*: she 'was sick with nerves'.[15] Her trepidation, Biala discovered, was without foundation. She had no quarrel with Bowen's portrayal of Ford which she described as 'a model of discretion, and generosity and kindness, and superhuman in its forbearance'.

The words 'discretion', 'generosity', 'superhuman in forbearance', are interesting. They seem appropriate when we remember that some five years after Bowen went to live with Ford, he brought Jean Rhys into their home and then into his bed; that in the United States in 1926-1927, he transferred much of his affection to Rene Wright and then wanted a menage whereby he spent half the year with Stella and Julie in Paris and half with Mrs Wright in America. In addition, Bowen's poverty and acute financial problems from the early 1930s resulted in large part from the investment of her small private income in their life in Paris, in the *transatlantic review,* and in the subsidies that were paid to Jean Rhys between 1925 and 1927. In a letter to Ford in 1927, Bowen observed that their outlay on Rhys and his mother equalled her income.[16]

Biala then had good reason to fear Bowen's account of her life with Ford, the more so in the context of the revenge that Violet Hunt had wreaked on Ford in *The Flurried Years.* But Bowen had equally good reason to give her extraordinarily sensitive, sympathetic and perceptive appreciation of her erstwhile and erring partner, to 'put things the way I wished'.[17] In *Drawn From Life,* Bowen mythologised Ford and her relationship with him. In doing so she secured her own identity and reputation. Thus, for example, she represented her meeting with Ford as taking place outside time and space (*DFL* 61-3). At no point in *Drawn From Life* did Bowen mention Hunt, who was still Ford's public partner when she met him; indeed, it seems very likely that the first meeting took place while Bowen was a guest at Hunt's country cottage. When in her turn, Bowen lost Ford to another woman, she wrote to him: 'I am not ashamed of any of it except the initial step of taking you away from an older woman. I wish with all my heart I had not done that'.[18] The focus in my discussion of Bowen's public story of her life with Ford is not, however, its beginning but its ending.

In *Drawn From Life,* there are two strands in Stella Bowen's story of the end: Ford's need to replenish his creative powers by the acquisition of new muses and her own growing desire for autonomy. Thus she portrays the Jean Rhys episode as an event which pushed her towards independence: 'it cut the fundamental tie between himself and me' (*DFL* 166). She found that she was in the not uncommon but banal position of being in love with someone who has fallen for someone else. But she also discovered, after a passage of time, that falling out of love could also be exhilarating; that she had a desire for freedom (*DFL* 168). Yet the letters that Bowen wrote to Ford during his five month visit to the United States in the autumn and winter of 1926 tell a different story and point to a woman shoring up her relationship at all costs. She asked him to 'get finished with any too-exacting intimacies' that he might have formed and to come back 'unentangled':

> Meanwhile, I continue to set our house in order – I am so dead keen on organising the flat properly and so *terribly* anxious that the prospect of domesticity will attract you sufficiently after all the trouble we have had to attain it. [19]

Bowen's efforts were to no avail. Ford's tendrils were wandering again and, by the end of 1927, she had suffered enough. She portrayed the ending of their relationship as civilised, dignified, and carried out with panache and style.

> Even when we were on the brink of separating, we could still go out and dine together and have a grand argument about Lost Causes, or the theory of the Infallibility of the Pope, or some such theme. (*DFL* 165)

In his biography of Ford, Alan Judd appears to have accepted Bowen's version of the ending. He wrote of Ford and Bowen managing their break up well: 'Gently, by stages, without any undue ruffles, they reached agreement as they always had'.[20] Max Saunders is rightly more sceptical: 'the separation from Bowen was as civilised as such things can be'.[21] There are hints enough in the letters of Bowen and Ford themselves – and it is important to note that the surviving correspondence has been censored by their daughter Julie – and in letters of others that the ending was managed not so much with grace and style but with all the quarrels and recriminations that normally accompany the event, quarrels over child access and rearing and over money, quarrels exacerbated by hurt and pain.

The letters that Stella Bowen received from Edith Sitwell, with whom her friendship was close in this period, are full of sympathy for her plight and admiration for the courage and dignity with which Bowen was coping. In November and December 1928, when Ford had returned to live in the same block of apartments in Rue Vaugirard as Bowen, and Rene Wright was in Paris, Sitwell told Bowen of the pain she felt for her in the 'dreadful' situation.[22] In the following March, she wrote that she hoped that Stella was 'at peace and freed from that nightmare of a continual presence'; 'that it won't be too dreadful and that he will go away soon': 'How can he give you any worry or extra cause of sadness after what you have been through. How can he?'[23] To her friend Jenny Bradley, Bowen wrote at this time:

> I have been having so much trouble with Ford and having received a long and very distressing letter from him here and I should awfully like to see you before I have to see him. It would help steady me. He made a great scene the night before I came away, on the grounds that my moving out of 32 was not giving him a fair deal and he would not be able to see Julie so much and that therefore I must let him take her to America. Says would never have agreed to separation if he hadn't thought would get dual control over Julie. Says his lady has given him the chuck because of the money and support he gives Julie and me. So you see its all a hateful mess and I've never felt before so much need of a few male relations.[24]

Things had deteriorated to such a point by May 1929 that Ford informed Stella from New York that since she was virtually precluding him from seeing Julie, he saw no reason to return to France. He simply did not know, 'being past caring'.[25] In the next year, Bowen related something of her situation to her brother Tom in Australia:

> I find his presence in Paris fairly trying. He expects to keep very Friendly, which is all right in theory, but he manages to bother me. However, this is a small thing compared to how things were.[26]

The situation went from bad to worse. In May 1933, Bowen's financial position forced her to leave Paris and move to London. Ford was unhappy about Julie's education in England, about the weakening of Catholic influences in her life and about her general development. His harping wore Bowen's patience:

> I am succeeding, after a period of harrowing insecurity and anxiety, in building up a new life and background for Julie – She is becoming acquainted with family and with people who have honourable standards of conduct . . . Instead of being thankful that I am so succeeding, your present rabid hatred of everything English causes you to view every aspect of our new life with fantastic suspicion . . . And here I must say that your anti-English influence is a real obstacle to this adaptation, and that I consider it to be an unfair addition to our difficulties.[27]

By 1934 Bowen and Ford were no longer on speaking terms. Bowen wrote to Jenny Bradley towards the end of the year:

> Also Ford and I are no longer on speaking terms so discussion with him is impossible. He behaved very badly to me when he was over here and we now correspond through Janice! Drat the man, he is impossible! I am, however, genuinely grieved not to have been able to maintain that decent outward friendship which helped sweeten an ugly situation and was certainly better for Julie.[28]

Bowen had informed Janice Biala earlier in the same year, that since Ford was not answering her letters, she was writing to Biala.[29] Indeed, from that time on there was little but the most formal contact between Ford and Bowen, and Janice Biala acted as the go-between on matters relating to money and Julie. Bowen did not see Ford when she took Julie to visit him in France just a few weeks before his death.

The ending of Stella Bowen's relationship with Ford Madox Ford was not, then, carried out with quite the style and panache that she suggested in *Drawn From Life*. But *Drawn From Life* was not the beginning of Bowen's mythologising of the last phases of her life with Ford. When Bowen and Ford separated early in 1928, she was already preoccupied with the writing of the public record. The official narrative was to be that they had separated by mutual consent and that they remained friends. She asked Ford that, if the news came out that they had parted because of Rene Wright, he stick by her story that he had not wanted to break with her outwardly, and that it was she who wanted to end it all. She also reminded him that he had agreed that she might tell people that they remained good friends; if Rene objected, she might be asked 'to be a sport about this' since Stella was making everything else easy for her.[30] For a time, the masquerade was sufficiently convincing to confuse observers. Allen Tate, who borrowed Ford's flat in 1928 was not certain whether Ford and Bowen were separated.[31]

Why was a public image of an ending marked by friendship, mutual consideration and dignity so important to Bowen? Jean Rhys, hardly an impartial observer, characterised the wife figure in *Quartet* as a conventional woman very much concerned with keeping up appearances. Impartial or not, Rhys was to a large extent accurate in her characterisation. Stella Bowen was a person to whom appearances and conventional morality mattered. She was no care-free Bohemian oblivious or contemptuous of conventions; in one of her first letters to Ford, she expressed her disapproval of the looser attitudes and behaviour of her flatmate, Phyllis Reid.[32] That the twenty-six year old Bowen should go and live with and bear the child of the married

Ford, who had been the subject of scandal and who was still associated with Violet Hunt, does seem extraordinary. It was the depth of her attraction to Ford, marvellously attested to in her letters, and the courage which she possessed in abundance that provide the clues to her action. But the same correspondence reveals her worries about the illegitimate nature of their relationship and her desire for privacy if not secrecy. This created problems when that relationship was coming to its end. What should they tell people? Should they give out the story that they were divorcing? At no point in *Drawn From Life* does Bowen suggest that she and Ford were married, but neither does she make explicit that they were not. Later she admitted in a letter to Katharine Lamb that this was the only deception in what she believed was an honest telling of her story.[33] Ironically, the legitimacy that eluded Bowen in life was given to her in death by Phyllis Reid Vallance, with whom her adventures had begun in Pembroke Studios during the First World War. Vallance filled in the details on Bowen's death certificate, identifying her as formerly the wife of Ford Madox Ford, now divorced. (Thus was initiated the long and fruitless chase by the editors of the *Australian Dictionary of Biography* for a marriage certificate.)

Stella Bowen was not only concerned that the irregularity of her relationship with Ford be hidden; she was also anxious in its ending that she should in no way present the image of a deserted wife, that she should not be associated with Hadley Hemingway and Olga Rudge in a 'Female World where everyone is a bit sore'.[34] In her concern that the public record should not present her as a deserted wife, Bowen had something in common with Violet Hunt's obsession with public appearances when Ford was leaving her for Bowen, an obsession to which Bowen was sensitive at the time. Ford had informed his mother in July 1919 that he continued to appear at Hunt's parties at Bowen's request: 'she wishes to save Violet the mortification of appearing officially deserted'.[35] But that was as far as Bowen's sympathy extended to her predecessor. Hunt had presented herself as a victim. This image was anathema to Bowen. When, in the early stages of here relationship with Ford, Hunt made a public spectacle of her desertion, Bowen wrote with distaste of Hunt's vulgarisation of intimate life and of her lack of pride.[36] Conversely, when Ernest Hemingway left his wife, Bowen wrote with admiration of Hadley Hemingway's 'superhuman efforts to go down with a smile and with dignity'.[37]

Image and appearances mattered to Stella Bowen in more subtle ways – ways that may have owed something to Ford. In a letter written to her in May 1919 when she was much preoccupied with what she should tell people and whom she should tell about their relationship, Ford wrote: 'Believe me, as in the Arts, so in life, Reticence is the first of all qualities'.[38] Bowen was reticent in her account of Ford's affair with Jean Rhys, referring to Rhys only as 'Ford's girl'. In *Drawn From Life*, she portrayed her own stance at the time as one of bravery, common sense, resilience, and herself as a person who felt no bitterness towards either her husband or his lover. Stoicism, dignity, style – especially when going down – were important to Bowen. This was the image that she created in *Drawn From Life*.

On a broader level, in her portrait of Ford, Bowen rationalised and elevated his wandering from her in terms of his genius.[39] While not ignoring Ford's idiosyncrasies – and who has made a better gloss than Stella Bowen on Ford's disregard for the normal canons of accuracy – these were always placed within the context of his passion for literature and his writing. His wandering tendrils, the difficulties and the messes of their years together, the submersion of her desire to paint and develop her own talents, the surrender of her only source of financial security were given meaning by her belief in Ford's genius and writing. She presented herself in retrospect as but the 'new object' that Ford needed to restore his belief in his powers after the war. As such she could make claims to success: *The Marsden Case*, the *transatlantic review* and *Parade's End* were the fruit of Bowen's time with Ford. To Janice Biala, Bowen wrote in 1935 that 'betting on his importance as a writer does after all represent quite a large slice of my life's energy and nothing can stop me taking pride in his success'.[40]

Stella Bowen was a painter for whom aesthetic satisfaction was the very essence of life, and art and the aesthetic were not restricted to brush and easel.[41] Self and surroundings were also works of art, the product of discipline, work and dedication. The decorative side of life, the conscious exercise of good manners, were not frivolous 'but had to do with style and form in living, like technique in painting':

> I have always adored carefully tended good looks, and I do not care how artificial they are. An appearance of this sort is a work of art, entailing skill, patience and discipline, and it must be carried off by the appropriate manner.[42]

And, in *Drawn From Life,* Bowen created herself indeed as a work of art, as the generous, discreet woman of superhuman forbearance who was only too aware of Ford's foibles but who also wanted to create a positive record of the relationship for which she had defied convention and which at its end left her deserted, broke and with a child to support. In placing a favourable biography of Ford at the centre of her memoirs, she secured her own identity and reputation and elaborated a personal myth. Indeed, Stella Bowen profited far more than Ford from the story she told of their relationship and its ending. In recommending *Drawn From Life* as a crucial source for Ford to the readers of the *Times* in 1966, Oliver Edwards went on to suggest that the very favourable image of Ford emerging from its pages might mainly be due to Stella Bowen herself, a woman 'with a fine nature and a sterling character'.[43] Julian Barnes in his review of Saunders' biography wrote of Bowen's 'clear and convincing voice', and that there was probably nothing more moving in the two volumes than Stella Bowen's 'truthful, honourable, heart-wrenched farewell to Ford'.[44]

That the ending of Bowen's relationship was not carried out with quite the dignity and style implied in *Drawn From Life* was the departure of life from the prepared script. She told it the way that she – and he – had wanted it to be. In a letter to Ford in April, 1928, reminding him that he had agreed that she might tell people that they remained good friends 'in spite of it all', she also told him of her pride in her connection with him, of her gratitude for the education he had given her, and of her hopes for his happiness. The letter concluded: 'and do let us stay friends'.[45]

As John Paul Eakin has observed, the making of the fictive self is not only the work of autobiography but the principal fact of existence. Victoria Glendinning has noted that the story of one's life is not only what happens and what one feels happens or what observers see happening but also what one wants it to be.[46] And what one wants it to be is as revealing of self as what happens. The self that Stella Bowen wrote about in *Drawn From Life* is not so very far removed from the Stella Bowen recalled by her friends. There is no doubt some basis to the bitchy presentations in the writing of Hemingway and Rhys, their characterisation of her as the provincial flattered to be moving among the talented and famous. And, indeed, the talented and famous do move through her memoirs. The incident which she chose to illustrate her colonial gaucherie when she arrived in Paris was Marcel Proust's funeral: on realising that she had to kiss the next of kin, she broke from the line of mourners and fled the church. What the reader remembers is not Bowen's self-identified gaucheries but the fact that she was present at Proust's funeral. And the Stella Bowen who in the later days of their friendship irritated Edith Sitwell with her common sense 'home truths' rings true.[47] But in earlier days, Sitwell had written to Bowen:

All I can say is that I am so happy that we are friends. Our friendship – (this sounds egotistic and egoistic) – is going to be one of the few happinesses in my life. I only wish I could be more worthy of it. The more I think of you and the more I know you, the more I realise just what a wonderful woman you are. Strength without hardness, sweetness without mawkishness, straightforwardness without cruelty, high ideals without coldness, all those you have got in high degree.[48]

In another letter, Sitwell wrote of her admiration for Bowen's 'beauty, gallantry, staying power, dash and understanding'.[49] Australian historian Keith Hancock, who knew Bowen in London during the war, spoke of her as 'the most courageous, vital and harmonious personality that I have ever known', of her 'genius for living', and of a laugh that 'was a great burst of joy or a trill of glee'.[50] Richard Church, in a letter to *The Times* prompted by Oliver Edward's article on Ford, expressed his pleasure that justice had been at last done to Stella Bowen: she was 'a woman of absolute commonsense and almost terse veracity, faithful in her friendships and factual in her demonstration of them'.[51]

The question remains of the role of Ford Madox Ford in the progressive creation of Bowen's fictive self. Joseph Wiesenfarth has shown the influence of Ford on the direction of Stella Bowen's painting and the style of her writing.[52] What of his influence in the making of her sensibility? In *Drawn From Life*, Bowen wrote that, from her life with Ford, she had obtained 'a remarkable liberal education, administered in ideal circumstances': 'to have the run of Ford's mind was a privilege for which I am still trying to say "thank you"' (*DFL* 64). She made the same point in a letter to Ford's daughter, Katharine Lamb, in 1947, when she recalled 'the tremendous attraction of his gorgeous mind'.[53]

If it was important to Bowen that the ending of her relationship with Ford be carried out with dignity and style, it was equally important that the ending of life be carried out in the same manner. Early in 1947, Stella Bowen wrote Jenny Bradley that her cancer was incurable:

I know you will be sorry to hear this, for it means, in effect, that I have received my notice to Quit . . . I am very sad Jenny, at the idea of not seeing you again . . . I grieve too at never seeing Paris again, nor the Midi .

.. And you can rest assured that if things were to go badly I should never allow myself to be dragged through any of the eventual ignominies practiced to prolong life – in fact if my renegade body becomes uninhabitable, I shall just quit![54]

At much the same time, Stella Bowen wrote to her daughter, Julie:

the time will come when you will have to arrange some sort of service for me at Golders Green or Brompton cemetery. Anyway don't wait for the ashes or any nonsense of that sort! Go and have a drink somewhere.[55]

By the end of the year Stella Bowen was dead.

NOTES

1. Edith Sitwell papers, Harry Ransom Centre, University of Texas, Austin.

2. On Bowen, see Lola Wilkins, 'Stella Bowen. Australian War Artist', *Art and Australia*, 28:4 (1991), pp 493-7; Ros Pesman, *Duty Free. Australian Women Abroad* (Melbourne: Oxford University Press, 1996), pp. 178-183; Ros Pesman, 'Autobiography, Biography and Ford Madox Ford's Women', *Women's History Review 8:4*, (December 1999), pp 655 - 670; Drusilla Modjeska, *Stravinsky's Lunch* (Sydney: Pan Macmillan, 1999).

3. Ford Madox Ford to Catherine Hueffer, 3 July 1919, Stow Hill Papers, BH Box 1, File 6, House of Lords Record Office, London.

4. Stella Bowen, *Drawn From Life* (London: Collins, 1941; Maidstone: George Mann, 1974) – henceforth *DFL*; Violet Hunt, *The Flurried Years* (London: Hurst & Blackett Ltd, 1926), published in a slightly different version in the United States as *I Have This To Say* (New York: Boni & Liveright, 1926).

5. Douglas Goldring, *The Last Pre-Raphaelite. A Record of the Life and Writings of Ford Madox Ford* (London: Macdonald & Co., 1948), p. vii.

6. Oliver Edwards, 'In Absentia', *The Times*, 28 July 1966.

7. Arthur Mizener, *The Saddest Story. A Biography of Ford Madox Ford* (London: The Bodley Head, 1972). On the role of partners in creativity, *Mothering the Mind: Twelve Studies of Writers and their Silent Partners*, ed. Ruth Perry and Martine Brownley (New York and London: Holmes and Meier, 1984); *Significant Others: Creativity and Intimate Partnership*, ed. Whitney Chadwick and Isabelle de Courtivron (London: Thames & Hudson, 1993).

8. Alan Judd, *Ford Madox Ford* (London: Collins, 1990), p. 314.

9. Max Saunders, *Ford Madox Ford. A Dual Life*, Vol. 2, *The After-War World* (Oxford: Oxford University Press, 1996), p. 331.

10. Bowen to Katharine Lamb, 22 June 1947, Bowen papers, Kroch Library, Cornell University.

11. Janice Biala to Bowen, 29 June 1940, Biala papers, Kroch Library, Cornell University.

12. Martien Kappers-den Hollander, 'A Gloomy Child and its Devoted Godmother: Jean Rhys, *Barred, Sous les verrous* and *In De Strik'*, *Autobiographical and Biographical Writings in the Commonwealth*, ed. Doireann MacDermott (Barcelona: Sabadell, 1984), p. 123. The other three accounts are Jean Rhys, *Postures*, 1928 (later editions *Quartet*); Edouard de Neve, *Sous les verrous* (1933) (Dutch version, *In De Strik*), Rhys's adapted English translation, *Barred* (1932); and Ford's *When the Wicked Man* (1931).

13. Julian Barnes, 'O Unforgettable Elephant', *New York Review of Books* (9 January 1997), 4.

14. Biala to Bowen, 29 June 1940, Biala papers.

15. Biala to Bowen, 15-17 September 1945, *Ibid.*

16. Bowen to Ford, 11 January 1927, *The Correspondence of Ford Madox Ford and Stella Bowen*, ed. Sondra J. Stang and Karen Cochran (Bloomington: Indiana University Press, 1993), p. 294.

17. Bowen to Biala, 31 July 1945(?), Biala Papers.

18. Bowen to Ford, 3 January 1928, *Correspondence*, p. 373.

19. Bowen to Ford, 11 January 1927, *Correspondence*, p. 294.

20. Judd, p. 375. See also David Dow Harvey, *Ford Madox Ford 1873-1939. A Bibliography of Works and Criticism* (Princeton: Princeton University Press, 1962), p. 497; Joseph Wiesenfarth, 'The Ford-Bowen Correspondence', *Review* , 17 (1995), 86.

21. Saunders, p. 329.

22. Sitwell to Bowen, 27 November, 6 December 1927, Edith Sitwell papers, Harry Ransom Centre.

23. Sitwell to Bowen, 7 March 1929, *Ibid.*

24. Bowen to Jenny Bradley, no date, but c. November 1928, Bradley Agency papers, Harry Ransom Centre.

25. Ford to Bowen, 16 May 1929, *Correspondence*, p. 397.

26. Stella Bowen to Tom Bowen, 19 November 1930, Stella Bowen papers, Adelaide.

27. Bowen to Ford, 1 February 1934, *Correspondence*, p. 433.

28. Bowen to Jenny Bradley, Bradley Agency papers.

29. Bowen to Biala, 26 July 1934. Biala papers.

30. Bowen to Ford, 18 April 1928, *Correspondence* pp. 379-80.

31. Saunders, p. 328.

32. Bowen to Ford, 24 April 1919, *Correspondence*, p. 99.

33. Bowen to Lamb, 22 June 1947, Bowen papers, Cornell.

34. Bowen to Ford, 22 November 1926, *Correspondence*, p. 234.

35. Ford to Catherine Hueffer, 3 July 1919.

36. Bowen to Ford, 26 April, 4 May 1919, *Correspondence*, pp. 104, 120.

37. Bowen to Ford, 9 November 1926, *Ibid.,* pp. 218-19.

38. Ford to Bowen, 2-3 May 1919, *Ibid.,* p. 115.

39. On the crucial importance of Ford as genius in the telling of Bowen's story, see Ros Pesman, 'Autobiography, Biography and Ford Madox Ford's Women'.

40. Bowen to Biala, 20 July 1935, Biala papers.

41. See for example, *Drawn From Life*, p. 99.

42. *Ibid.,* p. 55.

43. *The Times*, 28 July 1966.

44. Barnes, 'O Unforgettable Elephant', 24.

45. Bowen to Ford, 18 April 1928, *Correspondence*, p. 380.

46. Paul John Eakin, 'Writing Biography: A Perspective from Autobiography', *Shaping Lives. Reflections on Biography,* ed. Ian Donaldson, Peter Read and James Walter (Canberra: Humanities Research Centre, 1992), p. 201. See also Paul John Eakin, *Fiction in Autobiography. Studies in the Art of Self Invention* (Princeton: Princeton University Press, 1985); Glendinning quoted in Linda Wagner Martin, *Telling Women's Lives. The New Biography* (New Brunswick, N. J.: Rutgers University Press, 1994), p. 30.

47. Victoria Glendinning, *Edith Sitwell: A Unicorn Among Lions* (1981) (Oxford: Oxford University Press, 1983), p. 182.

48. Sitwell to Bowen, 5 May 1929, Edith Sitwell papers, Harry Ransom Centre.

49. Sitwell to Bowen, 18 July 1929. *Ibid.*

50. Clement Christesen, Notes of interview with Sir Keith Hancock, Clement Christesen papers, National Library of Australia, Canberra, MS 5019.

51. Richard Church, letter to *The Times*, 30 July 1966.

52. Joseph Wiesenfarth, 'Ford Madox Ford and the Pre-Raphaelites or how Dante Gabriel Rossetti Started the First World War, *REAL, Yearbook of Research in English and American Literature*, ed. Herbert Grabes, Winifried Fluck, and Jürgen Schlaeger (Tübingen: Gunter Narr, 1993): 9 (1993), pp. 129-131; 'The Battle of the Books. Violet Hunt, Jean Rhys, Stella Bowen, and Ford Madox Ford, unpublished paper, pp. 33-36.

53. Bowen to Lamb, 22 June 1947, Bowen papers, Cornell.

54. Bowen to Jenny Bradley 26 January (1947), Bradley Agency papers.

55. Quoted in Mizener, p. 462.

FORD MADOX FORD AND ERNEST HEMINGWAY IN THE LITERARY ARENA OF PARIS, 1924

Elena Lamberti

Allegorical introduction

The relationship between Ford Madox Ford and Ernest Hemingway has been largely neglected by Ford's and Hemingway's critics alike. With a few exceptions, scholars have underestimated the importance of this intriguing encounter.[1] In fact, it presents all the qualities of a 'cameo', standing for a whole series of literary and cultural issues as they started to develop after World War I. This essay will explore the significance of their encounter.

As a homage to Ford and his passion for 'imaginative writing', I will introduce my arguments through a literary allegory of Ford's and Hemingway's relationship as it was in 1924 in Paris, using an image which is well known to Hemingway's readers: bull-fighting. The allegory is of two bulls, a young one and an old one. Thanks to a witty toreador, they meet in a crowded arena and, as is their role, the noisy crowd urges them to fight. So they start the encounter. Yet, while the young bull takes the matter quite seriously, the old one seems more interested in his opponent's strategies than in the fighting itself. As the reader can guess, such an attitude really complicates the duel, so much so that the arbiters of the fighting are still discussing whom to announce as the winner.

Unfortunately, the two bulls simile is not my own: Nathan Asch, one of Ford's *transatlantic review* contributors, used it to describe young Hemingway's attitude towards older literary men.[2] Still, it seems appropriate, not only because of Hemingway's notorious passion for tauromachy (in fact, both writers wrote at length about bullfighting: Hemingway in *Death in the Afternoon* and in *Fiesta/The Sun Also Rises*; Ford in *Provence*), but also because Ford and

Hemingway's relationship can be read as a fascinating clash of two similar, yet different literary traditions, the British and the American. Moreover, the encounter took place in 1924 in Paris – at a time and in a town that, according to what Ford wrote in one of his most vivid memoirs, *It Was the Nightingale*, should have provided a perfect setting for his ideal (and idealistic) 'Republic of Letters', but, instead, proved to be rather a literary arena for a whole 'lost generation'. Inevitably, such a cultural setting conditioned Ford and Hemingway's encounter and forced them into a sort of 'dramatic role' which, in turn, affected their interaction.

Apart from the context, it is also evident that the different attitudes shown by Ford and Hemingway towards literary traditions and new artistic achievements ended by further conditioning their relationship, widening the gap between the two writers. This gap, for Hemingway, seemed also to be linked to a personal dislike focused not only on Ford as a Man of Letters, but also on him as a Private Person. In contrast, Ford always recognised Hemingway's achievements as a writer, and generously patronised him. In particular, Ford admired Hemingway's prose, his use of a plain language which was in line with one of the most important of Ford's impressionist tenets, the search for 'le mot juste'. Of course, Hemingway ended by developing a style of his own (after all, Ford himself always spoke of 'suggestions not dictates' when referring to his theories);[3] nevertheless, in Hemingway's prose it is possible to find evidence of his having been aware of several of Ford's technical guide-lines, possibly understood both through a direct reading of Ford's works and thanks to the mediation of Ezra Pound (the allegory's witty toreador). Indeed, it could be argued that Hemingway updated some of Ford's tenets to the 'new spirit' characterizing post-war society.

The encounter of the two bulls
Ford and Hemingway met in Paris early in 1924. Encouraged by Ezra

Pound, Ford took on the young Hemingway as an assistant editor for his *transatlantic review*. Yet, as previously suggested, the difficult relationship between Ford and Hemingway disguises something more than simply a daily quarrel between an editor and his assistant: it was truly an encounter between two different literary ages (the pre-war and the emerging post-war periods), and between two different traditions (the British and the American). Young Hemingway boxing, 'balancing on the point of his toes, feinting at (Ford's) head', as described by Ford himself,[4] provides another appropriate image for the confrontation.

As Meyers points out, when they met Ford was a middle-aged English writer, who seemed to be enjoying a new artistic vitality in post-war Paris. Hemingway was a twenty-five year-old American writer with a wife and a baby son to support, and was closer to the so called 'lost generation'. Nevertheless, despite their potential affinities,[5] and despite Pound and his attempt to mediate between the two men,[6] Hemingway never gave Ford the chance of a real friendship or, at least, of a real cultural interaction. Of course, such an attitude, deeply influenced the life of the *transatlantic review* itself, so that Ford, who would have enjoyed editing it according to the gentle rhythm of a sonata, couldn't but be led by Hemingway's frantic jazz-like tempo. Ford himself recognised that the *transatlantic review* was a 'rag-time affair where a great many things did go astray',[7] thus admitting that the review was overwhelmed by its own literary setting.

Many critics have underlined the importance of Paris in the twenties in the development of both British and American post-war literature, and *the transatlantic review* could be taken as a clear example of how things developed. With regard to Ford and Hemingway's relationship, the review also provided the boxing-ring, or, better, the arena for the encounter of the two bulls.

According to the circular presenting the newly-born review, the *transatlantic*'s aim was that of 'widening the field in which the

241

younger writers of the day [could] find publication [. . .] introducing into international politics a note more genial than that which almost universally [prevailed]' (Poli 37). It is clear that it was Ford's intention to establish a ground for what he liked to refer to as the 'Republic of Letters', namely an ideal literary Parnassus from which to start a revaluation of English Literature – something that, in Ford's opinion, was not simply made up of British productions. As he wrote in the circular: 'There is no British literature, there is no American literature: there is English literature which embraces alike Mark Twain and Thomas Hardy, with the figure of Mr. Henry James to bracket them' (Poli 37). Ford's attempt to produce a review with an editorial line very similar to that of his *English Review* is evident.[8] However, Paris in 1924 was quite different from Edwardian pre-war London, so that, despite Ford's declared wish to preserve an established and well-balanced editorial line, the review became more American than British, thus recognizing how the new 'English Literature' of the day was deeply influenced by Sylvia Beach's circle of friends.[9] If, as Samuel Putnam acknowledged, the *transatlantic review* 'was essentially the bringer of America to Europe',[10] it is also true, as both Poli and Meyers demonstrate, that this was mostly due to Hemingway's (and of course to Pound's) efforts. Ford himself, in *It Was the Nightingale,* declares that:

> through no volition of my own, but I dare say partly through the patriotic coercion of Mr. Hemingway, the *Review* was Middle Western as to a little more than half and a little less than one third French. The remaining sixth, mostly consisting of chronicles, came from the Eastern States, New York, and England.[11]

Despite Ford's attempt to justify such a situation by reference to the great 'level of excellence' of the Middle West productions, as well as both the lack of a 'great outstanding figure' in the French Arts of those days and the poorness of English contributions, it is evident that the *transatlantic review* exactly mirrors the frantic artistic reality of English-speaking expatriates in 1924 Paris (*IWN* 340). Having first set foot on European lands as warriors, the young Americans were now reinforcing their own artistic colony, establishing in Paris their main army camp, trying to transform their farewell to arms into a new sun also rising, a new fiesta. 'It was not merely Paris that was alive to the Arts: it was the whole world. . . . It was the real reaction from the war; the artist making his claim for glory as against the glory of the warrior', Ford wrote recalling that period, admitting that such a claim was much more American than British. In line with his well-known talent-spotting capability, Ford felt that 'a wave of literature' was to be born, a wave that 'in a few years produced . . . Mr. Hemingway's *A Farewell to Arms*, Mr. McAlmon's photographic reports on Berlin night life, Mr. Nathan Asch's *Love in Chartres*' (*IWN* 282, 339). It was a wave that was also to overwhelm Ford's editorial line, linked to what was beginning to appear an 'old-fashioned' literary perspective.

The urging crowd
In his first editorial for the review, Ford referred to the Paris motto, 'Fluctuat nec mergitur', which accompanies the town emblem, a ship upon the waves. Ford translated it as: 'She has her vicissitudes but does not sink'. In an almost prophetic decision, Ford took only the verb 'Fluctuat' as a motto for his review, leaving 'nec mergitur' to the readers.[12] It is well known that, unlike the Paris ship, the review sank, and that many of the highest waves came from Ford's naiveté as a business manager; yet the sinking was hastened thanks to the storms precipitated by Hemingway. Poli and Meyers have successfully shown that Hemingway's attacks on Ford's editorial choices were mostly due to the latter's attitude towards Tradition.

As many critics have acknowledged, Ford Madox Ford was an intellectual and a writer capable of bridging various literary and artistic eras thanks to his way of considering literature as a sort of great 'Work in Progress'. Ford's concept of literary tradition anticipated and was very close to Eliot's: it was based on the idea of a Republic of Letters formed by different and various 'individual talents', each adding something to the 'sacred fire of imaginative writing'. Flaubert, Dostoievsky, James, Conrad, and Hemingway himself were all to share Parnassus, despite their belonging to different traditions and ages. For this reason, Ford has been defined as a man of letters 'belonging to a time that was while being intensely aware of a time to be'.[13] However, if for today's readers such an attitude constitutes precisely the core of Ford's modernity, and if was to some extent shared by the young artists in pre-war London, it was seen as a problem by the 1924 Paris expatriates. It was certainly something that made them uneasy (Poli 82 ff.). It is worth remembering something that may seem a cliché now, but that was an undeniable reality at the time: that these expatriates arrived in Europe because of, or soon after, a world war which, in their minds, came symbolically to represent the extreme consequence of the degeneration of previous values, including the values of the pre-war artistic tradition. Hence the disruptive impact of writers coming from the 'new world' to the 'old' literary scene: who better than these angry people coming from an outside reality to turn Pound's motto 'make it new' into a concrete achievement?

There is no doubt that Hemingway was in line with this aspect of his time's inner feeling, if one is to credit not only what he wrote recalling that period, but also Nathan Asch's assertion that Hemingway 'could not function unless he fought and destroyed older men' (Poli 82). It is evident that Hemingway's approach to Ford was inevitably conditioned by such a cultural setting; certainly, in *A Moveable Feast*, he presents Ford as an out-of-date man of letters, who carelessly imposes his suffocating presence on the younger writers. Hemingway talks of the 'heavy, wheezing, ignoble presence of Ford himself',[14] thus transforming his physical repulsion for Ford into a cynical, literary metaphor used to manifest his contempt towards both the man and the artistic world he represents.

Hemingway seems to describe an old master portrait, faded by time, that, despite its hanging over the mantelpiece, clashes with the new sitting-room furniture.

However, Hemingway's attitude towards Ford and the artistic world he still represented was not an isolated one; even Nathan Asch felt that 'there was something unnatural about the mixing of generations' represented by Ford, presenting him as a 'walrus looking kind of stranger' (Poli 82). Ford himself confessed to his not being in tune with the younger artists' vehemence, recognizing that the gap was widening between him and the younger generation: 'they all shouted at me: I did not know how to write, or knew too much to be able to write, or did not know how to edit, or keep accounts, or sing *Franky & Johnny*, or order a dinner'.[15] Such a confession seems to clearly testify that Paris was, in fact, a crowded arena which inevitably influenced the encounter between Ford and Hemingway.

Two ways of fighting

The different spirit pervading Ford's and Hemingway's attitudes towards their time is clearly revealed in their books recalling those days, especially Ford's *It Was the Nightingale* and Hemingway's *A Moveable Feast* (even though it is possible to find memoirs of their Parisian experiences in many of their other books). While Ford describes Paris as a lively, charming city, as a 'sun' from which to establish relations with the world's 'furthest satellites', Hemingway's Paris seems more a place for penniless, desperate and alcoholic young American writers. Naively, Ford turned Paris and France into utopian lands: he deeply believed that Paris was a perfect setting from which to start the revaluation of English Letters (and of the Arts in general) due to its being the capital of a country, France, that esteemed 'the Art of Peace [. . .] above the science of warfare' (Poli 40). Conversely, for Hemingway, it seemed more a background for the young post-war artists' desperation and emptiness, as they tried to disguise existential anguish with frantic affairs and *fines à l'eau* (an image which immediately recalls those entangled and gloomy atmospheres described by other young writers of the period, as in Jean Rhys's *Quartet*). As previously discussed, the different perspectives displayed by the two writers were mostly due to their differing ages and cultural backgrounds. Both Poli and Meyers provide evidence of Hemingway's vehemence and Ford's diplomacy, some of it from the *transatlantic review* chronicles and letters. However, I would like to move to a deeper level of this complex encounter by discussing some of the artistic implications.

The comparison between Ford's and Hemingway's prose is to be carried out by constantly relating their poetic processes, that is their stylistic experiments and achievements, to their different perceptions of reality; in fact, all the tensions previously recollected contributed to shape their visions of the new 'world in progress', which were very much conditioned by their different epistemological approaches to both art and reality.

As far as their prose-styles are concerned, it is interesting to start by recalling and comparing Ford's criticism on Dostoievsky and Hemingway. In 1914, when reviewing Dostoievsky's *The Idiot*, Ford affirmed that 'what is to be aimed at in a style is something so unobtrusive and so quiet – so beautiful if possible – that the reader shall not know that he is reading, and be conscious only that he is living in the life of a book'.[16] Similarly, in his 1926 'Introduction' to Hemingway's *A Farewell to Arms*, he declared that:

> Hemingway's words strike you, each one, as if they were pebbles fetched fresh from a brook. It is a great quality. It is indeed the supreme quality of the written art of the moment [. . . .] This gift Hemingway has supremely [. . . .] Whilst you are reading it you forget to applaud its author. You do not know that you are having to do with an author. You are living.[17]

A similar account of Hemingway's *In Our Time* had already been published in the *transatlantic review*. Ford was praising

Hemingway's capability of presenting what Virginia Woolf would have called 'moments of being' through a plain prose refusing each superfluous word, so that the story went on beyond the written page. As previously suggested, it is evident that what Ford saw in Hemingway's prose style was the realisation of one of his fundamental impressionist tenets (which he himself arrived at after having 'pored over' Dostoievsky, Maupassant and Flaubert's prose).[18] He saw in Hemingway's work a recognition of the importance of questioning the 'form' of the novel, transforming both language and style into a tool the writer was to use in order to 'render his own time in the terms of his own time'.[19]

Hemingway's prose is well-known for its capability of avoiding any redundant word in order to compress emotions and life experience into a style which uses 'understatement' as a literary strategy. Possibly, his practice as a reporter helped him to develop such a style; yet, Hemingway's attitude towards a plain language, released from all exuberant rhetoric, is in line with Ford's demand for a 'clarity of diction',[20] as well as with his considerations on style, which, in turn, recall or, better, anticipate the famous 'A Few Don'ts by an Imagist' by Pound and Flint.[21] Here, it is important to underline Pound's role in Hemingway's literary training, as well as the fact that Pound was probably the only one among Ford's young protégés to always admit his debt towards 'Fordie'. In particular, it was Ford's language which impressed Pound, as, according to Pound, 'none [. . .] has found a more natural language than Ford did'.[22]

The reference to a 'natural language' is often made also by Hemingway's critics. For instance, Carlos Baker underlines how Hemingway learnt to write starting from daily experience, from the simplest facts.[23] The necessity of using a 'natural language' reflects both Ford's and Hemingway's need to render the poet's true observations of life; yet it is exactly the concept of 'truth', of 'reality', that is, ironically, at the basis of one of Hemingway's strongest criticism against Ford, namely that of being a liar (an accusation, as is well-known, which is a sort of 'leitmotiv' in many studies of Ford). Malcolm Bradbury, Vita Fortunati, Max Saunders in their work on Ford clearly investigate Ford's 'metaphysics', discussing how Ford and Conrad developed a new literary 'realism', and showing how their technical experiments were deeply connected with a new sensibility and a subtler idea of 'truth' aimed at deconstructing reality in order to 're-build' it.[24] The concept of 'imaginative writing' is used by Ford himself in order to define a literature whose goal is that of putting the reader into contact with the true spirit of his/her own time. To do this, sometimes the writer disregards the historical facts and develops illuminating 'visions'.[25]

Hemingway's mistrust of Fordian invention might make his own poetic seem closer to that of many writers of the Thirties, and to Lukács's later theories of realism. According to his Introduction to *Men at War*, the writer's duty is that of speaking the truth, reporting only what he sees, and not what he imagines seeing:

> A writer's job is to tell the truth. His standard of fidelity to the truth should be so high that his invention, out of his experience, should produce a truer account than anything factual can be. For facts can be observed badly; but when a good writer is creating something, he has time and scope to make it of an absolute truth.[26]

The writer's 'invention' or 'creation' is necessarily based not only on a 'true' experience, but also on 'true accounts' of that very experience; otherwise, the writer 'will never be at peace with himself because he has deserted his one complete obligation'.[27] It is this 'true account' which Hemingway considers as a fundamental tenet of his own poetic as both a writer and an editor. Accordingly, in 1942, he left out a selection from André Malraux's 'Man's Fate' from his collection of war stories because, despite its being 'a marvellous piece of writing', he was not sure about its accuracy. Malraux wrote about 'the suppression by Chiang Kai-shek of a communist revolt'. As

Hemingway recalls, in 1942 the 'Generalissimo Chiang Kai-shek' was one of the US allies; nevertheless he adds that:

> I still would have included the selection for its literary value if I had not, knowing Malraux in Spain, come to doubt his accuracy. If there was any doubt as to the truth of the incident, I felt it should not be published in this book while we were at war, no matter how well written it was. It was magnificently written.[28]

Nevertheless, the idea of 'invention' in order to make 'an absolute truth' reveals closer affinities with Ford's poetic than Hemingway may have wished to acknowledge.

Yet there are differences. Hemingway gives the term 'truth' and, therefore, the verb 'to see' a different meaning from Ford (and, of course, Conrad).[29] For both writers, the novelist's task is that of simply stating the truth through plain and natural language. Yet, while for Hemingway this means directly reporting 'facts', for Ford the new form aimed also at progressively revealing what lies below the surface, so that knowledge becomes not an immediate goal, but the result of a well calculated 'progression d'effet'.[30] Whereas Ford progresses within a line Flaubert had begun to trace and the symbolist poets had developed, Hemingway returns language to its plain referential level so that, despite the shared 'clarity of diction', the two writers represent two different epistemological approaches and poetics: Ford's 'to render' versus Hemingway's 'to report'.[31]

Inevitably, the different meanings linked to Ford and Hemingway's use of words such as 'realism' and 'true' raise important questions concerning both their social and political context, as well as the role of the novelist in a changing, post-war, society. In Ford's case, the novelist, faced with a shifting cultural environment, was elevated to the rank of a 'social historian' and was to show the real 'spirit of his own time', thus becoming the 'torch-bearer' of a new march towards a better society. In post-war Paris, Hemingway, for his part, was no longer forced to catch reality hidden under an opalescent surface, but to face the emptiness deriving from the war experience itself. As an 'obstinate, sentimental and old fashioned Tory', Ford deeply believed that art, especially good writing (that is the new, impressionist, 'imaginative writing'), would help people to recover a 'better standard of values'.[32] Ford's renewed society was still linked to an ideal brotherhood of artists and intellectuals, that is to a concept of society which was no more in tune with the new mass-society which had already started to form in the previous century, and which was about to consolidate in the immediate post-war period. In short, while Ford still believed in the possibility of improving society through art and literature (even though his *transatlantic review* editorials reveal a more pessimistic perspective than that displayed in the *English Review*), Hemingway did not. According to Italo Calvino, in his collection of essays *Perché leggere i classici* (*Why Read the Classics?*), Hemingway's plain prose hides 'the *horror vacui* of the existentialist vacuity'.[33] Hemingway does not write to help his reader recover ancient values, since, for him, those values are forever lost. Rather, he writes to fill the present-day emptiness and impotence through literary words. Calvino underlines how

> Hemingway's American expatriates are within the typhoon, body and soul. All that they can oppose to it is skiing well, shooting lions, having good relationships between men and women, that is to say trying to preserve all those techniques and virtues which will be alive in a better world, even though they do not believe in a better world themselves' (Calvino 279).

Whereas Ford preserves an ideal 'vision', which he tries to bring to bear upon the new society, Hemingway gives voice to a modern comedy of manners in which the characters seem to move more by inertia than because of real passion or inner strength .

It is above all the experience of war, and the way of perceiving and facing it, which differs in Ford's and Hemingway's novels. Apart from the evident brutality of the fighting itself, its violence and uselessness, Ford's war seems to be an element for both destruction and re-birth, as, in *Parade's End*, it symbolically brings Tietjens towards both a loss and a new life. Moreover, Ford still maintains the concept of 'chivalry', deeply connected to the gentleman-like code of good behaviour. Ford himself volunteered when he was forty-two, declaring that 'if one has enjoyed the privileges of the ruling class of a country all one's life, there seems to be no alternative to fighting for that country if necessary'.[34] As many critics have observed, the war itself was a truly cathartic experience for Ford as both a man and an artist, symbolically exemplified by his changing of name; nevertheless, if Ford Madox Hueffer died to give birth to Ford Madox Ford, the transubstantiation did not alter most of his traditional and artistic creeds.

By contrast, Hemingway's war becomes a landmark, a point of no return. 'The War is such a tremendous landmark that locally imposes itself upon our computations of time like the birth of Christ' – Wyndham Lewis wrote in *Blasting and Bombardiering* – 'We say 'pre-war' and 'post-war', rather as we say B.C. or A.D.'.[35] That's Hemingway's point of departure. As Calvino says wisely: 'Hemingway's fundamental perception was his having felt the war as being the truest image, the 'common' reality of the middle class in the imperialist age' (Calvino 284). It is not by chance that the 'fighting' image often recurs in his novels: men and bulls alike are urged to face their impotence, and the fighting ends by symbolising also their individual struggle, for the most difficult game to win, as Jake in *Fiesta* or the old man in *The Old Man and the Sea* secretly know, is the one to be played against oneself.

For this reason, Hemingway seems to take a stage further Ford's assertion that 'art comes only of the people and [. . .] the further it removes from people the less it flourishes'.[36] In post-war Paris, he no longer describes a changing world which (as in Ford's work) still recognises in art a possible heuristic function, but instead, a new mass society in which the post-war artist's impotence is evident. Paradoxically, only new wars will provide new vital impulses, as the Spanish Civil War proved. Many among Hemingway's critics spoke of the 'proletarianisation of literature in [his] prose'.[37] Atkins affirms that '[Hemingway] writes of the great majority who enjoy kitsch and comprise *Biedermeier kultur*, neither of which terms they have ever encountered'.[38] To acknowledge this is implicitly to assert that, while Hemingway's prose seems to maintain and investigate the impressionist considerations of novelistic form, in terms of language he ends by developing a new poetic which, nevertheless, was probably more in tune with post-war society than was Ford's.

Looking for an end

We should now complete the allegory and try to discover if either of the two bulls fighting could be declared the winner. According to a remark of Ford's, Hemingway should inevitably be considered as the winner simply for his being the younger:

> Those young men will survive you. They will be the judges when you are dead. So the young are always in the right [. . .] simply because with their inexperience they can get hold of a point of view and stick to it and shout about it. The middle aged are always in the wrong because they have learned caution [. . . .] Caution is no good: if a king desires rest, he abdicates.[39]

Certainly Hemingway knew how to 'get hold of a point of view' and push it vehemently: the ferocious portraits he gave of many of the 'middle aged' are still vivid icons forging what could be seen as a sort of post-war Paris index of (old) literary 'mythologies'. Nevertheless, now that both men have been outlived by their work, let's indulge in Ford's passion for 'imaginative writing' and challenge the reader by leaving an 'open ending' to the story. Imagine that, all of a sudden, the cautious old bull sits by the edge of the arena and, gently smiling, enjoys watching the new moves of the younger one. Despite a glimpse of sadness in its eyes, the old bull knows that you cannot stop the music and that, after the elegance of a minuet, there may follow the shock of a jazz band.

NOTES

1. In Ford's case, Bernard J. Poli's *Ford Madox Ford and the Transatlantic Review* (Syracuse, N.Y.: Syracuse University Press, 1967) – henceforth 'Poli', makes important comments on Ford and Hemingway's editorial co-operation; see also Jeffrey Meyers on 'Hemingway, Ford and *A Moveable Feast*', in *Critical Quarterly*, 25:4, (Winter 1983), 35-42; and chapter 11, '1924: *the transatlantic review*' in Max Saunders, *Ford Madox Ford. A Dual Life*, vol. 2 (Oxford: Oxford University Press, 1996). As far as Hemingway is concerned, his relationship with Ford is often simply mentioned *en passant* when talking of his artistic training and formative years.

2. Nathan Asch, 'Ford Madox Ford', a talk taped by station KPFA in Berkeley for radio broadcast, November 21, 1961; quoted in Poli 82.

3. Ford Madox Ford, *The English Novel: From the Earliest Days to the Death of Joseph Conrad* (Manchester, Carcanet, 1983).

4. Ford Madox Ford, 'Introduction to Ernest Hemingway, *A Farewell to Arms* (1932)', in Sondra J. Stang, ed. *The Ford Madox Ford Reader* (Manchester: Carcanet,1986), p. 249.

5. According to Meyers, 'Ford's personal qualities might also have appealed to Hemingway. Though Ford was over forty when the Great War broke out, he volunteered for service, had combat experience and was badly gassed in the summer of 1917. He had led a truly bohemian life before Left Bank expatriates made it fashionable. Despite his ungainly appearance, he conducted a number of sexual liaisons and he had the reputation of a ladies' man [. . . .]': 'Hemingway, Ford Madox Ford and *A Moveable Feast*', pp.35-36.

6. Hemingway himself admits such a mediation, even though he cannot but recall it sarcastically: 'I was trying to remember what Ezra Pound had told me about Ford, that I must never be rude to him, that I must remember that he only lied when he was very tired, that he was really a good writer and that he had been through very bad domestic troubles. I tried hard to think of these things, but the heavy, wheezing, ignoble presence of Ford himself, only touching-distance away, made it difficult': *A Moveable Feast* (London: Jonathan Cape, 1964), p. 77.

7. Ford Madox Ford, quoted by Frank MacShane in *The Life and Work of Ford Madox Ford* (London: Routledge and Kegan Paul, 1965), p. 160.

8. See Saunders, *Ford Madox Ford*, vol. 2, pp. 144ff.

9. Among others, Ford published works by Dos Passos, Hemingway, Gertrude Stein, William Carlos William, Pound, cummings, Nathan Asch, H. D., and Djuna Barnes. He also published an excerpt from Joyce's *Finnegans Wake* (Joyce himself was an habitué of Sylvia Beach's bookshop 'Shakespeare and Company'), as well as reproductions of some of the best visual artists and composers then in Paris (Picasso, Man Ray, Braque, Brancusi, Antheil). Therefore, Saunders is right when states that 'The *transatlantic review* stands up well as a discriminating cross-section of post-war international modernism': *Ford Madox Ford*, vol. 2, p. 145.

10. Quoted in Frank MacShane, *The Life and Work of Ford Madox Ford*, p. 164.

11. Ford Madox Ford, *It Was the Nightingale* (New York: The Ecco Press, 1984) – henceforth *IWN*; p. 340.

12. Ford Madox Ford, 'Editorial', *transatlantic review*, 1 (Jan.1924), 77-8.

13. Herbert Gorman, 'Ford Madox Ford: the Personal Side', *Princeton University Library Chronicle*, 9:3 (April 1948), 119.

14. Hemingway, *A Moveable Feast,* p. 77.

15. Ford, 'Introduction to Ernest Hemingway, *A Farewell to Arms* (1932)', p. 249.

16. Ford Madox Hueffer, 'Literary Portraits – XXIII: Fyodor Dostoievsky and "The Idiot"', *Outlook*, 33 (14 February 1914), 206-7.

17. Ford, 'Introduction to Ernest Hemingway *A Farewell to Arms* (1932)', pp.251-3.

18. See Joseph Wiesenfarth, ed., 'The Literary Life: A Lecture Delivered by Ford Madox Ford', in *Contemporary Literature*, 30:3 (Fall 1989); p. 177.

19. Ford, quoted in D. I. B. Smith, 'Ford Madox Ford and Modernism', in *University of Toronto Quarterly*, 51 (1981), 67.

20. See the circular written to advertise Ford's *English Review*, quoted in Nora Tomlinson, *Ford Madox Ford and The English Review*, (Hatfield Polytechnic: unpublished MA dissertation, January 1986), p. 10.

21. F. S. Flint, 'A Few Don'ts by an Imagist. (Interview with Pound)', *Poetry*, 1:6 (March 1913), 200-6. For a discussion of Pound's debt to Ford, see Robert Hampson, '"Experiments in Modernity": Ford and Pound', in Andrew Gibson, ed. *Pound in Multiple Perspective* (Basingstoke: Macmillan, 1993), pp. 93-125.

22. Ezra Pound in 'Homage to Ford Madox Ford', *New Directions*, no.7 (Norfolk, Connecticutt: New Directions, 1942), pp. 480-1.

23. Carlos Baker, *Ernest Hemingway: A Life Story* (London: Collins, 1969), p. 114.

24. See, for instance, the essays included in *Scrittura e Sperimentazione in Ford Madox Ford*, ed. R. Baccolini and V. Fortunati (Firenze: Alinea Editrice, 1994).

25. See Max Saunders, 'To Make you See: la metafisica della letteratura in Ford Madox Ford', in *Scrittura e sperimentazione in Ford Madox Ford*, pp. 59-90.

26. Ernest Hemingway, 'Introduction' to *Man at War: The Best War Stories of All Time*, ed. Hemingway (New York: Crown Publishers, 1942), p. xv.

27. *Ibid.*

28. *Ibid.*, p. xxx.

29. Cf. Conrad's Preface to *The Nigger of the 'Narcissus'*.

30. Cf. Vita Fortunati, *Ford Madox Ford. Teoria e tecnica narrativa* (Bologna: Patron Editore, 1975).

ELENA LAMBERTI

31. It is interesting to recall here a comment by Max Saunders which clearly reveals the way Ford continued to 'apply' his impressionist poetics also to Hemingway's new 'realism': 'As always for [Ford], literature and memory were inextricable. The highest praise he could give Hemingway was that he had achieved just that intricacy: "To read Mr. Hemingway is to be presented with a series of – often enough very cruel – experiences of your own that will in turn be dissolved into your own filmy remembrances" (the syntax itself dissolves Hemingway's subjects into Ford's experiences, not just with the engulfing parenthesis, but in the blurring of whether the experiences are Ford's only after he has read Hemingway, or whether Hemingway presents experiences that someone like Ford has already had)': *Ford Madox Ford*, vol. 2, p. 150.

32. As Ford told his readers in 1908: 'Speaking broadly, literature at the present day divides itself into two sharply defined classes – the imaginative and the 'factual' – and there is a third type, the merely inventive which, if it be not in any way to be contemned, has functions in the Republic nearly negligible': *English Review*, 1 (December 1908), 159.

33. Italo Calvino, *Perche' leggere I classici* (Milano: Arnoldo Mondadori Editore, 1991) – henceforth 'Calvino'; p. 279.

34. Ford, letter to his mother, quoted in A. Judd, *Ford Madox Ford* (London: Collins, 1990), p. 252.

35. Wyndham Lewis, *Blasting and Bombardiering. An Autobiography (1914-1926)* (1937) (London-New York: J. Calder / Riverrun Press, 1982), p. 1.

36. Ford Madox Ford, *transatlantic review*, 1:6 (June 1924), 450.

37. D. S. Savage quoted by John Atkins, *The Art of Ernest Hemingway. His Work and Personality* (London: Spring Books, 1952), p. 181.

38. John Atkins, *The Art of Ernest Hemingway: His Work and Personality* (London: Spring Books, 1952), p. 181

39. Ford Madox Ford, 'Mr. Wyndham Lewis and Blast', in *The Ford Madox Ford Reader*, p. 175.

FORD AND MAUPASSANT

W. B. Hutchings

Everyone acknowledges Maupassant as one of the nineteenth-century writers whom Ford regarded as true novelists, those who inherited the tradition which began with Richardson and then passed over the water to Diderot. This Anglo-French tradition Ford opposed to the English stream which began with the intrusive narration and moral duplicity of Fielding and led to the horrors of the nineteenth-century English 'nuvvle', described with customary Fordian vigour in *The English Novel* of 1929.

Ford quotes (or, rather, imaginatively misquotes) Maupassant in his essay on literary impressionism in *Poetry and Drama* (1914). Monsieur Cimme in 'La Reine Hortense', first published in *Gil Blas* on 24 April 1883 and collected in the volume *Clair de Lune* the next year, is Ford's example of how one strong impression, 'as hard and as definite as a tin-tack',[1] can fix a character. Maupassant's *conte* is a characteristically sardonic study of the death of an old woman, Hortense, who rules autocratically over her household of domestic animals. Her death-bed appeal for someone to take care of them falls on the deaf ears of her family, of whom Cimme is the key representative. He ends the story by entering the bedroom of the dead woman with the brutally short comment, 'That took less time than I would have thought'.[2] Cimme is introduced as 'a very fat, puffing character, who always came into a room first';[3] or, 'un monsieur à favoris rouges qui entrait toujours le premier' ('a man with red side-whiskers who always came into a room first'),[4] as Ford creatively reinvents him.

It is a novel by Maupassant that Ford cites in his dedicatory letter to Stella Bowen in *The Good Soldier*: 'I had in those days an ambition: that was to do for the English novel what in *Fort Comme la Mort*, Maupassant had done for the French' (*GS* 5). In Maupassant's work generally, and particularly in this late novel about the destruction of an artist (published in 1889, four years before his death), I would locate hard and definite connections between his art and that of the Francophile Ford. I shall divide these into definitions of impressionism, depictions of place and character, and specific parallels between Maupassant and *The Good Soldier*.

Maupassant and the derivation of impressionism

In his preface to the novel *Pierre et Jean* (1888), Maupassant articulates a principle of objectivity in opposition to writing which transforms reality. What he calls 'scrupulous resemblance' is achieved by means of a concatenation of small, well-defined, precise observations which constitute the vision by which is expressed the 'heart' of character and event. This perception of reality is thus an empirical and subjective process: 'Our eyes, our ears create as many truths as there are men on earth'.[5] Hence the novelist who tries to replicate how we encounter the world must primarily present intense perceptions, moments of vision through which the internal may be suggested. Action and gesture are our sole means of divining character, as in life we see just the body and can only guess at the heart.

This preface is commonly taken as a key text in late nineteenth-century French Realism/Naturalism (the Flaubert-Zola line). The influence of this tradition on English novels is supposed to be limited to those minor branches of early twentieth-century writing which Virginia Woolf disdainfully dismisses in her essay 'Mr Bennett and Mrs Brown'. Arnold Bennett 'would observe every detail with immense care [. . .] how Mrs Brown wore a brooch which had cost three-and-ten-three at Whitworth's bazaar; and had mended both gloves', but miss what Woolf calls 'life'.[6] Bennett, indeed, explicitly cited Maupassant's *Une Vie* as the source of *The Old Wives' Tale* in his preface to that novel (1908). But Maupassant's version of Realism is actually just as close to Ford's impressionism, to the strongly visual world of *The Fifth Queen* and *The Good Soldier*. In the latter, the search for the heart hidden beneath the exterior is Dowell's despair:

'Who in this world knows anything of any other heart – or of his own?' (*GS* 104).

Ford himself took up Maupassant's ideas in his preface to *Stories from Maupassant* translated by his wife, Elsie Martindale (1903). This early essay, preceding the better-known articles in *Poetry and Drama* by over ten years, serves as a focus for Ford's clear view of Maupassant's method and as a personal statement of intent. He praises his precision: 'a statement that is sharp, clear-cut, and trenchant';[7] and notes how this derives from his perception of concrete facts as illustrations of states of mind. This is the basis of Maupassant's art: 'The only thing of value is the concrete fact: the concrete fact is only of value as an "illustration" of a state of mind, a characteristic in an individual'. Ford goes on to praise his story 'Night' for its 'succession of concrete instances': 'the thing is simply there for you to take or leave: in its flawlessness it is as hard as a paving stone'.[8] This phrasing anticipates 'The impression is as hard as a tin-tack' in the *Poetry and Drama* article.

Theory to practice: narratives of place and character

Maupassant and Ford share a strong sense of place as a visual experience. In *The Soul of London* (1905), Ford is as much concerned with moments of temporary vision, with what it means to perceive, as he is with places as fixed objects. What we see is a product of how we see it: thus he writes not just of London, but of how we enter it, the movement rather than the object. Take the Mitcham bus to town and

> You find brown, black or red trams waiting for you in a very narrow Square of old, but not ancient, untidy, and probably 'doomed' shops. Rows of the small, red-brick, slate-roofed houses, with bow-windows to suggest a certain superiority, run at right angles to the highway. They whirl round and out of sight, as the tram advances, each moving vista ending in the screen of distant trees. Suddenly, on the highroad itself, there is a long block of buildings, white, and with green shutters above, liver-coloured brick below, slate roofed, rather startling and rather impressive.[9]

This whirling kaleidoscope of strong and precise impressions enforces a visual world locked into time: 'You live only with your eyes, and they lull you. So Time becomes manifest like a slow pulse, the world stands still'.[10] Max Saunders writes of these perceptions as frozen in time, 'moments of intense visual arrest'. The paradox is that, as with pictorial examples of impressionism such as Monet's series of paintings of the west front of Rouen cathedral, one receives a strong sense of fluctuation, and yet also of stillness.[11]

The visuality of impressionism is rightly acknowledged. Conrad's preface to *The Nigger of the Narcissus* is oft quoted: 'My task which I am trying to achieve is, by the power of the written word, to make you hear, to make you feel – it is, before all, to make you *see!*'[12] Dowell, recounting Ashburnham's description of one of the climactic moments of *The Good Soldier*, Florence's discovery of Nancy and himself on a bench outside the Casino, observes wryly, 'But the fellow talked like a cheap novelist. Or like a very good novelist for the matter of that, if it's the business of a novelist to make you see things clearly' (*GS* 76).

This emphasis comes straight out of Maupassant. For example, in a letter of 17 July 1885 or 1886, he praises the poet Maurice Vaucaire for having 'a mind which is highly receptive to impressions' and observes that 'everything depends on seeing'.[13] In his travel essay, *Sur l'Eau* (1888), set in Ford's favourite Provence, Maupassant describes the ideal novelist as an eye which takes in everything within its range: 'His eye is like a pump which mops up everything, like the hand of a thief always at work. Nothing escapes him; he gathers things up unceasingly; he picks up the movements, the gestures, the intentions, everything which passes and occurs in front of him; he gathers up the smallest words, the smallest actions, the smallest things'.[14] The eye is the active observer of a world in constant movement. And yet, as *Sur L'Eau* goes on to demonstrate, at key moments the eye fixes on an image of transfixing stillness, of arresting meaning. Maupassant, travelling alone, encounters a pair of lovers and gives a clear description of the woman, 'very elegant and simple with her grey travelling dress and her daring and coquettish felt hat'. Later Maupassant sees them at mealtime in the inn, talking apart as if secretly; then again on the sea-shore at night, when they have shrunk visually to 'silhouettes', 'shadows standing side by side' (*Sur L'Eau* 67-9). The movement is from day to night, certainty to obscurity. Maupassant's ability to picture them recedes as the light fades and he senses their separateness from him. The perceptions are precise, but subject both to the shifting of time, as night turns the lovers into figures of mystery, and to subjectivity, for Maupassant's sense of his own isolation is confirmed by his changing views of the lovers. The process actually shapes his own solitariness, the darkness within him.

Compare the scene in *The Good Soldier* which provokes Dowell's comment on seeing things clearly. Dowell summons up an image of Florence appearing behind Ashburnham and Nancy as they sit on the public bench in darkness, the Casino orchestra playing the Rakocsy march: 'there you have the picture, the immensely tall trees, elms most of them, towering and feathering away up into the black mistiness that trees seem to gather about them at night; the silhouettes of those two upon the seat; the beams of light coming from the Casino, the woman all in black peeping with fear behind the tree-trunk' (*GS* 77). The mixture of detail and obscurity fixes the moment as precise and dramatic, and yet expresses distance. Edward seems to be parting from Florence, and Florence from Dowell, as the trees recede into mistiness. Yet really this scene objectifies Dowell's own alienation from light and meaning. The blackness of night is ignorance, loss and – in Florence's case – death.

'Night' is both title and central symbol of one of the Maupassant stories translated by Elsie Martindale and noted by Ford in his preface to the volume. The *conte* is about the narrator's love for night, a love founded on a perception of the emptiness at its heart, as he acknowledges in Dowell-like tones: 'Death', reads Elsie Martindale's translation, 'lurks continually in the passion of a violent love. But how can I relate clearly what is happening to me? How can I explain even that I am able to tell you my tale at all? I do not know; I know nothing; I only know that it is so'.[15] The narrator then walks through Paris, becoming more and more disorientated by a loss of certainty in the deep darkness. His aimlessness and gradual loss of any notion of where he is produce in him a feeling of emptiness. His isolation creates fear, ending on an image of the almost frozen, almost dead Seine into which the narrator dips his hands: tactile contact in the absence of visual awareness, but only confirming him in the grip of an enclosing chill of mortality.

Characters in the fiction of both Maupassant and Ford are frequently associated with blackness. At the end of *Pierre et Jean*, Pierre, having discovered that his brother was actually the child of a relationship between his mother and a friend of the family, decides to leave his home. His mother visits him on board the ship that is to take him away from her. The discovery of her adultery has completely changed his life, disorientating him from normal perception of his habitual life. His vision now of his mother is stark and precise:

> He looked at her. She was dressed in black, as if she were in mourning, and he suddenly noticed that her hair, still grey the previous month, was now turning completely white.[16]

The sudden perception of her aging is his recognition of his distance from her, the death of his youth and youthful idealism, his parting from himself as well as from her.

With such a scene we may compare those moments of intense and stark visuality in *The Fifth Queen Crowned*, as the atmosphere closes in around the characters: Mary writing at her book-strewn table in a room whose bright and rich colours set off her black dress, or Katherine at her trial, 'a black figure in the bluish and stony gloom of the hall with the high roof a great way above her head'.[17] The static intensity of such moments renders them types of narrative metonymy, the picture – like that of Florence in darkness overhearing the conversation of Ashburnham and Nancy – fixing an image of the event or character as representative of the larger novel. A particularly striking example occurs in the last paragraph of *Privy Seal*, where

Katherine's response to the King's declaration is narrated as gesture, silent action:

> The light of the candles threw their locked shadows along the wall and up the ceilings. Her head fell back, her eyes closed, so that she seemed to be dead and her listless hands were open in her skirts.[18]

In its passivity, Katherine's gesture of acceptance merges into a gesture of defeat, proleptic of her eventual fate. The sharp image is that of a figure silhouetted against her own departure into shadow.

Maupassant and *The Good Soldier*
Some instances of Maupassant's impressionism take him close to the heart of *The Good Soldier*'s very theme. In 'Miss Harriet', published in *Le Gaulois* on 9 July 1883 and chosen by Maupassant as the title story of an 1884 collection, the narrator, a painter, is a guest at a Normandy inn, where a reclusive English spinster is also staying. The picture he is painting fascinates her, and he begins to observe in her something that he cannot understand:

> Her eye had a kind of madness, a mystical and violent madness [. . . .] It seemed to me that a battle was taking place inside her, her heart struggling against an unknown force [. . . .] What do I know? What do I know?[19]

The narrator, from this Dowell-like confession of ignorance as to what is going on in another's heart, rapidly adopts the Ashburnham role, flirting one evening with the servant-girl Céleste. He kisses her as the shadows of night fall beneath the trees, and then turns round with the sensation of someone watching. The silent observer is Miss Harriet, 'motionless as if looking at a ghost. Then she disappeared into the night'.[20] The next day her dead body is found in a well.

As in the scene when Florence overhears Edward's declaration to Nancy outside the casino, the dark trees form the setting for a moment of blinding revelation. The light of awful knowledge gleams in the dark ignorance of their lives, like the white hair set against the black dress of Pierre's aging mother. This is the 'picture' which defines the vision of the present moment. Dowell comments that Florence 'must have got it in the face, good and strong' (*GS* 77) before rushing back to the hotel to commit suicide.

The most striking instances occur in the novel to which Ford himself draws our attention. *Fort Comme la Mort* narrates how a man falls in love with young girl who occupies an ambiguously close relationship with him. Another painter, Olivier Bertin, after a long-lasting relationship with Anne, countess of Guilleroy, falls in love with her daughter.[21] The Livre de Poche editor, Marie-Claire Bancquart, comments that Bertin's feelings for Annette are close to incestuous because of the quasi-paternal situation he occupies towards the girl.[22] Maupassant had already written a provocative little story about incest called 'M. Jocaste', published in *Gil Blas* on 23 January 1883. A young man, Pierre Martel, becomes the lover of the wife of another, older man. She becomes pregnant, but dies in giving birth to a daughter. The suspicious husband brings the child up in secret, and Martel makes his separate way in the world. When, years later, he learns of the death of the husband, Martel looks for his daughter. At his first sight of her, he is stunned by her appearance, seeing in her the image of his lover: 'It was her! She was the same age, had the same eyes, the same hair, was the same height, had the same smile, the same voice'. Obsessed by her, 'loving her in memory of the other woman',[23] he yields to the desire to become her lover.

In *Fort Comme la Mort*, Bertin meets the countess through being commissioned to paint a portrait of her. He later finds her daughter Annette – little Anne – the image of this portrait. She seems to resemble the portrait more than she does her living mother: the daughter is the youth rather than the middle-age of her mother, the latter highlighting by contrast the former. Bertin's perception of the resemblance between Annette and the portrait encapsulates the nature of impressionism as both centrally revealing of idea and as itself complex in significance. The picture of Mme de Guilleroy fixes her in a precise moment, that of her first appearance in Bertin's studio:

> Her narrow black dress made her look very slim, gave her a young and serious look, however much this was contradicted by her smiling face illuminated by her fair hair. (*FCM* 69)

This image of innocence is also the sign of her ultimate defeat, for its youthful beauty will become that of the new generation, the child of six who comes into the studio with the count while Bertin is engaged on the portrait. The portrait's beauty will be recreated in the living Annette. Years later, the countess leaves Paris on account of her mother's death. Bertin, desperate to see her, travels to the country and is met at the station by Annette, who is dressed in black because of her grandmother's death. At the sight of her, Bertin is taken aback, as he exclaims on meeting his lover:

> She is your portrait which I painted, she is my portrait! It's you, just as when I met you long ago .... When I saw the little girl standing on the platform just now, dressed all in black, with the light of her hair around her face, my blood froze. (*FCM* 186)

Just as, back in his studio years ago, her mother's black dress had set off her face 'illuminated by her fair hair', so Annette's beauty is that of youth set against darkness. Light is set into relief by darkness, as the light from the casino illuminates Nancy's face beneath the dark trees of the park, and the candles, when Bertin sits at table with mother and daughter, shed golden light onto Annette's face.[24] Death highlights beauty, as the death of Bertin's love for the countess sets in relief the birth of his love for her daughter.

As in *The Good Soldier*, the heart is a motif which is both the subject and the mystery of *Fort Comme la Mort*. At the climax of the book, the countess forces Bertin to confess the love for Annette which he had until then himself only half recognised, and consoles him by saying, 'It's the fault of our hearts which have not grown old'. Bertin seeks to explain to her and to himself this repetition of the past in the present: 'I loved you as much as one could love a woman. I love her as I did you, since she is you; but this love has become irresistible, destructive, stronger than death' (*FCM* 284-5). On his death-bed after an accident which may have been an attempt at suicide, Bertin orders the countess to burn her letters to him. For her, this is like burning their two hearts, and, in the midst of the fire, they see what look like drops of blood coming 'from the very heart of the letters' (*FCM* 301-3). The fire is their passion, but also its death, lighting up both the figure of the countess, still in mourning for her mother, and the dying man: light surrounds black, like the blond hair which is set off by the black dress in the portrait.

As black is the colour of night, departure and death, so blue is the colour of day, light and life, as both exciting and perilous. Blue is the dominant colour of Maupassant's Provence, his landscape of vitality and intense experience. This is the marine world of Maupassant's travel writing, that Mediterranean coast where the sea scenes in Ford's *The Rash Act* take place and where Maupassant sets *Sur L'Eau* and the shorter 'Blanc et Bleu', which was published in *Gil Blas* in 1885. In these works, as in such celebrated *nouvelles* as 'Une partie de campagne' (1881), Maupassant is fascinated by the boat as movement, the sea as the trail of one's life. 'Blanc et Bleu' opens with a description of his boat, white with a blue streak along its side, sailing calmly on the deep blue sea, 'a transparent, liquid blue' (*Sur l'Eau* 183). As he sails along the coast he sees the vast white and menacing Alps, rearing up into the sky 'with every stroke of the oar which beat the blue water' (*Sur L'Eau* 185-6). The blue of the sea, the white of the snow, are both attractive and dangerous, the elements of human pleasure and human peril.

As a moment of perception of beauty and yet imminent danger, we may compare the scene in *The Rash Act* when Henry Martin luxuriates in the stillness of his becalmed boat before the arrival of the storm:

The sunlight grew whiter and more white. The day hung breathless. The sea was like a looking-glass: infinitely blue and getting bluer and ever more blue against the bright green of the promontory.[25]

As element is reflective of element, so the scene acts as a mirror for Henry's feelings. As he anticipates his suicide, his entry into eternity, the blue of the sea recedes into infinity, like images becoming ever smaller in reflecting mirrors. The moment of stasis fixes an image of life and its end. With sudden violence, the stillness is broken by the approaching storm, which turns the sea into an opaque chocolate colour and provokes Henry into instinctive, life-saving action. The still moment is at the same time the turning-point of the story.

Blue is also the colour of the very medium of visuality, of impression, the eye. A dramatic moment of narrative metonymy in *Fort Come la Mort* occurs when Bertin is staying with Anne and Annette at their country house. As the three of them walk through the countryside, Bertin offers to have a brooch made for Annette of precious stones in whatever colour she would like. She chooses the colour of the cornflowers she sees ('les bleuets'). Bertin, holding each by an arm, is trapped between them and sees 'their identical blue eyes, with small black dots, looking up at him' (FCM 200). Their blue eyes, the colour of daylight, of the opposite to night, reflect one another as will Bertin's love for each, which imprisons him, encloses him in a trap which only death can break.

So all those blue eyes in *The Good Soldier* (Florence, Leonora, Edward, Nancy, even the maid whom Edward comforts in the train) are both immensely attractive and strangely inscrutable to the observing Dowell, whose own eyes remain hidden from us. For example, Dowell remembers one vivid picture of Florence in her blue figured silk dress, with her broad Leghorn hat tied with a silk blue scarf: 'Yes, that is how I most exactly remember her, in that dress, in that hat, looking over her shoulder at me so that the eyes flashed very blue – dark pebble blue' (*GS* 22). The image combines attraction, self-consciousness and hardness. At Marburg, when Leonora looks Dowell straight in the eyes after Florence has laid one finger on

Ashburnham's wrist and shattered the world for ever, Dowell has for a moment 'the feeling that those two blue discs were immense, were overwhelming, were like a wall of blue that shut me off from the rest of the world' (*GS* 38). Blue is the colour of clarity, but also for Dowell of blankness, the imperceptibility of that which attracts, repulsion and attraction evenly balanced and irresolvable.

Thus Dowell associates blue with the calm sea which, like that which gives way to the storm in *The Rash Act*, represents a moment whose certainty sustains the white purity of human relationships:

> We were, if you will, one of those tall ships with the white sails upon a blue sea, one of those things that seem the proudest and the safest of all the beautiful and safe things that God has permitted the mind of men to frame. (*GS* 11)

The moment, one which appears to last for more than nine years, will vanish in four crashing days. This image, simultaneously of security and incipient danger, is recalled by Dowell's rhapsodic account of the eighteen-year-old Nancy's beauty:

> She was all in white, and so tall and fragile; and she had only just put her hair up, so that the carriage of her neck had that charming touch of youth and of unfamiliarity. Over her throat there played the reflection from a little pool of water, left by a thunderstorm of the night before, and all the rest of her features were in the diffused and luminous shade of her white parasol. Her dark hair just showed beneath her broad, white hat of pierced, chip straw; her throat was very long and leaned forward, and her eyebrows, arching a little as she laughed at some old-fashionedness in my phraseology, had abandoned their tense line. And there was a little colour in her cheeks and light in her deep blue eyes. And to think that that vivid white thing, that saintly and swan-like being – to think that ... Why, she was like the sail of a ship, so white and so definite in her movements. (*GS* 87)

The little pool of water is the small sign of the storm which will destroy Nancy's happiness, beauty and sanity, when the news of

Edward's suicide will reach her at Aden. The purity of Nancy's dress and parasol sets off her deep blue eyes, eyes which, when fixed in a 'dry and glassy' stare of madness, will fail to acknowledge the arrival of Dowell. In such intense moments of paradoxical vision, the external figures the internal, in its certainty and its uncertainty, and thus figures the very shape of the work of art.

NOTES

1. Ford Madox Ford, *The Good Soldier*, ed. Martin Stannard (New York and London: W. W. Norton & Company, 1995), pp. 261-2. Subsequent pages references given to this novel in the text are to this edition, abbreviated as *GS*.

2. Guy de Maupassant, *Contes et nouvelles*, Bibliothèque de la Pléiade, 2 vols (Paris: Gallimard, 1974), I, 809. Translations throughout are my own. References are given to the French texts so that readers can trace the quotations back to the originals.

3. Maupassant, *Contes et nouvelles*, vol. 1, p. 804.

4. Ford Madox Ford, 'On Impressionism', included in *GS*; p. 261.

5. Guy de Maupassant, *Pierre et Jean*, Livre de poche (Paris: Michel, n.d.), pp. 12-16.

6. Virginia Woolf, *Collected Essays*, 3 vols. (London: Hogarth Press, 1966), vol.1, p. 328.

7. *Stories from de Maupassant*, translated by E. M. with a preface by Ford Madox Ford (London: Jonathan Cape, 1927), p. 9.

8. *Stories from de Maupassant*, pp. 16-17.

9. Ford Madox Ford, *The Soul of London*, ed. Alan G. Hill (London: Dent, 1995), p. 36.

10. *The Soul of London*, p. 80.

11. Max Saunders, *Ford Madox Ford. A Dual Life*, 2 vols (Oxford: Oxford University Press, 1996), vol. 1, pp. 167-8.

12. Reprinted in *GS* 255.

13. Maupassant, *Contes et nouvelles*, vol. 1, p. xxxi.

14. *Sur L'Eau, Oeuvres Complètes de Guy de Maupassant*, vol. 21 (Paris: Conard, 1908), p. 30. Subsequent references to this edition are given in the text.

15. *Stories from de Maupassant*, pp. 211-12.

16. Maupassant, *Pierre et Jean*, p. 248.

17. Ford Madox Ford, *The Fifth Queen*, introduced by A. S. Byatt (Oxford: Oxford University Press, 1984), pp. 448, 585.

18. *The Fifth Queen*, p. 413.

19. Maupassant, *Contes et nouvelles*, vol.1, pp. 888-9.

20. Maupassant, *Contes et nouvelles*, vol. 1, p. 891.

21. The subject of male capacity for multiple loves, for polygamous desires, is recurrent in Maupassant. For example, 'La Rempailleuse' from *Contes de la Bécasse*, translated by Elsie Martindale as 'The Chair-Mender' and mentioned by Ford in his second 'Impressionism' article as well as in his preface to the translation, opens with a discussion of this issue: 'Most of the men maintained that the passion of love, like an illness, may attack the same person several times; and that it may bring him even to death's door, if an insurmountable obstacle opposes its course.' (*Stories from de Maupassant*, p. 79.)

22. Guy de Maupassant, *Fort Comme la Mort*, introduction et notes de Marie-Claire Bancquart (Paris: Librairie Générale Française, 1989) – henceforth *FCM*, p. 22.

23. Maupassant, *Contes et nouvelles*, vol. 1, p. 719.

24. *Fort Comme la Mort*, p. 189. At this stage Bertin remains ignorant of his growing feelings: 'Dieu! qu'elle est jolie en noir!' he exclaims naively to the comtesse.

25. Ford Madox Ford, *The Rash Act* (Manchester: Carcanet, 1982), p. 194.

THE EPISTEMOLOGICAL MALAISE OF THE NARRATOR CHARACTER IN FORD, CONRAD, PIRANDELLO AND SVEVO[1]

Vita Fortunati

Introduction

In the complex panorama of the early twentieth-century novel, I would like to trace an imaginary line that links Ford Madox Ford and Joseph Conrad to two Italian writers, Luigi Pirandello and Italo Svevo. What I want to suggest is that, although they came from very different historical and political environments (Edwardian England for Ford and Conrad, and Giolittian Italy for Pirandello and Svevo), they all anticipate some fundamental innovations in modernist fiction. And even if they lived in the same historical period, these writers never met, the only trace of Ford's possible knowledge of Pirandello's work being in the chronological table of *The March of Literature* (1938), his history of world literature, where the works of the Sicilian author are mentioned. These writers show surprising epistemological similarities, particularly in the central theme of many of their works, namely the conflict between appearance and reality, and in the use of the multiple point of view, the time-shift and the stream of consciousness.

The need for new narrative techniques and for a 'new form' comes for all these writers from the realization that modern life is chaotic, complex and heterogeneous: the faith in an ordered external world where rational knowledge is possible is replaced by the understanding that life is indeed elusive, multifaceted and ultimately unintelligible. What was once defined, organized and whole is replaced by the undefined, the disorganized, the fragmented. These writers are profoundly aware of the epistemological crisis which pervades their century: it is a malaise that leads them to revise realistic fiction altogether and develop a new kind of narrative which

Pirandello defined as 'romanzo da fare' (work in progress) and Ford and Conrad called the 'New Novel'. [2]

I will discuss the discomfort, that epistemological malaise which the narrator characters share: Dowell in Ford's *The Good Soldier*, Marlow in Conrad's *Heart of Darkness*, Serafino Gubbio in Pirandello's *Quaderni di Serafino Gubbio* and Zeno in Svevo's *La coscienza di Zeno*. All four novels were published between 1898, when in the pages of *Blackwood's Magazine* Conrad's novel appeared serialised in three parts, and 1923 when Svevo's novel was published. The characters of these novels are emblematic symbols of that malaise which is a recurring feature in many twentieth century novels – a malaise whose main features are loneliness, neurosis, inertia and lack of communication or, in other words, alienation.

Heart of Darkness records Conrad's search for a narrative strategy which is able to tell the truth in its complexity. From this need, in turn, derives the structure of the novel: an anonymous narrator remembers the occasion and the scene of the narration, thus introducing Marlow's character who filters other people's experiences, tales and points of view. Marlow is no longer an ordinary sailor; he is, above all, a man, who, like Dowell and Serafino Gubbio, has undertaken a painful, cognitive journey in the attempt to study the complex struggles of the human soul:

> Do you see the story? Do you see anything? It seems to me I am trying to tell you a dream – making a vain attempt, because no relation of a dream can convey the dream-sensation, that commingling of absurdity, surprise, and bewilderment in a tremor of struggling revolt, that notion of being captured by the incredible which is the very essence of dreams. [3]

One of the novel's most evident aspects is the frequent despair with which the narrator voices his inability to express through language an otherwise untellable experience. The text is full of uncertainties: many instances of 'perhaps', 'who knows', 'it seems', 'I don't know'. The human heart is obscure, dark and complex; man experiences only brief moments of illumination in which his ability to perceive reality is enhanced. Conrad's illuminations anticipate Joyce's epiphanies. There are brief moments in which the subject can catch the essence of objects and their ultimate meaning.

In all his novels, but especially in *Heart of Darkness*, Conrad discusses the inadequacy of language and of narrative devices in order to convey the horror and the anguish that exceed rationality. Exclamations, gestures, unfinished sentences, hints and sighs, all convey the exceptional nature of the experience – an experience that is so radical and extreme that it cannot be told:

> You can't understand. How could you? – With solid pavement under your feet, surrounded by kind neighbours, ready to cheer you or to fall on you, stepping delicately between the butcher and the policeman, in the holy terror of scandal and gallows and lunatic asylums – how can you imagine what particular region of the first ages a man's untrammelled feet may take him into by the way of solitude – utter solitude without a policeman – by the way of silence, where no warming voice of a kind neighbour can be heard whispering a public opinion? These little things make all the great difference. [4]

Also in Svevo's novels, which are closely linked with the new European fiction, characters from Alfonso Nitti in *Una Vita* to Emilio Brentano in *Senilità* and Zeno Cosini in *La Coscienza di Zeno* suffer from the twentieth century malaise: inertia, apathy, the inability to catch time.[5] In a brilliant article on Svevo[6] Claudio Magris states that already from its title, *Senilità*, the novel conveys an existential and physical fatigue or, better, the awareness of the fatigue which pervades European culture and bourgeois intellectuals. Old age becomes for Svevo a metaphor of the decay of a society whose protagonist is the apathetic intellectual who gives into indolence – the European malaise of which French and Russian writers had given memorable descriptions and that Svevo knew so well.[7]

Svevo's Zeno and Ford's Dowell belong to that group of pathological characters Lukács talks about.[8] These are characters who are incapable of living, whose life slips under their feet – characters who are inherently unable to catch time. They live only in the present. Svevo's novels, as G. De Benedetti has rightly said, are a 'slow but continuous succession of present-time moments'.[9] This is one way in which Svevo's novels differ from Proust's. For the French writer the recovery of the past is a totalizing experience; it is salvation from time; for Svevo, on the other hand, the recovery of the past is a means to enjoy the present, to use it.

Both Dowell and Zeno are examples of what Wayne Booth has defined as 'unreliable narrators'.[10] Both Ford and Svevo deal in their novels with the representation of a lie – a feature that becomes particularly complicated when he who narrates the story lies even if he swears he is telling the truth. Svevo lucidly depicts a narrator who lies, not because he uses a 'foreign language', nor because he wants to lie, but because he is confessing himself. That a confession, despite the good intentions of the person who confesses, is of itself false is a widely accepted truth in the twentieth century. Kafka, for example, wrote that 'Confessions and lies are the same. To confess one needs to lie. What one is, cannot be expressed, because one is like that; one can communicate but what we are not, that is, a lie'.[11] Svevo has, therefore, created a liar, an evasive, insidious and deceitful character, but his greatest merit lies in the fact that he has permeated the official confession, justification, defense/accusation with a hidden discourse. I would argue that, within *La coscienza di Zeno*, it is possible to a find a diffused and disorganized 'psychopathology of everyday life'. Svevo, then, makes use of psychoanalysis to solve the complex issue of the representation of lies in a narrative where there is no longer an omniscient narrator – rather, as we have seen, the story is told by 'an old liar who writes'. Like Ford's characters, Svevo's are inept men whose ineptitude is the psychological form of their displacement, of their split from the actions they perform or the words they say.

In these novels, reality is thus refitted into a mosaic of subjective visions; it is no longer what it appears to be, but it is the result of the juxtaposition of many points of view that clash and shed light on one another. It is precisely this technique of multiple points of view that produces an 'open' novel. The novel has only an apparent end, since questions remain unanswered for the reader, who finds himself inevitably involved in the disconcerting dilemmas of the various characters. The story does not come to an end precisely because Ford's, Svevo's and Pirandello's characters escape enclosure into rigid, stable and determined forms. The reader can never give a definite, unequivocal answer to a character's questions because it would mean the closure or definition of that character through some precise motive; these novels' characters, on the other hand, 'live' through this very multiplicity of questions and motives.

My focus is now on a detailed comparison between Pirandello's early novel, *Si gira*, which was published in 1915,[12] and *The Good Soldier* (1915) by Ford Madox Ford, which represents the best example of the new narrative techniques that Ford theorized, together with Joseph Conrad, during their collaboration (the years between 1898 and 1909). The narrative material of these two novels appears to resist 'tellability', being arranged in successive layers, continuous flashes forward and back, as well as tales-within-the-tale. Serafino Gubbio and John Dowell are two narrating voices of an 'affair', a plot, an 'arruffata matassa', as Pirandello defined it, of passions, betrayals and deaths; two narrating voices which dramatically express their awareness of the extreme relativity of their own points of view, since any one character acts on the basis of personal reasons which do not coincide with those of the other characters.

Both Dowell's and Serafino's narrations are continuously interrupted by sentences aimed to question the best way of relating facts, underlining a new relativistic conception of the world which needs a multiple point of view strategy. Accordingly, these two novels are structured on a fragmented time scheme which follows the flow of recollections that passes through the narrator's mind. By abandoning linear plots, Pirandello's and Ford's narrative writing mirrors existential disorder and chaos, moving forwards and backwards in time and space, following the flow of thoughts, mediations and reasoning of the writing self. Like Gide's *Les Faux-Monnayeurs*, both *Quaderni* and *The Good Soldier* record the efforts of the author who tries to build up a novel. It is precisely in the course of his search that the narrating self realizes that the novel escapes him and continuously reproduces itself as work in progress, that it might settle again in one, a hundred thousand or even no ways – to paraphrase the title of Pirandello's famous novel.

Thus, both novels show all the symptoms of a tension which was to be at the core of modernist writing: the tension deriving from the author's awareness that the creation of a novel is a problematic act. This dilemma of how to build up a novel gives way to a 'romanzo da fare', a work in progress that expresses the struggle between the search for a form and the awareness that life is, to say it with Ford's own words, 'so extraordinary, so hazy, so tenuous ... that it has become almost impossible to see any pattern in the carpet.' [13]

Similarly, Pirandello, at the end of his essay *L'Umorismo*, stresses again his gnoseologic relativism which frustrates the cognitive ambitions of the mind:

> Life is a continuous flux which we try to stop, to fix in stable forms that are determined within and outside ourselves [. . . .]The forms in which we try to stop, to fix for us this continuous flux, are the concepts and the ideals we would like coherently to stick to; all the fictions we created, on the other hand, are the condition and the state in which we tend to stabilize ourselves [. . . .] In some troubled moments, when the fictitious forms are hit by the flux, they miserably crumble. [14]

An analysis of the features of the two narrators, Serafino Gubbio and John Dowell, reveals the cognitive relativism characterizing the two writers' poetics and underlines both analogies and differences between them. Serafino Gubbio and John Dowell are dominated by alienation which derives from their inability to know their own identity; they are passive characters who do not act but, rather, are acted upon.

They are spectators, witnesses or, rather, *voyeurs* of the story they narrate. Both Dowell and Serafino Gubbio show a dissociated and divided inner self. On the one hand, they are passive witnesses (in this respect, Serafino Gubbio's job is emblematic, since he is a cameraman, the one who shoots and must be impassive):

> I study people while they are intent in ordinary tasks; I want to see if I can find in others what I lack when I set out to do something: the certainty, that is, that they understand what they are about to do. At first sight, it seems to me that many possess this certainty from the way in which they look at or greet one another, lost in their tasks or in their desires. But then, if I look at them in the eyes, with my own silent and willing eyes, a shadow passes over them. [15]

On the other hand, they play the philosopher, they judge the petty philistinism, and they criticize the sexual taboos of their society and the other characters, thus underlining the contradictory and multifaceted meaning of events. Thus, there is a contrast between sloth, hypocrisy, naiveté and the moral and sexual inertia which have characterized their part in the story and the clear conscience with which they judge society and the other characters. John Dowell and Serafino Gubbio end by being inevitably contradictory, a kind of blurred image of the authors themselves, thus revealing an almost imperceptible biographical identification. [16]

The stories narrated by Serafino and Dowell are not only their personal stories, but also those of the other characters. It is an analytic point of view that takes reality to pieces and, by fragmenting it, demystifies its false shapes and appearances. This aspect is clearly evident in the opening lines of the two novels. Serafino Gubbio says: 'It is always possible to go beyond. You can't or don't want to see it. But as soon as the "beyond" appears to my idle eyes, those eyes that observe you, you are confused, baffled or upset'.[17] And Dowell wonders: 'If for nine years I have possessed a goodly apple that is rotten at the core and discover its rottenness only in nine years and six months less four days, isn't true to say that for nine years I possessed a goodly apple?'[18]

The two novels are structured as an uneasy quest to reach the essence of reality. Pirandello's naturalistic need and Ford's impressionist need for objective representation turns into a desire to unmask the false 'values' and hypocritical behaviours of middle class society. As De Benedetti has said,[19] Pirandello's tragic expressionism becomes evident in the grotesque style he adopts to portray certain characters who appear ferociously ugly, revolting and disgusting, as is Simon Pau's case in *Quaderni*:

> He'd blow smoke out and then would remain still, listening to me with a wet, open mouth like an antique comic mask. His piggish, lively and cunning eyes looked like they had been trapped in the large, massive and rough face, the face of a naive but ferocious villain.[20]

The same deforming, grotesque point of view is used by Ford in certain descriptions, for example the episode in which Maisie Maidan's death is described, where his narrative impressionism, in its continuous search for the essence of reality, evolves towards a kind of expressionistic effect:

> [Leonora] had not cared to look round Maisie's rooms at first. Now, as soon as she came in she perceived, sticking out beyond the bed, a small pair of feet in high-heeled shoes. Maisie had died in the effort to strap up a great portmanteau. She had died so grotesquely that her little body had fallen forward into the trunk and it had closed upon her, like the jaws of a gigantic alligator [. . . .] Leonora lifted her up – she was the merest feather-weigh t– and laid her on the bed with her hair about her. She was smiling as if she had scored a goal in a hockey match. (*GS* 56)

278

The cognitive path followed by the two narrating voices goes through an awareness of the inescapable relativism of knowledge. At the end of the painful voyage in search of an inward understanding of the world, Serafino Gubbio and John Dowell must acknowledge and record the inevitable failure of knowledge itself to provide any univocal and reassuring certainty of what it is that regulates individual life, of what 'causes' can be said to lead to predictable and logical 'effects'.

After showing the epistemological malaise that runs through the characters of Ford's, Pirandello's and Svevo's novels, I would like to point to the differences between Ford's *The Good Soldier* and Pirandello's *I Quaderni di Serafino Gubbio operatore*. If a negative ending is common to both novels (Edward Ashburnham's suicide and Nancy's madness in *The Good Soldier*, Serafino's silence and the death of Vania Nestoroff and Aldo Nuti in *Quaderni*), Serafino, unlike Dowell, is characterized by a natural understanding, based on intelligence and human sympathy. Serafino expresses his need for understanding to the other characters by demonstrating intelligence and sympathy which, however, are constantly misunderstood and frustrated:

> I have always made an effort to go beyond my affections when judging others, to catch the noise of life, which is made mainly of crying rather than laughter, and to listen to as many sounds out of my feelings as I could.
> [21]

Serafino is the humorist-philosopher who, as Pirandello says: 'because of his essential, inner, process is bound to displace, *disarrange* and confuse' reality, thus unveiling the polyvalence and contradiction of facts.[22] However, the humorist-philosopher is also one who has an ironic detachment from reality and always sees the other side of things. At the same time he has also a strong 'sense of otherness' ('il sentimento del contrario'), that is a sense of personal and direct involvement, of understanding and empathy. Serafino's eyes are thus the compassionate filter of the 'odd phantasmagoria that is life':

> I wish never to speak; to contain everything and everyone in my silence – each cry, each smile; not to smile myself, I wouldn't be able to, nor to comfort the cry, I wouldn't know how; but so that each could find inside myself a tender pity for their pain and joy – a pity that would join them all, at least for a brief moment. [23]

Dowell, on the other hand, lacks this empathic understanding of the absurd destiny of the other characters, because he is completely concentrated on and absorbed by the paradoxical aspect of his story. *The Good Soldier* is permeated by a self-ironic approach to a tragic condition. In the end, this absurd character of an 'American millionaire' becomes aware of the fact that it is impossible to get to know things or, better, that the world is incomprehensible. The behaviour of 'good people' hides an unintelligible reality made of ruins and mourning, whose origin and meaning totally escape him. What remains is loneliness and an absurd and precarious fear: 'We are all so afraid, we are all so alone, we all so need from the outside the assurance of our own worthiness to exist' (GS 79-80).

Finally, I would like to discuss what I see as the basic difference between the two novels. The theatrical quality of Pirandello's narrative work is completely absent in Ford's novel, where, as we shall see, the oral aspect of the story prevails.[24] In fact, it is not by chance that the artistic fiction, clearly established and expressed by Dowell at the beginning of *The Good Soldier*, consists in imagining a narrator who tells the story to a friend (the 'silent reader')[25] in a natural way, as events come to his mind, without following a chronological order, but following instead the associative order of the mind caught in the act of remembering:

> So I shall just imagine myself for a fortnight or so at one side of the fireplace of a country cottage, with a sympathetic soul opposite me. And I

shall go on talking, in a low voice while the sea sounds in the distance and overhead the great black flood of wind polishes the bright stars. (*GS* 15)

As Simona Costa has recently noted, in her introduction to *Quaderni di Serafino Gubbio*, the work is deeply linked to the comedy *Ciascuno a suo modo*, published in 1924.[26] From the pages of *Quaderni* one can pass on to the stage of *Ciascuno a suo modo*, that, together with *Sei personaggi in cerca d'autore* (1921) and *Questa sera si recita a soggetto* (1929), makes up the trilogy of the 'Teatro nel teatro' ('play within the play'). The connection between Pirandello's theatrical and narrative work is not only thematic (a story of passion, betrayals and death), but also philosophical. Both works centre on the theme of the subjectivity of reality, the motives of which cannot be known since they are subjected to the most various interpretations – that is, 'to each his own', again to quote one of Pirandello's titles.

However, the aspect that most tightly links these two works is the deep need for renovation of structure. If *Quaderni* demystifies and denies the naturalistic *romanzo fatto* ('finished novel'), *Ciascuno a suo modo* contains a stronger provocation: the story's declared impossibility to tell any further produces incompleteness in the dramatic composition of the text which closes the second act. The *romanzo da fare*, the work in progress has thus turned into drama-in-progress: what matters, here, is not the actors' performance, nor the meaning of real life, but the unmasking of the mechanism, of the device, and the dismantling of the illusions of the scene and of the audience. The theatrical quality of the novel *Quaderni* is not only recognizable in the figurative language of the dialogues, but also and above all in Serafino's soliloquies. In fact, as Edoardo Ferrario has noted, these are full of vocative and deictic elements, such as, for example, 'i signori' ('you sirs') addressed by Serafino in his diaries, and the 'ecco qua' ('here it is').[27] Both elements imply the involvement of a reader-audience who is continuously addressed.

This intense theatrical quality is completely absent in *The Good Soldier*: its intensely aural disposition and meta-narrative quality turn Ford's novel into an artificial and sophisticated product. Thus, the continuous appeals to the reader in Ford's narrative imply, as in Pirandello's work, the narrator's precise will to involve the reader in the search for the truth of the characters' sad story. However, in Ford's novel, this game is subtler, because between Ford-Dowell and the reader there is an empathic complicity based on an implied, silent pact between the two; on the one hand, the reader is aware that what is being read constitutes a fiction; on the other, the author hides this fiction by means of a series of deliberate and astute rhetorical devices that can give the reader 'the illusion of reality'. It is almost a game based on tricks, ambiguous statements, concealment and revelations that bring the reader, on the one hand to be led and manipulated by the author, and, on the other, to be able to re-order the events of the story.

In conclusion, beyond the differences that I have tried to delineate, these two novels represent the end of the naturalistic novel in the panorama of early twentieth-century literature. In these novels, the function of the narrator character or of the playwright-interpreter becomes problematic, not only because life has become too complex and relentless, but also because the principle of the narrator's authority has begun to decline.

NOTES

1. Part of this essay appeared in *Journal of Anglo-Italian Studies*, 3 (1993), 180-9, with the title 'Cognitive Relativism and the Narrative Technique of Multiple Points of

View in Luigi Pirandello and Ford Madox Ford'. An earlier version of the whole essay appeared in *Interpreting/Translating European Modernism: A Comparative Approach*, ed. Elena Lamberti (Bologna: COTEPRA and the University of Bologna, 2001).

2. My attempt to find a shared 'Zeitgeist' in the European writers of the turn of the century situates itself in a line of critical work in comparative studies. I am thinking of G. De Benedetti's study *Il romanzo del Novecento* (Milan, 1971), M. Lavagetto's work on the relationship between Svevo, Joyce and Proust and the volume by G. Mazzacurati *Pirandello nel romanzo europeo* (Bologna, 1987). In particular, Mazzacurati has convicingly shown to what extent the Sicilian writer is involved in the European avant-garde debate on the 'romanzo da fare'.

3. Joseph Conrad, *Heart of Darkness* (Torino: Mursia, 1978), p. 86.

4. *Ibid.,* pp. 144-6.

5. In Svevo's last novel, *Il Vecchione*, the protagonist states: 'I don't know how to move with certainty in time' (my translation) in *Romanzi. Italo Svevo*; a cura di M. Lavagetto, con la collaborazione di F. Amigoni, N. Palmieri e A. Stara (Torino: Einaudi-Gallimard, 1993).

6. Claudio Magris, 'La scrittura e la vecchiaia selvaggia: Italo Svevo', in *Anello di Clarisse* (Torino: Einaudi, 1984).

7. Compare the beginning of *Senilità* where the dispassionate eye of the writer thus describes Emilio Brentani, the character who wanders along the rainy streets in Trieste: 'He faced life passively; he avoided all dangers as well as joyful moments and happiness. He was 35 and felt in his soul the lack of love and pleasure, already the bitterness deriving from not having experienced love, and in his brain he experienced a great fear of himself and of his weak nature, a weakness rather suspected than experienced. [...] He lived by waiting impatiently for something that was to come from his brain, something that was supposed to come from outside – fortune, success – as if the time of energy hadn't disappeared'. Italo Svevo, *Senilità* (Firenze: Frassinelli, 1995) pp. 5-6. (My translation.)

8. G. Lukács, M. Bachtin e altri, *Problemi di teoria del romanzo* (Torino: Einaudi, 1976); Georg Lukács, *Studies in European Realism*; with an Introduction by Alfred Kazin (London: Hillway, 1950).

9. G. De Benedetti, *Il romanzo del Novecento* (Milan:Garzanti, 1971).

10. Wayne Booth, *The Rhetoric of Fiction* (Chicago: University of Chicago Press, 1961).

11. M. Lavagetto, 'Introduzione' a *Romanzi. Italo Svevo* (Torino: Einaudi-Gallimard, 1993).

12. The book was then reprinted in 1924 with the title changed into *Quaderni di Serafino Gubbio operatore*.

13. Ford Madox Hueffer, *Henry James. A Critical Study* (London: Martin Secker, 1914), p. 150.

14. Luigi Pirandello, *L'Umorismo* (Milano: Mondadori, 1986) p. 159. (My translation.)

15. Luigi Pirandello, *Quaderni di Serafino Gubbio operatore*, p. 4. (My translation.)

16. On the connections between Pirandello and Serafino, see G. De Benedetti, *op. cit.,* p. 275ff; on those between Ford and Dowell, see Alan Judd, *Ford Madox Ford* (London: Collins, 1990), and Max Saunders, *Ford Madox Ford: A Dual Life*, 2 vols (Oxford: Oxford University Press, 1996), vol. 1.

17. Luigi Pirandello *Quaderni di Serafino Gubbio operatore*. (My translation.)

18. Ford Madox Ford, *The Good Soldier*, ed. Martin Stannard (New York and London: W. W. Norton & Company, 1995), p. 12. Subsequent references to this edition appear parenthetically in the text using the abbreviation *GS*.

19. See G. De Benedetti, *Il romanzo del Novecento* (Milano: Garzanti, 1971).

20. Pirandello, *Quaderni di Serafino Gubbio operatore*, pp. 9-10. (My translation.)

21. Pirandello, *Quaderni di Serafino Gubbio operatore*, p. 65.

22. Pirandello, *L'Umorismo*, p. 57.

23. Pirandello, *Quaderni di Serafino Gubbio operatore,* p.91. (My translation.)

24. See Sondra J. Stang and Carl Smith, 'Music for a While: Ford's Compositions for Voice and Piano', *Contemporary Literature*, 30: 2 (Summer 1989), 183-224.

25. On the figure of the 'silent reader', see V. Fortunati, *Ford Madox Ford. Teoria e tecnica narrativa* (Bologna: Patron, 1975).

26. Simona Costa, 'Introduzione', Luigi Pirandello, *Quaderni di Serafino Gubbio*.

27. E. Ferrario, in S. Costa 'Introduzione', p. xxviii.

FORD MADOX FORD
AND THE UNNOTICEABLE THINGS

Paul Skinner

Halfway through *Some Do Not . . .*, Christopher Tietjens and
Valentine Wannop are approaching the disastrous end of their night
ride when Tietjens catches sight of Icklesham Church, just above
Mountby:

> Rising out of the mist on a fantastically green knoll, a quarter of a mile
> away, was an unnoticeable place of worship; an oak shingle tower roof
> that shone grey like lead; an impossibly bright weathercock, brighter than
> the sun. Dark elms all round it, holding wetnesses of mist.[1]

'Carefully examined', Ford wrote in the year of *Some Do Not . . .*'s
publication, 'a good – an interesting – style will be found to consist in
a constant succession of tiny, unobservable surprises'.[2] The only
business of style is 'to make work interesting', and a style interests
when 'it carries the reader along'. Conversely:

> *Too* startling words, however apt, *too* just images, too great displays of
> cleverness are apt in the long run to be as fatiguing as the most over-used
> words or the most jog-trot cadences. (*JC* 193)

How much does the reader, 'carried along', actually notice of the
paragraph first quoted? We might point to 'fantastically' as a 'tiny'
surprise. With its suggestion of caprice or fancy, it hints at an
observing, judicial consciousness, and 'impossibly' functions in the
same way. 'Dark elms all round it' economically affords naturalistic
grounds for the contrasted impression of extreme brightness, while
also completing the 'frame', in a modified chiasmus: the paragraph
begins and ends in mist, which encloses, both on the page and in the
'real' world, knoll and elm which, in turn, frame the actual building.

The phrase 'place of worship' is no mere circumlocution – the perceiving eye and mind register the 'worth-ship' not only of building but of context, *place*. The paragraph's ultimate return to its first amorphous element ('mist'), the choice of 'holding' and the grouped sibilants combine to imply a suspension, a lastingness. For Tietjens, this is indeed the case and, if we recall 'fantastically' once again, bearing in mind its root meaning of 'make visible', there are evident connections with the image of Bemerton which occurs part-way through *A Man Could Stand Up*–: 'the church that the dawn was at that moment wetly revealing' (*PE* 566).

The cadence of the paragraph is that of the speaking voice – but the actual diction? Is there – to recall Pound's words – 'nothing that you couldn't, in some circumstance, in the stress of some emotion, actually say'?[3] Such judgements are inescapably subjective – and hedged around with all manner of cultural assumptions – but I would say that yes, one *can* hear a voice, recounting the story of that moment, use all these words as Ford uses them, with the probable exception of 'unnoticeable'. Is this a tiny Fordian joke, that the word 'unnoticeable' is precisely that until we speak the passage aloud or otherwise focus our attention upon it? Tietjens notices that 'unnoticeable place of worship' because he is 'an exact observer' (*PE* 128), although he is also in a state of heightened awareness, having so recently experienced that 'all but irresistible impulse' towards Valentine (*PE* 137). To those who are not exact observers, such a place is indeed 'unnoticeable'; while to Tietjens it will serve as a talismanic image, a luminous and representative particular of England and 'Englishness'.

The significance of 'unnoticeable' is confirmed by both earlier and later textual instances. Tietjens recalls his first impression of Valentine as 'an unnoticeable young female who had announced herself as being a domestic servant, and wore a pink cotton blouse...' (*PE* 87), while, to Edith Ethel Duchemin, Tietjens himself is 'a large, clumsy, but otherwise unnoticeable being' (*PE* 92). In the important conversation with Sylvia early in Part Two of *Some Do Not. . .*, Tietjens alludes to the deaths of his two brothers and his sister: "'Unnoticeable people. But one can be fond of unnoticeable people...'".[4] Elsewhere, Ford recalled his conviction that 'you could employ the words "he said" as often as you like, accepting them as being unnoticeable, like "a", "the", "his", "her" or "very"' (*JC* 188). 'Unnoticeable' or – like those 'tiny surprises' – 'unobservable', then, but hardly unimportant; nor was it merely such little words but style in general: 'the first province of a style is to be unnoticeable', Ford remarked as late as *The March of Literature*.[5]

'[T]he first' province rather than 'the only'. Nevertheless, what does it mean to say that a style is 'unnoticeable', and to what end is such a style employed? To induce in us, as Ford often seems to suggest, the illusion that we are engaged with 'life' rather than reading a book? It was Ford's admired Flaubert who proposed style as a way of seeing.[6] And of being seen? *Le style, c'est l'homme*? 'I want to pass unnoticed in the crowd that life is', Ford wrote in 1914, 'because to be noticed interferes with my train of thought'.[7]

'Unnoticed' or 'unnoticeable': it seems odd to apply either word to Ford, so visible that he appears to crop up in every twentieth-century literary memoir we come across. Yet how often is it Ford the novelist or the poet, the writing self who produced those eighty books, rather than Ford the editor, the 'unreliable' raconteur, the party host, that self which recurs in courtrooms and German spas? Is the complex nature of that relationship between prosaic self and *prosateur* mirrored by the disparities between, say, the words on the page and the effects of the process of reading them? Because Valentine Wannop, like Icklesham Church, is unnoticeable yet *has been noticed*: by the author, the narrative voice, the character Tietjens and, finally, by the reader. Or consider:

> When other Bards sing mortal loud, like swearing,
> Like poor Dan Robin, thankful for your crumb,

289

If the wind lulls I try to get a hearing.

So Ford 'once wrote in a poem I never published', that small aside thus publishing it – on several occasions, in fact.[8] To place in a text is to publish, to make visible, to make noticeable: but how noticeable, exactly? A word on a page is there, may be seen and noted, just as an object is in the world and may be seen and noted. Yet, just as we look without seeing, so too we read without noting. Or rather, we note what we are prepared to note. And by prepared, I mean in both senses: not just willing – but also able, enabled.

We are enabled by our character, our history, above all, perhaps, by our education, that inexplicable, haphazard and always unfinished process. How we learn to read, yes, but we learn or relearn this many times. We may also be enabled by our foreknowledge of what we are about to read and, of course, our reasons for doing so.

One fact still often lost sight of in consideration of Ford's writings is the extent to which he utilizes the associational force of individual words and phrases, a force derived less from conventional usage, such as Eliot's 'swaddled' (indistinguishable in our culture from allusions to the Christ-child) than from instances of usage in the text itself.[9] Where it has been missed in Ford's work, it is generally because it has not been allowed for. Joyce is *that* sort of writer, as is Pound, and we study their works accordingly. Pound wrote once about 'a sort of counterpoint...in which sounds hang in the auditory memory'.[10] And, in Ford's work, those sounds are often, ostensibly, quite small and commonplace ones: *The Good Soldier*'s 'heart' and 'know' are probably the most familiar examples. At what point, after how many repetitions, in how many different local contexts, do we *begin to take notice*? It seems so simple: not mythological figures or historical allusions or complex images – just ordinary, quite unexceptional words. Yet each repetition, subtly placed and subtly different, carries with it that not quite conscious memory of each previous instance, and so on, back to the beginning of that book – or the one before.

And, with a greater familiarity with Ford's work, increasingly, we go forward, we go back. The fact is that literally scores of words and images can be tracked, instructively and often revealingly, through Ford's texts, just as they can be through *Ulysses* or *The Cantos*. Is this important? Yes, if it helps to refute charges that Ford was an habitually careless or slapdash writer; and yes, if it helps to persuade resistant readers of the remarkable coherence of his *oeuvre*. And yes, perhaps most of all, if it helps us to focus on Ford's ideas of writing and reading, and on the inextricable natures of these activities, or the nature, rather, of this duplex activity.

One of the most significant features of Ford's best work is his use of the time-shift. And his concern with the *effect* of this technique – *and* his concern for the reader – are, I think, indicated in *The Good Soldier* and *Parade's End* in comparable ways. Dowell's stated wish that he could 'put it down in diary form',[11] to somehow combat the maddening lack of co-operation displayed by both characters and chronology in the story taking shape beneath his pen, seems to foreshadow one of *Parade's End*'s most suggestive moments, that in which Tietjens attempts to state 'the facts of the story' in the form of a military report. The reader may seize upon this undertaking with eager relief: but it is short-lived. What the report – or the intention to write it – has left out of account is precisely the central feature of the experiences it seeks to order: the crises of perception, language, social and sexual relations, chronology and, indeed, history, which render conventional linear narrative both ineffectual and untrue (*PE* 345ff).

But Tietjens is also enacting the discovery of that endlessly intriguing and often frustrating phenomenon familiar to all – not just professional – writers: that however definite the image, or the memory, or the course of events may seem in your mind prior to writing, they cannot be carried over onto paper without being changed by the act – the process – of writing. Just so, the words on a page, definite and discrete as they seem, cannot be carried from text to reader without subtle changes being effected in and by the act of reading. Dowell and Tietjens, then, explicitly writing, explicitly notice the difficulties, or at least complexities, of the task in which we are engaged. They focus, that is, on effect and on process.

'We agreed', Ford writes of Conrad and himself, 'that the general effect of a novel must be the general effect that life makes on mankind' (*JC* 180). It is customary now to register profound unease at such apparently casual equating of art and life. Yet those two words, 'general' and 'effect', surely resist the interpretation put upon Ford's theories of novel-writing by more than one critic, that he seeks, or believes possible, some perfect verisimilitude. 'The general effect' – that is probably vague enough to signal anything one likes, and none of us can legislate for others as to its meaningful senses. Yet I shall propose one, in an attempt to focus attention on *how* we see: 'life' is odd, is bewildering, is deceptive, is ultimately mysterious. And we know this but there are tremendous pressures exerted upon us to act as though it were ordered, rational, explicable and largely predictable. So we tend, for the most part, to set aside that complex of tiny, unsolved mysteries, glimpses, dreams and disappearances, coincidences, snatches of overheard conversation which eerily echo our thoughts. But in some frames of mind, at some times of life, under some pressures of circumstance, we focus directly upon them – and the world shifts. In Ford's work, the world often shifts.

One of the anecdotes that most recurs to me when reviewing Ford's writings is that of Podmore's brother, whose special talent is to distract the mind in order to deceive the eye. Ford's example involves giving a box of matches to a friend and then talking so enthrallingly that you are able to take them from his hand without his being in the least conscious that the matches are gone. That is the trick of Impressionism, Ford adds, and we hardly need to substitute 'sympathetic listener' or 'reader' for that friend to get the point: talking on and on, in a low voice, while a reader loses his grasp on what he thought was safely held.[12] And, given Ford's way with puns, it seems reasonable to regard his use of the phrase 'matchless prose' a little warily.[13]

So John Dowell can say that 'You have the facts for the trouble of finding them' (*GS* 120) – a wonderful assertion in which almost every word needs to be weighed and questioned – this from an author who has always had for facts 'a most profound contempt'.[14] And it's not only the nature of 'a fact' that is at issue here: it is the plural, 'them'. Trouble arises less from deciding what is or is not 'a fact' than from the need of such 'facts' to share space – in our minds, on a page, in the world – with other such 'facts'. We should add that Ford's contempt does not extend to impressions, or, let us say, the impressions of facts. Because such impressions do much to furnish our minds. Furniture or *bric à brac*? '[H]aving no taste for bric a brac,' Ford wrote to Pound, 'you hate to have to read about this passion…But it is one of the main passions of humanity…You might really, just as legitimately object to renderings of the passion of LOVE, with which indeed the FURNITURE passion is strongly bound up…'.[15]

That 'furniture' connotes, yes, comfort and familiarity: it also stands between us and the contemplation of stark and naked space. And its very familiarity renders such 'furniture' oddly compliant, an accomplice in disorientation, when, for example, the mind becomes uneasy or disturbed. So Nancy Rufford regards with mounting panic the 'andirons with the brass flowers' and the burning logs, as her world shifts on its axis (*GS* 141). So, in our own minds, it is less the outlandish or the self-assertively unfamiliar that unsettles us, than minute shifts in the aspects of what we assumed to be reliable, even innocuous . . . say, the 'ordinary' words.

Ford's writing, even at its most bravura and provocative, does not significantly impede the reader: yet, while we read, we become half-aware of dozens of echoes, hints, associations, details from some other time or text – most often, of course, one of Ford's own texts, often, indeed, the one we are actually reading – almost subliminal, increasingly unsettling. The fluency of the prose makes us reluctant to stop, to concentrate on remembering, each time this happens. So there is a cumulative sense of something building, widening, all the time we read, something which must be faced and interrogated at some point. But not just yet. Behind Dowell's exclaiming: 'Permanence? Stability! I can't believe it's gone' (*GS* 11), we can sense Ford's knowledge that it had always already gone, although after the Great War it had gone rather more evidently and completely. Joseph Brodsky has suggested that 'in the business of writing what one accumulates is not expertise but uncertainties. Which is but another name for craft'.[16] From the unstable excitement of the months before the outbreak of war to that recognition of the 'merest film' stretched across 'the abysses of Chaos',[17] Ford accumulated, considered and rendered uncertainties. His prose does not simply 'defamiliarize' the familiar in order to make strange: it asserts and confirms the peculiarity of what has become, or what we believe to be, the familiar – the shock of recognition which he often provokes in us comprises our acknowledgement of what, with part of our minds, we always knew to be the case.

What is, in a sense, 'unnoticeable' is often, rather, hidden in plain sight. One example is the name of the Fordian hero. I won't rehearse the minor mystery of John Dowell – to rhyme with 'trowel' or 'roll'? – but try the name 'Tietjens': strange at first view when attached to a man so 'peculiarly English' (*PE* 178). Yet not, it turns out, strange after all, because it's originally 'foreign', explicitly Dutch. But then again – like others, no doubt, I have trawled uncomprehendingly through Dutch reference books and other remote places, looking for suggestive instances, discarding the odd opera singer and a German or two . . . only to end up with an early Kipling story, 'The Return of Imray', in which Strickland's deerhound, whom 'the natives' treat with 'the great reverence that is born of hate and fear', is named Tietjens: which seems much more like the real, right Fordian thing.[18] Partly because the story was published in 1891 – and because it *is* a story – and Ford's 'oldest literary recollection' is of reading Kipling, in a railway carriage, when he was eighteen; because several versions of the genesis of *Parade's End* – and much else: the deaths of Conrad and Lord Kitchener and Holman Hunt, the outbreak of war – involve trains; because of the increasingly intricate series of puns on training, entraining, in training, train of thought; and perhaps because this sentence can only really end in ellipsis . . .[19]

It must end in ellipsis not merely because of limitations of space, here, in this essay – a conventional enough disclaimer – but because such a limitation of space results inescapably from Ford's practice. Ezra Pound, who tended, in his estimates of Ford, to get some things partially right some of the time, remembered trying to make a note on a point raised in Ford's *Ancient Lights*: 'I thought it would go on the back of an envelope and found to my young surprise that I couldn't make the note in fewer words than those on Ford's actual page. That set me thinking . . .'.[20] Well, yes. But it is more than a local 'problem' of style, an apparently leisurely manner of writing that *seems* capable of compression or abbreviation. Ford's punning, for example – if that word will still serve – is less on single words than on whole networks of image, phrase and figure, characteristically constructed in and by his work, drawing with great skill upon scores of comparable instances within the Fordian *oeuvre*, many of them 'simple' and 'ordinary' in themselves. So the habitual observation that Ford needs 'space', that he lacks compression – the sort of remark which Ford himself is slyly prone to making – is revealed as a half-truth, or at least a truth that provokes a counter-truth. And Ford's writing itself constructs that counter-truth: that the reading (or interpretation or unfolding) of the Fordian work *necessarily* entails reaching over huge areas of the body of his writings; that the reader – whom Ford himself constantly foregrounds – cannot legitimately (or fairly, to the work under discussion) contract and condense while maintaining critical accuracy. There is, indeed, 'compression' in that work; but on a scale, or of a kind, that frequently eludes a scrutiny schooled only in Poundian/Imagiste aesthetics or the neat models of the New Criticism.

So the careful reader's attention is frequently rewarded at different viewing distances, *Parade's End* in particular prompting, indeed requiring, both the Great View (of architectonics and larger symbolic structures) and the closer view of individual details, those tiny instances of accurate and sounded syllables, since Ford is a master of both. And, indeed, of the two combined. *The Good Soldier*'s first word is 'This', an assured demonstrative, however subsequently problematic; its last word 'it', a tellingly brief and brutal pronoun, referring explicitly to Nancy's telegram, the briefest and most brutal text contained in this text of 'The Saddest Story'. Reappearing in the opening pages of *No Enemy*, 'it' signifies, more portentously, The War. In *Last Post*, the first word is 'He'; the last, in quotation marks, in inverted commas, is 'I'. As the novel moves from third-person narrative voice to the individual consciousness, so does the whole tetralogy, which commences with a very definite article; even, we may say, 'the modern Novel', because *Parade's End* is, among so much else, an examination of the development of the Novel from late nineteenth century realism to the age of *Ulysses*, including Ford's own part in that development, by praxis, enacting the search for fictional forms able to address the threatening landscape of the postwar world and the terrible knowledge inscribed upon it, demonstrating both how the modern novel evolved and what it was that modernist strategies were responding to, what actually brought them into being.

But Ford's best work was produced during the High Modernist Period when style was most often announcing itself in tones of thunder. Open Joyce's *Ulysses* and you find: 'The heaventree of stars hung with humid nightblue fruit.'[21] That's *style*. But open *The Good Soldier,* and you find: 'I just wanted to marry her as some people want to go to Carcassone' (*GS* 84). Or this: 'I console myself with thinking that this is a real story and that, after all, real stories are probably told best in the way a person telling a story would tell them.

They will then seem most real' (*GS* 120). And though Ford could turn on the style when he wanted to, perhaps his real danger – which he didn't always evade – was precisely a too great facility, a remarkable fluency which he realized the need to restrain.

Yet it seems that Ford's success in what he terms 'keying [his] prose down' (*TR* 52) has tended to work against him, or against his posthumous reputation. Perhaps because of the apparently innocuous surface of his prose, the rarity of outlandish words or tortured syntax, his insistence on a succession of tiny surprises rather than shocks, there was a long history of Ford's being read carelessly. The absence of more noticeable 'modernist' features from his pages has in fact tended to divert critical scrutiny to more obviously rewarding texts, so that while Eliot, Joyce, Lewis, Woolf and Pound have been the objects of extensive and sustained scholarly attention, serious work on Ford was begun rather belatedly. So those who laboriously began counting instances, in various forms, of the verb 'to know' in the pages of *The Good Soldier* were a little surprised to find, in this electronic age, that there are 289 such occasions.[22]

Reading Pound's *Cantos*, we are armed with Carroll F. Terrell's *Companion*, with guides by Cookson or Brooker.[23] Reading *Ulysses*, we can prop open Don Gifford's *Ulysses Annotated* or Blamires' *The Bloomsday Book*. Companions, of course, explain the problematic but in doing so assert what exactly *is* problematic, what our attention should address or at least pause upon. And reading Ford? We have Max Saunders' exemplary biography and several fine critical books and essays. Yet they're not readers' cribs and the whole point, of course, is that Ford doesn't require guides or readers' companions. Readers *as* companions, yes. He is a remarkably – some would say bewilderingly – readerly writer. And our best preparation for reading Ford is so sensible, so fundamental, so – I'm tempted to say – old-fashioned, that it seems almost invisible, almost unnoticeable, seems to be no preparation at all. Yet though the big words have gone, just as the Great Figures have gone, here are words juxtaposed or recurring, over greater and greater bodies of text, which we could, if we wished, write Fordian histories of: engrossment, scarlet, rest, immense, adumbrate, sanctuary, affair. Ford may have implied that he merely wrote for 'men of goodwill' *(hominibus bonae voluntatis)* and asserted that 'you should ask of your reader no knowledge whatever except that of the exact sense of words'.[24] But since it is precisely that sense which is constantly and subtly brought into question, it is clear that Ford actually makes considerable demands upon his readers – though they are often the kinds of demands that twentieth century literary history, the history of literature as it is taught, has somehow rendered unnoticeable.

Perhaps this brings us a little closer to the paradox of why such a readerly writer is less read than other modern masters, who are now, in any case, almost exclusively, *studied.* Ford's 'difficulties' are not signalled in what have come to be seen as appropriate ways, while many of his virtues are, in a real sense, unnoticeable: he requires those trained observers. Joyce wrote for people who would read Joyce. Pound wrote for intending poets and later, perhaps, for adepts. Ford writes for people who read as Ford reads: with sympathy, with appreciation of the writer's skills, with an acute historical awareness, above all, with engrossed attention. The whole corpus of his work is intended to give pleasure, yes, but also 'the province of literature', he wrote, 'is to educate – so that the reader may be stirred to the perception of analogies or to the discovery of the sources of pleasure within himself.'[25]

This connects, I think, with what Sven Birkerts, in his *Gutenberg Elegies*, refers to as 'deep time', the 'associative mechanisms . . . constantly operative'.[26] Ford shows us many examples of his ideal reader: Grocer Rayner, who read the works of Crane, Conrad and James, Ford says, 'with the passionate engrossment of a man in deep isolation' (*RY* 157); children reading in the twilight; Ford himself; or, to shift the focus a little to those not literally readers, Rosalie Prudent, centred, focused, concentrated (*NE* 267-8).

The body of Ford's writings offers us an engrossing and never quite grasped network of – often implicit – echoes, shadow memories, teasing yet ultimately strengthening connections, held in productive tension by, let us say, that self rarely to be found in *salons* and courtrooms. Reading him, our minds necessarily range more and more widely, but always returning, retracing, recalling, as we engage in the gradual process of noticing what was, at first, unnoticeable, of becoming trained observers. 'There was too much to think about', Ford writes in *No More Parades*, '. . . so that nothing at all stood out to be thought of' (*PE* 378).

Awareness of that larger context increasingly discovers congruity, coherence, an ultimate shapeliness and grace. There *are* remarkable scenes in Ford's fictions, fantastic or dramatic, or scenes of high comedy. And there are many striking and resonant phrases. Ford – like his most memorable character, Tietjens – is not, by most criteria, unnoticeable. Yet what Ford thinks of as the virtues of his prose are often, certainly by High Modernist norms, unnoticeable, as are many of the characters whom he obviously regards as 'heroes': Meary Walker, in whose biography 'you could find traces of great benevolence and of considerable heroism', but who generally attracted 'no attention at all' (*RY* 146, 151), or the old Tommy of the Lincolns (*NE* 184-9). '[S]o beastly normal', Stella Bowen said of Valentine Wannop,[27] but that surely was the point. Ford's version of the twentieth century hero is that compound character, the writer/reader: one might say, rather, the artist, but only in the conscious knowledge of the range of Ford's artists, of those who honour the *métier*, and attend to littlenesses of finish, as well as those who honour the life of the mind. The ideal Fordian reader is, then, something a little like a Fordian character: engrossed, with body in one place and mind in another; or gazing into that glass and seeing, superimposed upon the scene outside, a reflection of ourselves. Because, of course, when the prose works, the 'passionate engross-ment' works, for all our postmodern self-consciousness. A vigorous attention, care for 'the exact sense of words' – and high rewards for those who do the reader's share.

NOTES

1. Ford Madox Ford, *Parade's End* (London: Penguin, 1992), p.139. Subsequent references in the text are to this edition, using the abbreviation *PE*.

2. Ford Madox Ford, *Joseph Conrad: A Personal Remembrance* (London: Duckworth, 1924) – henceforth *JC*; p. 197.

3. Ezra Pound, *Selected Letters 1907-1941*, edited by D. D. Paige (New York: New Directions, 1971), p. 49.

4. *PE* 177. See also Ford Madox Hueffer, 'Literary Portraits – LXVIII. Et in Terra Pax', *Outlook* (London), XXXIV (26 December 1914), 823, on Verviers, 'unnoticeable and filled with such unnoticeable people', yet stricken by the war.

5. Ford Madox Ford, *The March of Literature* (London: George Allen & Unwin, 1939), p. 843.

6. Flaubert to Louise Colet, 16 January 1852. He actually suggested that 'from the standpoint of pure Art one might almost establish the axiom that there is no such thing as subject – style in itself being an absolute manner of seeing things.' See *The Letters of Gustave Flaubert: 1830-1857*, selected, translated and edited by Francis Steegmuller (Cambridge, Massachusetts and London: Harvard University Press, 1980), p. 154.

7. Ford Madox Hueffer, 'Literary Portraits – XLVII. Mr. W.R. Titterton and "Me As a Model"', *Outlook* (London), XXXIV (1 August 1914), 143. See also Ford Madox Hueffer, *Thus to Revisit* (London: Chapman and Hall, 1921) – henceforth *TR*; p. 202; Ford Madox Ford, *Return to Yesterday* (London: Victor Gollancz, 1931) – henceforth *RY*; p. 303.

8.. Ford to Harold Monro, 30 May 1920: *Letters of Ford Madox Ford*, ed. Richard M. Ludwig (Princeton: Princeton University Press, 1965), p. 99. See also *TR* 213; Ford Madox Hueffer, *The Critical Attitude* (London: Duckworth, 1911), p. 181; Ford Madox Hueffer, *Between St Dennis and St George* (London: Hodder and Stoughton, 1915), 180; *Critical Writings of Ford Madox Ford*, edited by Frank MacShane (Lincoln, Nebraska: University of Nebraska Press, 1964), p. 156.

9. T. S. Eliot, 'Gerontion', *Collected Poems 1909-1962* (London: Faber and Faber, 1963), p. 39.

10. 'William Atheling' [Pound], 'Music', *New Age*, XXVI, 24 (15 April 1920), reprinted in *Ezra Pound and Music*, edited by Murray Schafer (London: Faber, 1978), p. 224.

11. Ford Madox Ford, *The Good Soldier*, ed. Martin Stannard (New York and London: W. W. Norton & Company, 1995) – henceforth *GS*; p. 142.

12. *TR* 138-9. See Ford Madox Hueffer, 'Literary Portraits – XXXI. Lord Dunsany and "Five Plays"', *Outlook* (London), XXXIII (11 April 1914), 494: 'And that, you know, is the real triumph of an art – to make the hand deceive the eye though the eye knows all the while what the hand is doing'.

13. See, for instance, his remarks in E. R. [Ford], 'The Work of W.H. Hudson', *English Review*, II (April 1909), pp. 161-2.

14. Ford Madox Hueffer, *Memories and Impressions* (New York: Harper, 1911), p. xviii.

15. See *Pound/Ford: The Story of a Literary Friendship*, edited by Brita Lindberg-Seyersted (London: Faber, 1982), pp. 44-5. Pound's 'Canto VII', borrowing a few 'furniture' phrases from Flaubert, draws on precisely the passage of 'Un Coeur Simple' which Ford had specified seven years earlier: '"Un Coeur Simple"', *Outlook* (London), XXXV (5 June 1915), 738-9; *Between St Dennis and St George*, p. 203.

16. Joseph Brodsky, 'Less Than One', in *Less Than One: Selected Essays* (New York: Farrar, Straus & Giroux, 1986), p. 17.

17. Ford Madox Ford, *It Was the Nightingale* (Philadelphia: Lippincott, 1933), p. 64.

18. Rudyard Kipling, 'The Return of Imray': *Life's Handicap* (London: Macmillan, 1891), pp. 226-7.

19. *RY* 3-4; on the genesis of *Parade's End*, see *It Was the Nightingale*, pp. 187-91, 200, 207; on Conrad, see *JC* 32-3; on Lord Kitchener, see *No Enemy* (New York: The Macaulay Company, 1929) – henceforth *NE*; pp. 29-34; on Holman Hunt, see *Memories and Impressions*, pp. 231-2; on the outbreak of war, see *RY* 434-5. On trains, see Sara Haslam's essay in this volume, pp. 35-46.

20. Ezra Pound, 'Ford Madox (Hueffer) Ford: Obit', in *Selected Prose 1909-1965*, edited by William Cookson (London: Faber, 1973), p. 432.

21. James Joyce, *Ulysses*, edited by Hans Walter Gabler (Harmondsworth: Penguin, 1986), p. 573.

22. See Thomas C. Moser's introduction to the World Classics edition of *The Good Soldier* (Oxford: Oxford University Press, 1990), p. xx, citing C. Ruth Sabol and Todd K. Bender, *A Concordance to Ford Madox Ford's "The Good Soldier"* (New York: Garland, 1981).

23. Carroll F. Terrell, *The Companion to the Cantos* 2 vols (University of California Press, 1980); William Cookson, *A Guide to the Cantos of Ezra Pound* (London and Sydney: Croom Helm, 1985); and Peter Brooker, *A Student's Guide to the Selected Poems of Ezra Pound* (London: Faber, 1979).

24. Ford Madox Hueffer, 'Literary Portraits: XXII. London Town and a Saunterer', *Tribune* (21 December 1907), 2; 'Literary Portraits – XXIV. Miss May Sinclair and "The Judgement of Eve"', *Outlook* (London), XXXIII (2 May 1914), 600. Cf. *TR* 93, where the 'technical rule' ascribed to Conrad (and to Flaubert) duplicates this wording.

25. Ford Madox Hueffer, 'Thus to Revisit: III. The Serious Books', *Piccadilly Review* (6 November 1919), 6.

26. Sven Birkerts, *The Gutenberg Elegies* (London: Faber, 1994), pp. 75, 113.

27. Stella Bowen to Ford, 14 October 1927: see *The Correspondence of Ford Madox Ford and Stella Bowen*, edited by Sondra J. Stang and Karen Cochran (Bloomington and Indianapolis: Indiana University Press, 1994), p. 331.

THE CONTRIBUTORS

Sally Bachner is Assistant Professor of English at Wesleyan University. She is currently at work on a project about the prestige of violence in post-War fiction and theory.

Bernard Bergonzi is Emeritus Professor of English at the University of Warwick. He has written extensively on modern British literature; his latest books are the collection of essays, *War Poets and Other Subjects* (Aldershot: Ashgate, 2000); and *A Victorian Wanderer: The Life of Thomas Arnold the Younger* (Oxford: Oxford University Press, 2003).

Dennis Brown is Emeritus Professor of Modern Literature at the University of Hertfordshire, specialising in twentieth-century poetry, and a Fellow of the English Association. His publications include *The Modernist Self in Twentieth-Century English Literature* (Basingstoke: Macmillan, 1989), *Intertextual Dynamics within the Literary Group – Joyce, Lewis, Pound and Eliot: The Men of 1914* (Basingstoke: Macmillan, 1990), *The Poetry of Postmodernity* (Basingstoke: Macmillan, 1994), and *John Betjeman* (Plymouth: Northcote House, 1999). He is currently working on the relationship between poetics and (British School) psychotherapy.

Robert L. Caserio is Professor of English and Head of the Department of English at the Pennsylvania State University, University Park. His previous publications include *Plot, Story, and the Novel: From Dickens and Poe to the Modern Period* (Princeton University Press, 1979) and *The English Novel 1900-1950: Theory and History* (Twayne–Simon & Schuster Macmillan, 1999). His previous essays on Ford have appeared in *Antæus* and in *Contemporary Literature*.

Giovanni Cianci is professor of English at the Università Statale of Milan. He is the author of *La Scuola di Cambridge* (on the literary criticism of I. A. Richards, William Empson, and F. R. Leavis: Bari, Adriatica, 1970), and *La fortuna di Joyce in Italia* (Adriatica, 1974). He edited Quaderno no. 9 (a special issue on Futurism/Vorticism, Palermo, 1979) and the international collection of essays *Wyndham Lewis: Letterature/Pittura* (Palermo: Sellerio, 1982). Co-editor of the annotated bibliographical guide to *Letterature Inglese e Americana* (Milano: Garzanti, 1989), he has also edited *La città 1870-1930* (on the impact of the city on literature: Fasano: Schena, 1991) and *Modernismo/Modernismi* (on the English avant-garde: Milano: Principato, 1991). He co-edited *Ruskin and Modernism* with Peter Nicholls (Basingstoke: Palgrave, 2001) and *Il Cézanne degli scrittori, dei poeti e dei filosofi* with Elio Franzini and Antonello Negri (Milano: Bocca Editori, 2001).

Cornelia Cook is Dean of the Faculty of Arts at Queen Mary, University of London. Her fields of publication are English literature of the nineteenth and early twentieth centuries, and rhetorical strategies in Biblical writing.

Vita Fortunati is Professor of English Literature at the University of Bologna, and co-ordinator of the European Network on Cultural Memory, ACUME. She is the author of *Ford Madox Ford: teoria e tecnica narrativa* (Bologna: Patron, 1975); and the editor, with Rafaella Baccolini, of *Scrittura e Sperimentazione in Ford Madox Ford* (Florence: Alinea Editrice, 1994). She has also co-edited two volumes with Elena Lamberti: a collection of Ford's critical essays, *Il Senso critico. Saggi di Ford Madox Ford* (Florence: Alinea, 2001); and a volume of essays from the 2001 Bologna conference, *Ford Madox Ford and 'The Republic of Letters'* (Bologna: Clueb, 2002). She is the editor (with Raymond Trousson) of *Dictionary of Literary Utopias* (Paris: Champion, 2000). Her recent interests involve literature and aging ('The Controversial Female Body: New Feminist

Perspectives on Ageing', in *Textus*, XII [2001]), and she is currently editing *The Controversial Women's Body: Images and Representations in Literature and Art* (Bologna: Bononia University Press, 2003).

Robert Hampson is Professor of Modern Literature and Head of the Department of English at Royal Holloway, University of London. He is the author of *Joseph Conrad: Betrayal and Identity* (Basingstoke: Macmillan, 1992), and *Cross-Cultural Encounters in Conrad's Malay Fiction* (Basingstoke: Palgrave, 2000). He co-edited (with Peter Barry) *New British Poetries: The scope of the possible* (Manchester: Manchester University Press, 1993), and (with Andrew Gibson) *Conrad and Theory* (Amsterdam: Rodopi, 1998). He is a former editor of *The Conradian,* and has been textual editor and/or editor of a range of works by Conrad and Kipling: *Lord Jim* (Harmondsworth: Penguin, 1986), *Something of Myself* (Penguin, 1987), *Victory* (Penguin, 1989), *Soldiers Three / In Black and* White (Penguin, 1993), *Heart of Darkness* (Penguin, 1995), and Nostromo (London: Wordsworth, 2001). He is currently editing *The Arrow of Gold* for the Cambridge Edition of the Collected Works of Joseph Conrad.

Sara Haslam completed her Ph.D., on Ford, at King's College London in 1997. She was a Lecturer in English at Chester College of Higher Education, and is currently Lecturer in Literature at the Open University. She has published articles and essays on Ford, James, and modernism, and her book, *Fragmenting Modernism: Ford Madox Ford, the Novel and the Great War*, was published by Manchester University Press in 2002. With pedagogy another of her interests, she produced a multi-media CD-ROM on the poetry of Thomas Hardy in 2001 (a search engine, the *Complete Poems*, plus numerous essays included). Current projects include an edition of Ford's *England and the English* trilogy for Carcanet Press. She is a founder member and Treasurer of the Ford Society.

Philip Horne is Professor of English Literature at University College London. He is the author of *Henry James and Revision: the New York Edition* (Oxford: Clarendon, 1990); and the editor of James's *The Tragic Muse* (Harmondsworth: Penguin, 1995); *Henry James: A Life in Letters* (London: Allen Lane / Penguin, 1999); and Dickens' *Oliver Twist* (London: Penguin Classics, 2002).

W. B. Hutchings is Senior Lecturer in English Literature at the University of Manchester. He is Programme Editor of the Carcanet Press Millennium Ford project, for which he has edited *The Good Soldier* and *Return to Yesterday*. He is author of *The Poetry of William Cowper* (London: Croom Helm, 1983) and co-editor of *Thomas Gray: Contemporary Essays* (Liverpool: Liverpool University Press, 1993). He was awarded a National Teaching Fellowship in 2000.

Sir Frank Kermode has been Lord Northcliffe Professor of Modern English Literature at University College, London, King Edward VII Professor of English Literature at Cambridge, and Charles Eliot Norton Professor of Poetry at Harvard. The most recent of his many books is the acclaimed *Shakespeare's Language* (London: Penguin, 2000).

Elena Lamberti teaches Anglo-American Literature at the University of Bologna. She has specialized in English and Canadian Literature, in particular Anglo-American Modernism, as well as literature and technology. She has written various articles on Ford Madox Ford, on Marshall McLuhan, as well as on literature, technology and culture. She is the author of *McLuhan: Tra letteratura, arte e media* (Milan: Mondadori, 2000), co-editor of a collection of Ford's critical essays, *Il Senso critico: Saggi di Ford Madox Ford* (with Vita Fortunati, Florence: Alinea, 2001), editor of *Interpreting/Translating European Modernism. A Comparative Approach* (Bologna: Compositori

Grafiche, 2001), co-editor of *Ford Madox Ford and The Republic of Letters* (with Vita Fortunati, Bologna: Clueb, 2002).

Caroline Patey teaches English Literature at the Università degli Studi in Milan. Her research focuses on both Renaissance and Modernist literature with a comparative approach and a special interest in the visual arts. She is currently editing a book on James Joyce and the question of memory and preparing a book on Henry James and London. Among her other publications are *Tempi difficili: Su Joyce e Proust* (Milan: Marcos y Marcos, 1991), and *Manierismo* (Milan: Editrice Bibliografica, 1996).

Robin Peel is a Principal Lecturer in English at the University of Plymouth. His interest in Ford's rewriting of himself developed during research for a pamphlet on *Literary Oxted and Limpsfield: the Edward Garnett Years*, and his doctoral thesis on representations of rootlessness in English prose 1910-15 includes a chapter on Ford. He is currently writing a book with the working title *Apart from Modernism : Edith Wharton, Fiction and Politics*, and has recently published a study of *Writing Back: Sylvia Plath and Cold War politics* (London: Associated University Presses; Madison, WI: Fairleigh Dickinson Press, 2002). His other recent study, *Questions of English,* with Annette Patterson and Jeanne Gerlach (London and New York: Routledge, 2000) explored the relationship between literature, education, and the formation of subjectivity.

Ros Pesman is Professor in History and Pro-Vice-Chancellor of the College of Humanities and Social Sciences at the University of Sydney. She has published on early sixteenth-century Florentine politics and government, Italian migration to Australia and the overseas travel of Australians. She is presently working on the writings of late Victorian and Edwardian women on Italian history and art. Her recent studies include *Duty Free: Australian Women Abroad* (Melbourne: Oxford University Press, 1996); the co-editorship of *The Oxford Book of Australian Travel Writing* (Melbourne: Oxford University Press, 1996); and *Pier Soderini and the Ruling Class in Renaissance Florence*, Biblioteca Eruditorum, 31, (Goldbach: Keip Verlag, 2002).

Davida Pines is an Assistant Professor of Humanities and Rhetoric at Boston University in the College of General Studies. She received an M.Phil. in English Romantic Studies from St. Catherine's College, Oxford University in 1993, and a Ph.D. in Modern British and American Literature from Brandeis University in 1999. She is completing a book on 'Marriage and Modernism, 1880-1939'.

Roger Poole was until recently Reader in Literary Theory in the Department of English at the University of Nottingham. His book *The Unknown Virginia Woolf* (Cambridge: Cambridge University Press, 1978), caused a good deal of contention, but went through four editions, the last in 1995. In recent years he has been Visiting Professor at the University of Sussex, Visiting Fellow at the University of Warwick, and is currently a Visiting Fellow at the University of Cambridge.

Max Saunders is Professor of English at King's College London, where he teaches British, American and European literature. His two-volume biography, *Ford Madox Ford: A Dual Life*, was published by Oxford University Press in 1996. He has edited three volumes for the Millennium Ford series: *Selected Poems* (Manchester: Carcanet, 1997); *War Prose* (Carcanet, 1999); and a selection of the *Critical Essays* (with Richard Stang: Carcanet, 2002). He was guest editor for the *Agenda* special double issue devoted to Ford (1989-90), and has written and lectured on Ford, other modernists – notably Conrad, Joyce, Pound, and Lawrence – and on autobiography and biography. He is chairman of the Ford Madox Ford Society.

Paul Skinner has taught at the University of the West of England and the University of Bristol. His doctoral thesis was on Ford Madox Ford and Ezra Pound. He edited Ford's *No Enemy* (Manchester: Carcanet, 2002) and has published articles on Ford, Pound and Rudyard Kipling. He lives in Bristol, where he works in publishing, and is currently writing a book on Ford, centred on *Parade's End*.

Martin Stannard is Professor of Modern English Literature at the University of Leicester. His *Evelyn Waugh: The Critical Heritage* (London: Routledge, 1984) was followed by a two-volume biography: *Evelyn Waugh. The Early Years: 1903-1939* (London: Dent, 1986) and *Evelyn Waugh. No Abiding City: 1939-1966* (London: Dent, 1992). His most recent book is the Norton Critical Edition of Ford's *The Good Soldier* (London and New York, 1995). He is currently writing the authorised life of Muriel Spark.

Joseph Wiesenfarth is Professor Emeritus at the University of Wisconsin-Madison. He has written extensively on Ford and on the English novel. His book *Gothic Manners and the Classic English Novel* (Madison, Wisconsin: University of Wisconsin Press, 1989) includes a chapter on *Parade's End*. He was guest editor for the special issue, on 'Ford Madox Ford and the Arts', of *Contemporary Literature*, 30:2 (Summer 1989). His most recent book, on Ford and his personal and artistic involvement with Violet Hunt, Jean Rhys, Stella Bowen, and Janice Biala, will be published by Wisconsin in the near future.

ABBREVIATIONS

The following abbreviations have been used for works cited several times, whether in the text or in the notes. The list is divided into two alphabetical sections: works by Ford and by others. A full list of abbreviations to be used in future volumes can be found on the Ford Society web site.

(i) Works by Ford

CA   *The Critical Attitude* (London: Duckworth, 1911)

Call   *A Call: A Tale of Two Passions*, with an Afterword by C. H. Sisson (Manchester: Carcanet, 1984)

GS   *The Good Soldier*, ed. Martin Stannard, Norton Critical Edition (New York and London: W. W. Norton & Company, 1995)

IWN   *It Was the Nightingale* (Philadelphia: J. B. Lippincott, 1933; London: William Heinemann, 1934)

JC   *Joseph Conrad* (London: Duckworth, 1924; Boston: Little, Brown, 1924)

'On Impressionism'   'On Impressionism', *Poetry and Drama*, 2 (June and December 1914), 167-75, 323-34

PE   *Parade's End* (one volume edition of all the Tietjens novels: *Some Do Not. . ., No More Parades, A Man Could Stand Up –,* and *Last Post*) (New York: Alfred A. Knopf, 1950). Same pagination as Viking, Penguin and Carcanet paperback editions.

ABBREVIATIONS

SL *The Soul of London* (London: Alston Rivers, 1905); new edition, ed. Alan. G. Hill (London: J. M. Dent, 1995)

SLL *The Simple Life Limited*, [pseudonym: Daniel Chaucer] (London: John Lane, 1911)

SP *The Spirit of the People* (London: Alston Rivers, 1907)

TR *Thus to Revisit* (London: Chapman & Hall, 1921)

RY *Return to Yesterday* (London: Victor Gollancz, 1931)

(ii) Works by Others

DFL Stella Bowen, *Drawn from Life* (London: Collins, 1941)

Calvino Italo Calvino, *Perche' leggere I classici* (Milano: Arnoldo Mondadori Editore, 1991)

FCM Guy de Maupassant, *Fort Comme la Mort*, introduction et notes de Marie-Claire Bancquart (Paris: Librairie Générale Française, 1989)

FY Violet Hunt, *The Flurried Years* (London: Hurst & Blackett, [1926])

GB James G. Frazer, *The Golden Bough. A Study in Magic and Religion*, edited by R. Fraser (Oxford: Oxford University Press, 1994),

Green Robert Green, *Ford Madox Ford: Prose and Politics* (Cambridge: Cambridge University Press, 1981)

Poli   Bernard J. Poli, *Ford Madox Ford and the Transatlantic Review* (Syracuse, N.Y.: Syracuse University Press, 1967)

Saunders Max Saunders, *Ford Madox Ford: A Dual Life*, Two Volumes (Oxford: Oxford University Press, 1996)

THE
FORD
MADOX
FORD
SOCIETY

Ford c. 1915   ©Alfred Cohen, 2000   Registered Charity No. 1084040

This international society was founded in 1997 to promote knowledge of and interest in Ford. Honorary Members include Julian Barnes, A. S. Byatt, Samuel Hynes, Alan Judd, Sir Frank Kermode, Ruth Rendell, Michael Schmidt, John Sutherland, and Gore Vidal. There are currently over one hundred members, from more than ten countries. The Society organizes an active programme of events. Besides regular meetings in Britain, it has held major international conferences in Italy, Germany, and the U.S.A. In 2002 it launched the annual series, International Ford Madox Ford Studies, which is distributed free to members. The first issues include: a reappraisal of Ford's diversity; 'Ford Madox Ford's Modernity'; 'History and Representation in Ford'; and 'Ford and the City';. If you are an admirer, an enthusiast, a reader, a scholar, or a student of anything Fordian, then this Society wants to hear from you, and welcomes your participation in its activities.

The Society aims to organise at least two events each year, and to publish one or two Newsletters. It has also inaugurated a series of Ford Lectures, which have been given by Martin Stannard, Alan Judd, David Crane, Sergio Perosa, and Oliver Soskice.

To join, please send your name and address (including an e-mail address if possible), and a cheque made payable to 'The Ford Madox Ford Society', to:

Sara Haslam, Department of Literature, Open University, Walton Hall, Milton Keynes, MK7 6AA.

Annual rates:

Pounds sterling: Individuals: £12; Concessions £6; Member Organisations £25
US Dollars: Any category: $25

For further information, either contact Sara Haslam (Treasurer) at the above address, or Max Saunders (Chairman) on e-mail at: max.saunders@kcl.ac.uk

The Society's Website is at : **www.rialto.com/fordmadoxford_society**

Virtual Geographies.
Cyberpunk at the Intersection of the Postmodern and Science Fiction.

Sabine Heuser

Amsterdam/New York, NY 2003. XLV, 257 pp.
(Postmodern Studies 34)
ISBN: 90-420-0986-1   EUR 50.-/US $ 60.-

Virtual Geographies is the first detailed study to offer a working definition of cyberpunk within the postmodern force field. Cyberpunk emerges as a new generic cluster within science fiction, one that has spawned many offspring in such domains as film, music, and feminism. Its central features are its adherence to a version of virtual space and a deconstructivist, punk attitude towards (high) culture, modernity, the human body and technology, from computers to prosthetics

The main proponents of cyberpunk are analyzed in depth along with the virtual landscapes they have created - William Gibson's Cyberspace, Pat Cadigan's Mindscapes and Neal Stephenson's Metaverse. Virtual reality is examined closely in all its aspects, from the characteristic narrative constructions employed to the esthetic implications of the 'virtual sublime' and its postmodern potential as a discursive mode.

With its interdisciplinary approach *Virtual Geographies* opens up fresh perspectives for scholars interested in the interaction between popular culture and mainstream literature. At the same time, the science fiction fan will be taken beyond the conventional boundaries of the genre into such revitalizing domains as postmodern architecture and literature, and into cutting-edge aspects of science and social thought.

USA/Canada: One Rockefeller Plaza, Ste. 1420, New York, NY 10020,
Tel. (212) 265-6360, Call toll-free (U.S. only) 1-800-225-3998,
Fax (212) 265-6402
All other countries: Tijnmuiden 7, 1046 AK Amsterdam, The Netherlands.
Tel. ++ 31 (0)20 611 48 21, Fax ++ 31 (0)20 447 29 79
Orders-queries@rodopi.nl   **www.rodopi.nl**
Please note that the exchange rate is subject to fluctuations

Posting the Male

Masculinities in Post-war and Contemporary British Literature.

Edited by Daniel Lea and Berthold Schoene.

Amsterdam/New York, NY 2003. 171 pp. (Genus 3)
ISBN: 90-420-0976-4 € 38,-/US $ 45.-

The essays collected in *Posting the Male* examine representations of masculinity in post-war and contemporary British literature, focussing on the works of writers as diverse as John Osborne, Joe Orton, James Kelman, Ian Rankin, Carol Ann Duffy, Alan Hollinghurst, Ian McEwan, Graham Swift and Jackie Kay. The collection seeks to capture the current historical moment of 'crisis', at which masculinity loses its universal transparency and becomes visible as a performative gender construct. Rather than denoting just one fixed, polarised point on a hierarchised axis of strictly segregated gender binaries, masculinity is revealed to oscillate within a virtually limitless spectrum of gender identities, characterised not by purity and self-containment but by difference and alterity.

As the contributors demonstrate, rather than a gender 'in crisis' millennial manhood is a gender 'in transition'. Patriarchal strategies of man-making are gradually being replaced by less exclusionary patterns of self-identification inspired by feminism. Men have begun to recognise themselves as gendered beings and, as a result, masculinity has been set in motion.

Rodopi

USA/Canada: One Rockefeller Plaza, Ste. 1420, New York, NY 10020,
Tel. (212) 265-6360, Call toll-free (U.S. only) 1-800-225-3998,
Fax (212) 265-6402
All other countries: Tijnmuiden 7, 1046 AK Amsterdam, The Netherlands.
Tel. ++ 31 (0)20 611 48 21, Fax ++ 31 (0)20 447 29 79
Orders-queries@rodopi.nl www.rodopi.nl
Please note that the exchange rate is subject to fluctuations

Culture and Cooperation in Europe's Borderland.

Edited by James Anderson, Liam O'Dowd and Thomas M. Wilson.

Amsterdam/New York, NY 2003. 250 pp.
(European Studies 19)

ISBN: 90-420-1085-1   Bound € 60,-/US $ 71.-

Scholarly interest in the study of state borders and border regions is growing in Europe, keeping pace with the remarkable changes associated with the transformation of old borders and the creation of new ones in the European Union and beyond over the last fifteen years. Social scientists have increasingly examined cross-border co-operation as one way to understand the changes which affect European borderlands. Ironically, given the recent turn to issues of culture and identity in the social sciences, one of the most neglected aspects of the critical and comparative analysis of cross-border co-operation has been culture. *Culture and Co-operation in European Borderlands*, the first collection of essays to provide multidisciplinary perspectives on these issues in European borderlands, presents three modes of analysis of culture and cross-border co-operation as a tentative way forward to redress this imbalance. These overlapping perspectives, on cultures of co-operation, co-operation about culture, and the impact of culture on forms of co-operation, are offered as possible strategies in the comparative social science of European borderlands.

USA/Canada: One Rockefeller Plaza, Ste. 1420, New York, NY 10020,
Tel. (212) 265-6360, Call toll-free (U.S. only) 1-800-225-3998,
Fax (212) 265-6402
All other countries: Tijnmuiden 7, 1046 AK Amsterdam, The Netherlands.
Tel. ++ 31 (0)20 611 48 21, Fax ++ 31 (0)20 447 29 79
Orders-queries@rodopi.nl   **www.rodopi.nl**
Please note that the exchange rate is subject to fluctuations

"Trading Magic for Fact," Fact for Magic
Myth and Mythologizing in Postmodern Canadian Historical Fiction

Marc Colavincenzo

Amsterdam, New York, NY 2003. XXII, 239 pp.
(Cross/Cultures 67)

ISBN: 90-420-0936-5   Bound EUR 60,-/US$ 71.-
ISBN: 90-420-0926-8   Paper EUR 29,-/US$ 35.-

This study brings together three major areas of interest - history, postmodern fiction, and myth. Whereas neither history and postmodern fiction nor history and myth are strangers to one another, postmodernism and myth are odd bedfellows. For many critics, postmodern thought with its resistance to metanarratives stands in direct and deliberate contrast to myth with its apparent tendency to explain the world by means of neat, complete narratives.

There is a strain of postmodern Canadian historical fiction in which myth actually forms a complement not only to postmodernism's suspicion of master-narratives but also to its privileging of those marginal and at times ignored areas of history. The fourteen works of Canadian fiction considered demonstrate a doubled impulse which at first glance seems contradictory. On the one hand, they go about demythologizing - in the Barthesian sense - various elements of historical discourse, exposing its authority as not simply a natural given but as a construct. This includes the fact that the view of history portrayed in the fiction has been either underrepresented or suppressed by official historiography. On the other hand, the history is then re-mythologized, in that it becomes part of a pre-existing myth, its mythic elements are foregrounded, myth and magic are woven into the narrative, or it is portrayed as extraordinary in some way. The result is an empowering of these histories for the future; they are made larger than life and unforgettable.

USA/Canada: One Rockefeller Plaza, Ste. 1420, New York, NY 10020,
Tel. (212) 265-6360, Call toll-free (U.S. only) 1-800-225-3998,
Fax (212) 265-6402
All other countries: Tijnmuiden 7, 1046 AK Amsterdam, The Netherlands.
Tel. ++ 31 (0)20 611 48 21, Fax ++ 31 (0)20 447 29 79
Orders-queries@rodopi.nl   **www.rodopi.nl**
Please note that the exchange rate is subject to fluctuations

The Politics of English as a World Language.
New Horizons in Postcolonial Cultural Studies. ASNEL Papers 7.

Edited by Christian Mair.

Amsterdam/New York, N.Y. 2003. XXI, 497 pp. (Cross/Cultures 65)
ISBN: 90-420-0876-8   Bound € 110,-/US$ 131.-
ISBN: 90-420-0866-0   Paper € 55,-/US$ 65.-

The complex politics of English as a world language provides the backdrop both for linguistic studies of varieties of English around the world and for postcolonial literary criticism. The present volume offers contributions from linguists and literary scholars that explore this common ground in a spirit of open interdisciplinary dialogue.
Leading authorities assess the state of the art to suggest directions for further research, with substantial case studies ranging over a wide variety of topics - from the legitimacy of language norms of lingua franca communication to the recognition of newer post-colonial varieties of English in the online *OED*. Four regional sections treat the Caribbean (including the diaspora), Africa, the Indian subcontinent, and Australasia and the Pacific Rim.
Each section maintains a careful balance between linguistics and literature, and external and indigenous perspectives on issues. The book is the most balanced, complete and up-to-date treatment of the topic to date.

USA/Canada: One Rockefeller Plaza, Ste. 1420, New York, NY 10020,
Tel. (212) 265-6360, Call toll-free (U.S. only) 1-800-225-3998,
Fax (212) 265-6402
All other countries: Tijnmuiden 7, 1046 AK Amsterdam, The Netherlands.
Tel. ++ 31 (0)20 611 48 21, Fax ++ 31 (0)20 447 29 79
Orders-queries@rodopi.nl   **www.rodopi.nl**
Please note that the exchange rate is subject to fluctuations

Literary Culture and Female Authorship in Canada 1760-2000

Faye Hammill

Amsterdam/New York, NY 2003. XXIV,245 pp. (Cross/Cultures 63)
ISBN: 90-420-0915-2
Bound € 54,-/US$ 64.-
ISBN: 90-420-0905-5
Paper € 28,-/US$ 33.-

"There are two ladies in the province, I am told, who read," writes Frances Brooke's Arabella Fermor, "but both are above fifty and are regarded as prodigies of erudition." Brooke's *The History of Emily Montague* (1769) was the first work of fiction to be set in Canada, and also the first book to reflect on the situation of the woman writer there. Her analysis of the experience of writing in Canada is continued by the five other writers considered in this study – Susanna Moodie, Sara Jeannette Duncan, L.M. Montgomery, Margaret Atwood and Carol Shields. All of these authors examine the social position of the woman of letters in Canada, the intellectual stimulation available to her, the literary possibilities of Canadian subject-matter, and the practical aspects of reading, writing, and publishing in a (post)colonial country.

This book turns on the ways in which those aspects of authorship and literary culture in Canada have been inscribed in imaginative, autobiographical and critical texts by the six authors. It traces the evolving situation of the Canadian woman writer over the course of two centuries, and explores the impact of social and cultural change on the experience of writing in Canada.

USA/Canada: One Rockefeller Plaza, Ste. 1420, New York, NY 10020,
Tel. (212) 265-6360, Call toll-free (U.S. only) 1-800-225-3998,
Fax (212) 265-6402
All other countries: Tijnmuiden 7, 1046 AK Amsterdam, The Netherlands.
Tel. ++ 31 (0)20 611 48 21, Fax ++ 31 (0)20 447 29 79
Orders-queries@rodopi.nl
Please note that the exchange rate is subject to fluctuations
www.rodopi.nl

Borderlines.

Autobiography and Fiction in Postmodern Life Writing.

Gunnthórunn Gudmundsdóttir

Amsterdam/New York, NY 2003. VII, 294 pp.
(Postmodern Studies 33)

ISBN: 90-420-1145-9   € 60,-/US $ 71.-

Borderlines. Autobiography and Fiction in Postmodern Life Writing locates and investigates the borderlines between autobiography and fiction in various kinds of life-writing dating from the last thirty years. This volume offers a valuable comparative approach to texts by French, English, American, and German authors to illustrate the different forms of experimentation with the borders between genres and literary modes. Gudmundsdóttir tackles important contemporary concerns such as autobiography's relationship to postmodernism by investigating themes such as memory and crossing cultural divides, the use of photographs in autobiography and the role of narrative in life-writing. This work is of interest to students and scholars of comparative literature, postmodernism and contemporary life-writing

USA/Canada: One Rockefeller Plaza, Ste. 1420, New York, NY 10020,
Tel. (212) 265-6360, Call toll-free (U.S. only) 1-800-225-3998,
Fax (212) 265-6402
All other countries: Tijnmuiden 7, 1046 AK Amsterdam, The Netherlands.
Tel. ++ 31 (0)20 611 48 21, Fax ++ 31 (0)20 447 29 79
Orders-queries@rodopi.nl   **www.rodopi.nl**
Please note that the exchange rate is subject to fluctuations

Literature on the Move

Ottmar Ette

Translated by Katharina Vester

Amsterdam/New York, NY 2003. 316 pp.
(Internationale Forschungen zur Allgemeinen und Vergleichenden
Literaturwissenschaft 68)

ISBN: 90-420-1155-6   € 62,-/US $ 74.-

Literature on the Move formulates a new aesthetics for the altered conditions and challenges of the new century. The point of departure for examining a bordercrossing literature on the move is travel literature, from which the view opens up unto other spaces, dimensions and patterns of movement which will shape the literatures of the 21th Century. And these will become - one needs no prophetic gift to see - for a major part *literatures with no fixed abode*. Signposts of this journey through literature proposed by this book are texts by, among many others, Balzac, Barthes, Baudrillard, Borges, Calvino, Condé, Cohen, Diderot, Goethe, A.v. Humboldt, Kristeva, Reyes, Rodó or Stadler. This book will specially appeal to an audience interested by comparative literature, literary theory, and travel literature and will be of interest to anybody who delights in «literary journeys».

USA/Canada: One Rockefeller Plaza, Ste. 1420, New York, NY 10020,
Tel. (212) 265-6360, Call toll-free (U.S. only) 1-800-225-3998,
Fax (212) 265-6402
All other countries: Tijnmuiden 7, 1046 AK Amsterdam, The Netherlands.
Tel. ++ 31 (0)20 611 48 21, Fax ++ 31 (0)20 447 29 79
Orders-queries@rodopi.nl   **www.rodopi.nl**
Please note that the exchange rate is subject to fluctuations

Two Hundred Years of Pushkin

Volume II Alexander Pushkin: Myth and Monument

Edited by Robert Reid and Joe Andrew

Amsterdam/New York, NY 2003. X, 211 pp.
(Studies in Slavic Literature and Poetics 39)
ISBN: 90-420-0874-1   vols. I-III
ISBN: 90-420-1135-1   € 45,-/US $ 54.-

Pushkin's status as the founding father of Russian literature owes much to his stylistic and linguistic innovations across a wide range of literary genres. But equally important is the influence he exerted on his successors via his exploitation of myth in its widest sense. His poetry, prose and drama frequently draw upon myths of classical antiquity, myths of modern European culture – grand narratives such as the Don Juan legend and Dante's *Inferno* – as well as uniquely Russian myths, particularly those associated with St Petersburg and its founder Peter the Great. It was through the elaboration of such myths that Russia attained to a sense of both its cultural uniqueness and its inscription in the broader context of European culture. The contributors to *Alexander Pushkin: Myth and Monument* explore these myths from a variety of critical viewpoints and highlight the specific ways in which Pushkin uses myth – among these his recurrent emphasis on the symbolism of monuments and statuary, famously referred to by Roman Jakobson as Pushkin's 'sculptural myth'.

Alexander Pushkin: Myth and Monument is the second volume devoted to Pushkin published in the SSLP series, the first being *'Pushkin's Secret': Russian Writers Reread and Rewrite Pushkin*. A third volume – *Pushkin's Legacy* will follow.

USA/Canada: One Rockefeller Plaza, Ste. 1420, New York, NY 10020,
Tel. (212) 265-6360, Call toll-free (U.S. only) 1-800-225-3998,
Fax (212) 265-6402
All other countries: Tijnmuiden 7, 1046 AK Amsterdam, The Netherlands.
Tel. ++ 31 (0)20 611 48 21, Fax ++ 31 (0)20 447 29 79
Orders-queries@rodopi.nl   www.rodopi.nl
Please note that the exchange rate is subject to fluctuations

Huysmans l'inchangé
Histoire d'une conversion

Marc Smeets

Amsterdam/New York, NY 2003. 239 pp.
(Faux Titre 237)
ISBN : 90-420-1075-4   € 48,-/US $ 57.-

Même si elle a fait l'objet de nombreux commentaires déjà, un mystère plane encore sur la conversion au catholicisme de Joris-Karl Huysmans (1848-1907). L'homme, certes, se convertit, mais qu'en est-il de l'œuvre ? Un grand écrivain peut-il en même temps être un bon converti ? En d'autres termes encore, comment gérer deux vocations, deux parcours dont le moins que l'on puisse dire est qu'ils sont difficilement compatibles ? A travers documents personnels et œuvres littéraires nous essaierons de retracer le trajet particulier d'un écrivain « décadent » qui renoue avec Dieu. Nous aurons à nous pencher plus précisément sur ce que nous appellerons un mélange bizarre de fidélité à soi-même et de volonté de rupture, mélange qui, croyons-nous, est au cœur d'une problématique qui n'a pas eu l'attention qu'elle mérite. Lacune à laquelle nous voulons remédier ici. Peut-on brûler ce que l'on a adoré ? Quelque chose, semble-t-il, condamne l'écrivain à revenir toujours à ses anciennes amours. Huysmans, de ce point de vue, est l'homme qui n'a pas vraiment su faire peau neuve.

USA/Canada: One Rockefeller Plaza, Ste. 1420, New York, NY 10020,
Tel. (212) 265-6360, Call toll-free (U.S. only) 1-800-225-3998,
Fax (212) 265-6402
All other countries: Tijnmuiden 7, 1046 AK Amsterdam, The Netherlands.
Tel. ++ 31 (0)20 611 48 21, Fax ++ 31 (0)20 447 29 79
Orders-queries@rodopi.nl   **www.rodopi.nl**
Please note that the exchange rate is subject to fluctuations.

Cultural Expressions of Evil and Wickedness
Wrath, Sex, Crime

Edited by Terrie Waddell

Amsterdam/New York, NY 2003. XVIII, 226 pp.
(At the Interface/Probing the Boundaries 3)

ISBN: 90-420-1015-0   € 50.-/US $ 60.-

Cultural Expressions of Evil and Wickedness: Wrath, Sex, Crime, is a fascinating study of the a-temporal nature of evil in the West. The international academics and researchers who have contributed to this text not only concentrate on political, social and legally sanctioned cruelty from the past and present, but also explore the nature of moral transgression in contemporary art, media and literature. Although many forms and practices of what might be called 'evil' are analysed, all are bound by violence and/or the sexually perverse. As this book demonstrates, the old news media axiom, 'if it bleeds it leads,' also extends to the larger pool of popular culture. This absorbing volume will be of interest to anyone who has ever pondered on the exotic, extraordinary and surreal twists of human wickedness.

USA/Canada: One Rockefeller Plaza, Ste. 1420, New York, NY 10020,
Tel. (212) 265-6360, Call toll-free (U.S. only) 1-800-225-3998,
Fax (212) 265-6402
All other countries: Tijnmuiden 7, 1046 AK Amsterdam, The Netherlands.
Tel. ++ 31 (0)20 611 48 21, Fax ++ 31 (0)20 447 29 79
Orders-queries@rodopi.nl   **www.rodopi.nl**
Please note that the exchange rate is subject to fluctuations.